The Grosset Secretarial Handbook

The Most Up-to-Date Book for Today's Secretary

The Grosset Secretarial Handbook

edited by **John Clement**

Grosset & Dunlap
A Filmways Company
Publishers   New York

Acknowledgments

The editor expresses his appreciation to the following for permission to use the stationery in the illustrations on pages 108, 109, and 110: Crane Fine Papers; Harvey & Tracy Associates, Inc.; The Lehman Corporation; and Secretarial Systems, Inc.

Copyright © 1980 by Grosset & Dunlap, Inc.
All rights reserved
Published simultaneously in Canada
Library of Congress catalog card number: 79-50418
ISBN 0-448-12657-5
First printing 1980
Printed in the United States of America

Contents

General Office Practice

1. Calendars, Reminders, and Follow-up Systems 1
2. Filing 7
3. Typing 18
4. The Telephone 24
5. Telegraph and Other Long-Distance
   Communication 35
6. Mail and Postal Information 42
7. Travel Arrangements and International Business 72

Letter Writing

8. Guidelines for Good Letters 104
9. Forms of Address 144
10. Model Letters 176

Correct English Usage

11. Capitalization 195
12. Punctuation 243
13. Spelling 270
14. Abbreviations 277
15. Troublesome Words and Phrases 330
16. Numbers 336

Special Secretarial Functions

17. Keeping Minutes of Meetings 342
18. Legal Secretarial Practice 349
19. Medical Secretarial Practice 366

Useful Information

20. Weights and Measures 383
21. Signs and Symbols 388
22. Proofreading 390
23. Further Information 393

Index 399

The Grosset Secretarial Handbook

General Office Practice

1. Calendars, Reminders, and Follow-up Systems

Calendars

Your own calendar. The best choice for your own desk calendar is usually a diary-type yearbook, sometimes also called a day-at-a-glance calendar. Each page represents one day of the year and is broken down into 15- or 30-minute intervals.

Use the calendar to keep track of your own appointments and activities as well as to note your employer's appointments. Also make notes of things you have to remind your employer about. If you are responsible for carrying out a long, time-consuming project, make notations in your calendar sufficiently ahead of the deadline to permit you to finish the task in time.

Your employer's calendar. A day-at-a-glance yearbook is also a good choice for your employer's desk calendar. In some cases, a week-at-a-glance diary might be sufficient. Because these calendars are in book form, they may be easily closed by your employer when he or she does not wish their contents to be visible to visitors.

You are responsible for keeping the employer's calendar up to date. Enter all dates which are important to him or her: appointments, deadlines, birthdays, social occasions, etc. You should

2 GENERAL OFFICE PRACTICE

also be aware of dates which the employer himself or herself enters in the calendar; transfer these dates to your own calendar so that no conflicts will arise.

Employer's pocket memo book. Your employer will probably want to carry a small pocket memo book when out of the office for meetings, appointments, trips, and the like. This memo book should contain the dates of your employer's important appointments and meetings for the near future. He or she will thus be able to make new engagements without fear of conflict with existing engagements.

Recurring calendar items. Certain items recur yearly, monthly, or weekly. You should be sure that all of them are noted in your employer's calendar. Here is a checklist of the most common recurring items:

Meetings

- Board meetings
- Annual stockholders' meeting
- Committee meetings
- Business and professional association meetings
- Club meetings
- Luncheons

Holidays

- Christmas. Make a note at least four to six weeks before Christmas regarding gifts to be purchased and Christmas cards to be sent.
- Religious holidays. Your employer may want to note special observances.
- Valentine's Day.
- Family Dates
  - Birthdays
  - Anniversaries
  - Father's Day and Mother's Day
- Tax Dates
  - Income taxes. Make advance notations of due dates so that taxes are paid on time.

Renewal Dates
  Driver's license and auto registration
  Subscriptions to newspapers and periodicals
  Hunting and fishing licenses
Payment Dates
  Insurance premiums
  Mortgage payments
  Loan payments
Pledged contributions
Periodic payments, such as tuition payments and wages to servants

When to start the next year's calendar. Start the next year's calendar in October, unless your employer makes appointments far in advance, in which case you may start it even earlier. Go through the calendar month by month, entering all the items listed above as well as any appointments for the coming year which your employer has already made.

Reminders

Tickler file. A tickler file of 3-by-5-inch cards is a useful complement to your regular desk calendar. It contains additional information on all recurring items.

A tickler file has two sets of tabbed guides: 12 guides, one for each month; and 31 guides, one for each day of the month. The daily guides are placed behind the guide for the current month. Thus, in January, the January guide is at the front of the file, followed by the 31 daily guides. The guides for February, March, April, and the rest of the months are placed at the back of the file.

Memoranda are made on 3-by-5-inch cards and the cards are filed behind the proper daily guide according to the date on which the matter is to be brought up. For instance, if a mortgage payment is due on the first of the month, place a card with the relevant information behind the guide for the first day of the month. Thus, if a check is to be mailed monthly, you can make one card and move it up from month to month, instead of making 12 entries in your calendar.

4 GENERAL OFFICE PRACTICE

The tickler file cards should contain all necessary information. In the above example, for instance, if mortgage payments are due monthly, the card should show: (1) due dates, (2) amount of payment, (3) name and address of bank, (4) loan number, and (5) the name of the mortgaged property.

You will thus always have an accurate record of your employer's obligations. This is especially important when you are absent from the office, i.e., if you are ill. With the tickler file, you will be assured that your substitute will be able to conduct your employer's business smoothly until you return.

You should note that the tickler file does not take the place of the calendar for noting appointments. The calendar should contain all appointments, even ones that recur regularly. If it does not, you will find that whenever you want to make an appointment for your employer, you are wasting time looking not only at the calendar but also at the tickler file.

Reminders for indefinite dates. Your employer will often have obligations for which no specific date has been set, such as "meet Mr. Jones in September" or "go over stock file as soon as possible." Although these instructions cannot be entered in the employer's calendar, you must keep track of them yourself. Here are two useful methods:

1. Note the item on a card in your tickler file and move the card up every week or so.
2. Make a pencil notation on your own calendar at frequent intervals.

Contact file. This file is a record of your employer's personal "contacts." If your employer meets many people in the course of business, he or she may not be able to remember them all. Yet it may be very important for him or her to be able to recall these names and connections. (Politicians and salespeople frequently find themselves in this situation.) The contact file is a useful aid.

A small looseleaf notebook, perhaps the 4-by-6-inch size, is handy for the purpose. Enter the names of all the persons your employer wants to remember, together with their affiliations and the circumstances of the meeting. You might note, for instance, that your employer met "Mr. Stephen Bishop, president of U.S.

Forge, Inc.," on "May 15" at the "Civic Society luncheon." Include any additional items that will help your employer remember the contact. If your employer wants to contact this person at some time in the future, make a note to that effect as well.

You may find it helpful to make more than one entry for each contact. For instance, if your employer met Mr. Jones of the Dennison Company in Chicago, you might make an entry under "Jones," "Dennison," and "Chicago." Thus, if your employer meets with officials of the Dennison Company, he or she will have a record of each of these officials whom he has met personally. Or, if he or she makes a business trip to Chicago, the file entry under "Chicago" should contain a list of all contacts in that city.

Follow-up

Certain items usually call for follow-up. Orders placed and received, letters sent, and requests made are examples of such items. You must keep careful records of these matters so that they are not neglected or forgotten.

Simple follow-up system. Whenever you type a letter that may require a follow-up—for instance, an order, a request for information, or a sales letter—type a carbon copy and file it in a special "follow-up" folder. Go through the follow-up folder frequently to determine which letters require further action.

Large-scale follow-up system. When you find that one folder is not sufficient to hold all your follow-up material, you will have to expand your follow-up system.

The most efficient system requires a file drawer and file folders. You will need 13 file guides, one for each month of the year plus one labeled "Future Years," plus 31 file folders, one for each day of the month. Arrange the file drawer so that the most current file is at the front. For instance, on May 15, the folder marked "15" should be at the front of the drawer, followed by "16", "17," etc. up to "31." After "31," the file guide for the next month, i.e., June, should appear. The remaining "day" folders are inserted after the "June" guide, in this case, the folders marked "1" through

"14." The remaining "month" guides are grouped at the back of the file drawer.

Every day you will adjust the follow-up file so that the current date appears at the head of the file. In this manner, you will always have a 31-day record of all material that requires following up.

Preparing material for follow-up. Type a carbon copy of all letters and memoranda that require follow-up. Make a note on the carbon of the date on which the material is to be followed up, and file the material under the proper date.

If you have no carbon copy of the material requiring follow-up, type a brief memo for the follow-up file. For example, if your employer places an order by telephone and tells you to follow up on it at a certain date, type a memo giving the relevant information and file it under the proper date.

Indefinite follow-up. Certain material will have no definite follow-up date. Move this material forward from week to week until a definite follow-up date is established or until the matter is settled.

2. Filing

Pros and Cons of Various Filing Systems

Alphabetical. The alphabetical filing system is easy and straightforward. Names and subjects are simply filed in alphabetical order, often in the same file drawer but sometimes in separate drawers if the files are voluminous. The only difficulty that is likely to arise is the proper selection of the subject categories: unless you decide carefully which subjects are truly important, the files may become chaotic. You will often find yourself faced with a choice of files: should Mr. Robertson's letter be filed under ACCOUNTS RECEIVABLE or JOBS IN PROGRESS? This problem can be overcome by the use of judicious cross-referencing, however, and it is a small price to pay for the convenience and orderliness of alphabetical files.

Geographic. This system may be useful to sales organizations which are more concerned with activity in any given territory than with particular company names. Under the geographic system, material is filed: first, according to the name of the state; second, according to the city or county; third, by the name of the correspondent or branch office. Standard sets of guides which consist of these classifications are available from office supply

8 GENERAL OFFICE PRACTICE

firms. The principal difficulty of this system is that you will also have to maintain a cross-index of names in the form of a card file. This index will tell you that Mr. Jefferson's letters are filed under Cincinnati and that the Ideal Toy Company's letters are filed under Bakersfield.

Numeric. This filing system is primarily of interest to firms whose jobs or clients are all given numbers (Job Numbers, Order Numbers, Invoice Numbers, etc.). The files are maintained in strict numerical sequence and are thus very accurate and very easy to use. Their principal disadvantage is that they require a cross-index card file to be maintained in addition. This auxiliary file is necessary to let you know that U.S. Steel's correspondence is filed under Job No. 555.44.30 and that Applied Leasing's letters may be found under Order No. 39809-56.

Repairing File Guides

Staggered tabs or straight-line tabs? When organizing a new file, you may have to decide whether to use folders with staggered tabs or folders with tabs all in the same position. "Straight-line" tabs are usually easier to use and easier to read: there is less chance of misfiling, and your eyes do not have to dart back and forth over the file drawer when you are looking for a specific file.

Guide categories. Filing is easier if the file drawers contain guide letters to tell you where the As begin, the Ms begin, etc. You may use an ordinary alphabetical guide system, one guide for each letter of the alphabet; but you will often find that this is not entirely satisfactory because some sections may be very short while others run to several drawers.

You should use more or fewer divisions depending on how many drawers of filed material you have. Alphabetical index guides are available from office supply firms in divisions of from 25 to 2,000.

> For 1 drawer . . . . 25 divisions
> For 2 drawers . . . . 40 divisions
> For 3 drawers . . . . 60 divisions

Filing 9

```
For  5 drawers  . . . . . . . . . . . . . . .  100 divisions
For  8 drawers  . . . . . . . . . . . . . . .  160 divisions
For 10 drawers  . . . . . . . . . . . . . . .  200 divisions
For 20 drawers  . . . . . . . . . . . . . . .  400 divisions
```

Some examples of alphabetical guides.

20 Divisions	40 Divisions		60 Divisions	
A	A	Ro–Rz	A–Am	Le–Li
B	Ba	S–Sc	An–Az	Lo–Ly
C–Cl	Be–Bj	Se–Sk	Ba	M–Map
Co–Cz	Bl–Bo	Sl–Sq	Be	Mar–May
D	Br–By	St–Sz	Bi–Bl	Mc
E–F	C–Ce	T	Bo	Me
G	Ch–Cl	U–V	Br	Mi–Mop
H	Co–Cz	W–We	Bu–By	Mor–My
I–J–K	D–De	Wh–Wi	C–Ce	N
L	Di–Dz	Wo–Z	Ch–Cl	O
M–Mc	E		Co–Cor	P–Pen
Me–My	F–Fl		Cos–Cz	Peo–Pi
N–O	Fo–Fy		D–De	Pl–Q
P–Q	G–Gl		Di–Do	R–Re
R	Go–Gy		Dr–Ek	Rh–Rol
S–Sl	Ha		El–Fa	Rom–Ry
Sm–Sy	He–Hi		Fe–Fl	Sa
T–U–V	Ho–Hy		Fo–Fy	Sc
W–Wh	I–J		G–Ge	Se–Sh
Wi–Z	K–Ki		Gi–Go	Si–Sm
	Kl–Ky		Gr–Gy	Sn–Sta
	L		H–Har	Ste–Sty
	Ma		Has–Hek	Su–Te
	Mc		Hel–Hi	Th–Ty
	Me–Mi		Ho	U–V
	Mo–My		Hu–I	Wa
	N–O		J	We
	P–Ph		K–Ke	Wh
	Pi–Q		Ki–Ky	Wi
	R–Ri		La	Wo–Z

GENERAL OFFICE PRACTICE
Preparing Material for Filing

Special problems arise in very large organizations, especially when all the files of the organization are maintained by a special central office. In such cases, material to be filed should usually be plainly marked, perhaps with a FILE or RELEASE stamp, so that it will not be mislaid or lost.

Retention codes may also be used as an aid for the filing personnel. The codes should indicate how long the filed material should be retained (30 days, 90 days, 2 years, etc.). In addition, the code may also indicate whether the material is to be transferred to microfilm or placed in computer storage.

Cross-references. You will often have a question as to which file a given piece of material should go into; that is, Mrs. Joseph's purchase agreement might be filed either under *Joseph* or under *Purchase Agreements.* Short of flipping a coin, there are several ways you can solve this problem.

First, you can copy the material and file a copy under each category. However, with large documents or bulky material this will not be convenient, and it will be impossible when you are trying to choose among three or four possible file categories.

Better, you can use a cross-reference. Type a cross-reference sheet and put one in each file where you want to leave a reminder. The cross-reference sheet will be more visible if you type it on colored paper and put CROSS-REFERENCE at the top. (Such sheets are available, already printed, from office supply firms.)

```
              CROSS REFERENCE

    JOSEPH, Alfred J., Mrs.

    Purchase agreement letter 8 Jan 79

    SEE

    PURCHASE AGREEMENTS
```

How to Control Material Taken from Files

When files are borrowed frequently from file drawers, you will need a system to keep track of them. *Out guides, out folders,* and *on call* guides are designed for this purpose.

Out guides. When a file folder is removed for any length of time, it should be replaced with an out guide. This is a colored cardboard sheet with lines on it for the notation of the date, material borrowed, borrower, etc. When the file is returned, the out guide is removed and the notations are crossed out or erased.

Out files. These are the same as out guides, except that they are folders instead of single sheets. They serve as receptacles for records that are to be stored while the original folder is charged out. Out folders contain the same notations on the front as out guides.

On call guides. An on call guide is sometimes used in place of an out folder. The on call guide indicates to the filing personnel that they should send any incoming material to the person listed on the on call guide. The on call guide is not removed from the file until the original folder, plus all the added material, is returned.

DATE	MATERIAL	DATE REMOVED	RETURN BY	CHARGED TO	REMARKS

12 GENERAL OFFICE PRACTICE
Rules of Indexing and Alphabetizing

Arrangement of personal names. Names of individuals are always arranged in the following manner: surname, first name or initial, middle name or initial.

   Sones, John Paul   Miller, L. James
   Jefferson, J. K.   Forsythe, Mary K.

Arrangement of company names. Company names that include the name of an individual are written with the first name or initials immediately after the surnames.

   Jones, A. W., & Co.
   Melville, John, & Sons
   Gaynor, Fred, Inc.
   Haviland, George, Co.
   Holt, T. J., Company, The
   Strauss, J., & Bros., Ltd.

However, if the company is well known in its given form, it need not be broken down.

   Marshall Field & Company
   John Hancock Mutual Life Insurance Company
   Roger Smith Hotel
   Sarah Lawrence College

Indexing personal names. When there are several entries with the same surname, as *Smith*, alphabetize according to the first name, as *Amanda* before *Betsy*. If the first names are also the same, alphabetize according to the middle name or initial. The indexing adage "Nothing before something" indicates that a shorter name always precedes a longer one, as *K.* before *Kate*.

   Smith, (Mr.)
   Smith, K.
   Smith, K. L.
   Smith, K. Landon
   Smith, Kate

Smith, Kate L.
Smith, Kate Landon
Smith, Katharine

Indexing company names. Company names are indexed according to the first word. If the first word is the same, alphabetize according to second word, etc.

Ame, Lois, & Co.
Amerada Hess Oil Company
American Auto Stores
American Automobile Club
American Factors of Greenwich
American Factors of Smithville
Americana, Ltd.
Ames, Joseph D.
Amex & Co.

Ampersand. The ampersand symbol (&) is disregarded when filing.

Jones & Jones, Inc.
A & B Company

treat as:

Jones Jones, Inc.
A B Company

Hyphenated words. Hyphenated words are treated as one word.

A-B-C Company
Up-Stairs Shoes, Ltd.
Eynsford-Hill, Freddy
Hi-Ho Greeting Cards

treat as:

ABC Company
Upstairs Shoes, Ltd.
Eynsfordhill, Freddy
Hiho Greeting Cards

14 GENERAL OFFICE PRACTICE

However, if the two hyphenated words can stand separately by themselves, it may sometimes make more sense to treat them as two words.

>Chicago-Cincinnati Trucking Company
>American-European Friends of Music, Inc.

>*treat as:*

>Chicago Cincinnati Trucking Company
>American European Friends of Music, Inc.

Apostrophes. Apostrophes are disregarded when filing. Thus, *Fred's* is treated as *Freds*, and *Jones'* is treated as *Jones*.

>Robert, Alfred D.
>Robert's Auto Repair, Inc.
>Roberts, Ava
>Roberts' Bar & Grill
>Robert's Barber Shop
>Roberts, Joseph
>Robertson, A. V.

Names with little words. Little words such as *the, and, by, for, of, on, from,* and *to* may be disregarded when filing, but modern usage tends to prefer that they be considered in full.

>Bryants, Franklin
>Bryants of Philadelphia, Inc.
>Players Press, Ltd.
>Players, The
>Society for the Aged, The
>Society of Arts and Sciences
>Tavern Equipment Company
>Tavern on the Green

Titles. Titles in most cases are disregarded for filing purposes but are added after the name for clarity.

>Johnson, John J., Jr.
>Dodson, W. W., Rev.

Filing 15

    Fox, Solomon, Dr.
    Orsini, Giancarlo, Count
    Grayson, Howard, III, Prof.
    Olivier, Lawrence, Sir

However, if a firm name contains a title, consider the title as the first word.

    Madame Fifi Apparel
    Prince George Hotel
    Mr. Big, Inc.

Names with "Mc" and "Mac." *Mc* and *Mac* are best handled by filing them together in a section separate from the rest of the *M* category. Do not distinguish between *Mc* and *Mac;* treat them as if they were spelled the same.

    MacArthur, Bob
    McArthur, Douglas
    McDonald, James
    MacDonald, Terence

Numbers in names. When numbers occur in names, alphabetize them as if the numbers were spelled out.

    The 21 Club
    3-4-5 Jiffy Mix
    900 First Ave., Inc.

file as:

    Twenty-One Club, The
    Three-Four-Five Jiffy Mix
    Nine Hundred First Ave., Inc.

Abbreviations in names. File *Mt., St., Pt.,* and *Ft.,* as though they were spelled out: "Mount," "Saint," "Point," "Fort."

    Mt. Hood Ice Cream
    St. Vincent's Hospital
    Ft. Sutter Jewelry Co.

16　GENERAL OFFICE PRACTICE

treat as:

Mount Hood Ice Cream
Saint Vincent's Hospital
Fort Sutter Jewelry Co.

Letter names. Firms whose names consist of single letters or multiple letters are grouped together at the beginning of a classification; letter names precede word names.

E & B Bakeries
E Systems, Inc.
E.A.T. Club
EEEEE Shoes, Inc.
ETV of Lansing
EXTRA, Inc.
Earl, Elizabeth
Ebbing, Kraft, & Sons

Names with particles. When names have particles such as *da, de, della, la, le, van,* or *von,* treat the entire name as one word.

d'Amato, Franco
D'Antuono, Eleanor
De Forest, J.
da Costa, Morton
de la Mole, M.
El Camino Club
La Paix Modes
Ten Eyck, Rudy
van der Pool, P.
Von Kerstein, B. B.

treat as:

Damato, Franco
Dantuono, Eleanor
Deforest, J.
Dacosta, Morton
Delamole, M.
Elcamino Club
Lapaix Modes

Teneyck, Rudy
Vanderpool, P.
Vonkerstein, B. B.

Names that include compass points. When compass points are part of a name, index under *north, south,* etc.

South Bronx, N.Y.
North California

not Bronx, South, N.Y.
not California, North

Names with words or phrases. When common words or phrases such as *Estate of* or *Trustees of* appear in titles, the title should be inverted and filed under the principal name.

Kreeger, Lloyd J., Estate of
Harvard University, Trustees of

School names. File schools, colleges, and universities under the principal name.

California, University of (Davis)
William and Mary, College of
Holy Cross, College of the

Governmental departments. When you have numerous files of governmental departments, file by the name of the chief governing body.

United States Government	California (State of)
Defense (Dept. of)	Highway Department
Munitions Bureau	Roads (Division of)
Nassau (County of)	Eureka, California
Commissioner's Office	City Planning Commission

3. Typing

Measuring and Spacing on the Typewriter

How to get the same number of lines on each page. If your typewriter has a numbered strip at the left edge of the platen, feed each successive page into the machine in alignment with the number one. Make a note of the numbers at which you begin and end your model page, and type the rest of the pages in accordance with the same numbers.

If your typewriter does not have a numbered strip, use this method. Type the first sheet and remove it from the typewriter. Align it with the next sheet to be typed and lightly mark with pencil the correct lines at which to begin and end typing.

Useful measurements.

    10 spaces of pica type equal 1 inch.
    12 spaces of elite type equal 1 inch.
    A sheet of paper 8½" x 11" has 85 spaces of pica type per line.
    A sheet of paper 8½" x 11" has 102 spaces of elite type per line.
    A sheet of paper 8½" x 11" has 66 lines.
    6 lines equal 1 inch (for both pica and elite type).

Ruling by typewriter. To make vertical lines, on a typed sheet, release the variable line-spacer. Turn the knob while holding a pencil firmly in the desired position. (Some typewriters have a special place to insert a pencil for this purpose.)

You can also use the apostrophe for vertical lines, while using the underscore for horizontal lines.

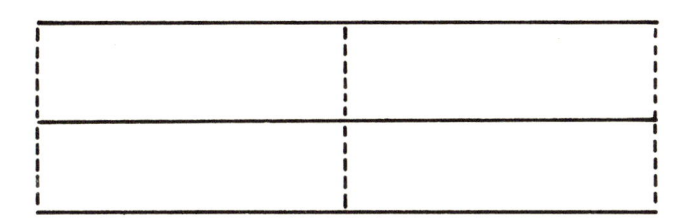

Vertical centering. For accurate placement of typed material, follow this procedure: (1) Count the number of lines and spaces in the material to be typed; (2) Subtract this number from the number of lines on the sheet (standard 8½" x 11" paper has 66 lines); (3) Divide the remainder by two. This represents the number of lines that will be left blank at the top and bottom of the page.

How to Type Tables.

Setting tabs. Tabs for the following table would be set in this manner.

BALANCE SHEET

	First Quarter		Six Months Ended June 30	
	1980	1979	1980	1979
Cash	$ 1,007	$ 950	$ 7,800	$ 9,000
Accounts Receivable	99,430	78,456	200,550	156,789
Plant and Equipment	15,783	16,700	15,783	16,700
Deferred Taxes	150	7,909	150	7,909
Goodwill	1	1	1	1
Prepaid Insurance	1,400	200	1,400	200

20 GENERAL OFFICE PRACTICE

1. Count the longest items in each column and record the number of spaces in each. (Be sure to include the dollar sign.) In this example, the longest lines in each column are, respectively, Accounts Receivable; 99,430; 78,456; 200,550; and 156,789. Including four dollar signs, we have a total of 49 spaces.
2. Consider your margins. If you are typing on an elite typewriter and your margins are at 15 and 88, your margins are consuming 15 spaces at the left side of the page and 14 spaces at the right (102 minus 88), for a total of 29.
3. Add the column total to the margin total: 49 + 29 = 78.
4. A full line of elite type contains 102 spaces. 78 are already accounted for. Thus 24 are left to apportion as spaces between the columns of the table.
5. There are five columns (one of words and four of figures) and therefore there will be four "space" columns.
6. 24 spaces divided between 4 columns gives 6 spaces, which indicates that 6 spaces will be left between each column in the table.
7. Set tabs by counting columns consecutively from the left margin, setting tabs as you go.

Proper alignment for columns. Columns of Roman and Arabic numerals should be aligned so that the right-hand edge is even. When typing sums of money or decimal figures, the decimal points should be aligned.

XIII	3,987,000	$9,345.00
V	99	56.24
XIX	34,444	777.28
MM	345	500.00
III	3	.95

Standard Rules for Spacing after Punctuation

One space:

after a comma
after a semicolon

after a period following an abbreviation
before and after an x, as in 8½" x 11"
between the initials of a name, as F. O. Simpson
on envelopes, between the elements of the last line of the address, as Milwaukee WI 95672

Two spaces:

after a colon
after each sentence
after the numbers in an enumeration, as
   1. Fortitude
   2. Honesty

No spaces:

before or after a dash (sometimes written as two hyphens)
before or after a hyphen
between the initials of an abbreviation, as R.F.D. or F.O.B.
between quotation marks and the quoted words

Making Corrections

Corrections tricks. Use an erasing shield (available from typewriter dealers) for correcting small areas without smudging.
   Use a soft pencil eraser for correcting carbon copies.
   White chalk may be used to cover an unsightly erasure; it is barely discernible on white paper.

Crowding and spreading. When it is necessary to erase one word and insert a longer or shorter word in its place, you will have to crowd or spread.

Spreading:	This misstake was ...
	This mistake was ...
Crowding:	This mistak was ...
	Thismistakewas ...

In both crowding and spreading, the back-space key is slightly depressed while striking each letter of the word. In crowding, begin the inserted word *one* space from the previous word in the sentence; in spreading, begin the inserted word *two* spaces from the previous word. This procedure is unnecessary on typewriters that have a half-space key. Simply use the half-space key to position the first letter of the corrected word at the indicated starting position.

Correcting errors at the bottom of a page. It is difficult to keep sheets and carbon copies aligned when making erasures at the bottom of a page. To remedy this, roll the paper *backward* in the typewriter until the line to be corrected is easily reached at the top of the roller.

Making corrections on pages bound at the top. Legal documents are often bound at the top. To correct an error on one page of a bound packet, use the "back feeding" method. Insert an ordinary sheet of paper into the typewriter as for typing. Insert the bottom of the sheet to be corrected between the blank page and the front of the platen. Then roll the platen backward to draw the desired sheet into the proper position for correction.

Special Problems

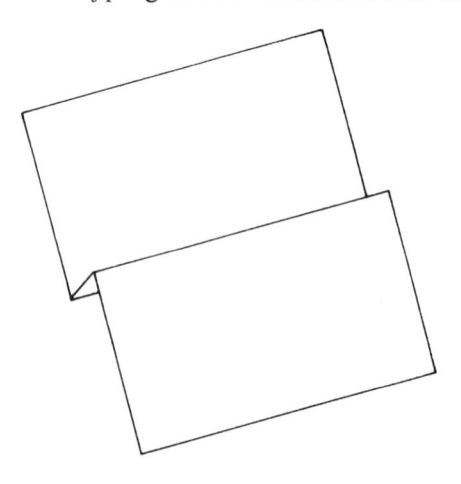

How to type thin labels. Cards and labels which are too small to be held in place for typing can be handled in this manner: Fold a sheet of paper in the indicated manner. Insert it into the typewriter; the pleat will neatly hold your card or label. (The pleated paper may be inserted into the typewriter either right side up or upside down, depending on whether you want to type on the top or bottom of the label.)

Shortcuts for typing envelopes. When you have many envelopes to address, you can save time by "chain-feeding." In chain-feeding, one envelope is inserted into the typewriter before the previous envelope is removed, so that one twist of the platen knob removes the first envelope while automatically bringing the next one into position to be typed. (Be sure to insert the envelopes with the flaps *open* so as to avoid bunching and clogging.) When using the chain-feeding system, even more time may be saved by preparing envelopes in groups of threes for insertion into the typewriter.

Inserting heavy carbon packs. To insert a pack of four to six carbons into the typewriter without losing alignment, fold a strip of paper over the top of the pack. This will help guide the pack into the machine.

How to separate carbon copies easily. When typing more than three or four carbons at a time, cut a small triangular piece off one of the upper corners of the carbons. Then when you grasp this corner, you are grasping the writing paper but not the carbons. This makes separation easier. (This technique is used mostly with colored or specially treated forms of carbon paper, as ordinary carbon paper usually has the corner already cut.)

What to do if your back aches at the typewriter. Your feet should be flat on the floor; if they are not, adjust your chair. When you are typing, your forearms should be roughly horizontal; if they are not, adjust the height of your typewriter.

Relax your shoulders completely; they should not be tight or hunched. Try to sit straight. Get a stronger chair if this is impossible. Do not thrust your elbows out; they should be held easily against your sides. Do not let your wrists droop as you type or you will put a strain on your hands and arms.

4. The Telephone

Business Telephone Etiquette

Placing calls for your employer. When you place a call for your employer, you will usually be connected to the secretary of the person your employer is trying to reach. There is a perennial question as to which executive is to come on to the line first. Ordinary business etiquette says that when *you* place the call, it is your privilege to get the other executive on the line before connecting your employer. Conversely, if a call is placed to you, it is the privilege of the calling party to get your employer on the line first.

Thus, when you are placing a call for your employer, Mr. Executive, the conversation may proceed as follows. You have placed a call to another executive, Mr. Bigshot, and have gotten Mr. Bigshot's secretary on the wire. You say, "Is Mr. Bigshot there, for Mr. Executive of ABCD Company?" Mr. Bigshot's secretary will put Mr. Bigshot on the line and he will say "Hello" or "Yes?" You will then say to him, "Here is Mr. Executive, Mr. Bigshot," and immediately put your employer on the line.

There are several exceptions to this procedure. The most important occurs when your employer wants to call an old friend or a person in a high official capacity. Your employer will not want to run the risk of offending the party he is calling, so he should be the first to get on the wire; he should pick up his phone as soon as you have reached the secretary at the other end of the line.

Another common problem arises when you and your employer are the same sex: people on the telephone will mistake you for your employer. For example, when placing a call for your employer, if you simply say to the secretary at the other end of the line, "Is Mr. Smith there, for Mr. Jones of XYZ Company?", the secretary will often assume that you are Mr. Jones. She will put Mr. Smith on the line and he will say heartily, "Hello there, Mr. Jones!" You will then have the task of admitting to an embarrassed Mr. Smith that you are *not* Mr. Jones. The simple solution to this problem is to identify yourself at every opportunity. When placing a call, you should say, "This is Mr. Secretary in Mr. Jones' office at XYZ Company. Is Mr. Smith there to speak to Mr. Jones?"

You will occasionally contact secretaries who refuse to put their executives on the line until the caller is on the line. They are probably acting under their employers' orders. Do not get into an argument with such a secretary. Simply put your employer on the line first.

Screening calls. If your employer prefers to have his or her calls screened, you will answer the phone and ask, "May I tell Mr. Brown who is calling, please?" In most cases, the caller will tell you his or her name. If, in response to your repeated inquiries, the caller will not give you a name, you have little recourse but to say, "I'm terribly sorry, sir, but if you cannot tell me who is calling, it might be better to send Mr. Brown a letter marked PERSONAL."

When your employer does not want to take the call. If, after telling your employer that Mr. Blank is on the line, you find that he does not want to talk to Mr. Blank, you will have to make an excuse. In most business offices, the standard excuses are:

"I'm sorry, Mr. Blank, but Mr. Hightson is on another call."
"I'm sorry, he's on long distance."
"I'm sorry, he's away from his desk."
"I'm sorry, he's in conference."

26 GENERAL OFFICE PRACTICE

If you are acting as private secretary to an executive or individual, you may be responsible for answering a residence phone rather than a business phone. You will often encounter this conversation:

> You: "Mr. Whately's residence."
> Caller: "Is Mr. Whately in?"
> You: "May I ask who is calling, please?"
> Caller: "This is Mr. Blank."
> You: "Just a moment, Mr. Blank. I'll see if Mr. Whately is in."

If your employer, Mr. Whately, then decides that he would rather not talk to Mr. Blank, you may have difficulty in finding an excuse to give to Mr. Blank. The traditional office excuses ("another call," "away from his desk," "in conference") will not be appropriate. You run the risk of gravely offending Mr. Blank if you merely say, "I'm sorry, Mr. Blank, but Mr. Whately is not in." Mr. Blank will assume, rightly or wrongly, that Mr. Whately is brushing him off. Depending on the time of day, you can tell Mr. Blank that your employer is at breakfast, lunch, or dinner; is taking a nap; or has gone to bed. Or you can say that Mr. Whately has company or is conferring with his accountant, lawyer, or doctor.

Discretion on the telephone. Never volunteer unnecessary information on the telephone. Stick to generalities. Even such an innocuous statement as "Mr. Jones is in Kalamazoo today" may, in certain instances, give the caller important information.

Too informative:	*Sufficient:*
"He's in Kalamazoo today."	"He's out of town today."
"He is sick."	"He will not be in today."
"He's on a trip to Saudi Arabia."	"He is away on a trip."
"He's playing tennis."	"He won't be back to the office today."

"He can be reached at the Senate Office Building."

"He hasn't come in yet."

"I can get in touch with him and have him call you."

"He isn't here at the moment."

Soothing annoyed callers. If you work in a large corporation (and especially if you work in a government office), you will occasionally receive calls that have been transferred from other offices in the organization. Such calls are often transferred several times, and by the time the call comes to your number, the caller is irritated. This problem is often unavoidable in big organizations, but it will not enhance the organization's image. If you receive such a call from an annoyed caller, apologize for the inconvenience. Then, if you are not able to answer the question yourself, ask for his telephone number and say you will call him back in a few minutes. Find the name of the person in your organization who can answer the question, and then return the call, giving the name and telephone number of this person.

Telephone Services

The following special types of telephone calls may be useful in certain circumstances.

Conference calls. Up to ten telephones in different cities can be connected in a conference call. No special equipment is required. Your employer can talk with up to ten different people at a time from his regular telephone. To make a conference call, ask the operator to connect you with the conference operator and give her the numbers you want to reach.

Messenger calls. Use a messenger call to reach someone who does not have a phone. The operator at the other end of the line will dispatch a messenger for the person you are trying to reach. You pay person-to-person rates for the call as well as paying the fee for the messenger whether or not the messenger has succeeded in locating the person you desired to reach.

28 GENERAL OFFICE PRACTICE

Appointment calls. An appointment call is simply a person-to-person call which you ask the operator to put through at a specified time. She will place the call at the exact time and will ring you when she has the other party on the line. Charges are the same as for a regular person-to-person call.

Mobile calls (air-land-sea). Use a mobile call to reach a ship, plane, automobile, or truck. Ask the operator to connect you to the mobile, marine, or high seas operator and give her the name and number of the party you are trying to reach.

International Direct Distance Dialing (IDDD). From certain locations in the U.S. you can dial international calls directly, without operator assistance. To dial international calls, dial in sequence:

  The international access code—011
  The Country code—a two or three digit number
  The City Routing code—a one to five digit number
  The local telephone number
  The "#" button (if you are dialing from a Touchtone phone)

For example, to call Frankfurt, Germany, you would dial:

011	+	49	+	611	+ 45 06 87 +	#
International Access Code		Country Code		Routing Code	Local Number	(on Touchtone phones only)

Following is a listing of the most frequently used Country and City Routing codes. More detailed listings are available from local phone company business offices.

Australia—country code 61		Austria—country code 43	
Adelaide	8	Bad Gastein	6434
Brisbane	72	Graz	3122
Canberra	62	Innsbruck	5222
Melbourne	3	Kitzbühel	5456
Perth	92	Linz, Donau	7222
Sydney	2	Salzburg	6222
		Vienna	222

Belgium—country code 32

Antwerp	31
Bruges	50
Brussels	2
Ghent	91
Liège	41
Louvain	16
Mons	65
Namur	81
Ostend	59

Brazil—country code 55

Belo Horizonte	31
Brasilia	612
Curitiba	412
Niterói	21
Recife	812
Rio de Janeiro	21
Salvador	712
Santos	132
São Paulo	11

Denmark—country code 45

Copenhagen	1 or 2

France—country code 33

Bordeaux	56
Cannes	93
Cherbourg	33
Le Havre	35
Lyons	78
Marseille	91
Nancy	28
Nice	93
Paris	1
Rouen	35
Toulouse	61

Germany, West—country code 49

Berlin	30
Bonn	2221
Cologne	221
Düsseldorf	211
Frankfurt	611
Hamburg	411
Heidelberg	6221
Munich	89
Stuttgart	711

Great Britain—country code 44

Belfast	232
Birmingham	21
Cardiff	222
Edinburgh	31
Glasgow	41
Liverpool	41
London	1
Manchester	61
Sheffield	742
Southampton	703

Greece—country code 30

Athens	21
Piraeus	21

Guatemala—country code 502

Guatemala City	61

Hong Kong—country code 852

Hong Kong	5
Kowloon	3

Ireland—country code 353

Cork	21
Dublin	1
Galway	91

GENERAL OFFICE PRACTICE

Israel—country code 952

Haifa	4
Jerusalem	2
Tel Aviv	3

Italy—country code 39

Bologna	51
Florence	55
Genoa	10
Milan	2
Naples	81
Rome	6
Trieste	40
Venice	41

Japan—country code 81

Kobe	78
Kyoto	75
Nagoya	52
Niigata	252
Osaka	6
Tokyo	3
Yokohama	45

Netherlands—country code 31

Amsterdam	20
Rotterdam	10
The Hague	70
Utrecht	30

Norway—country code 47

Bergen	5
Oslo	2

Philippines—country code 63

Manila	2

South Africa—country code 27

Cape Town	21
Durban	31
Johannesburg	11
Pretoria	12

Spain—country code 34

Barcelona	3
Cadiz	56
Granada	58
Madrid	1
Malaga	62
Seville	52
Torremolinos	52
Valencia	63

Sweden—country code 46

Göteborg	31
Malmo	40
Stockholm	8
Uppsala	18

Switzerland—country code 41

Baden	56
Basel	61
Berne	31
Geneva	22
Interlaken	36
Lausanne	21
Lucerne	41
Lugano	91
Zurich	1

Taiwan—country code 86

Taipei	2

Venezuela—country code 58

Caracas	2
Maracaibo	61

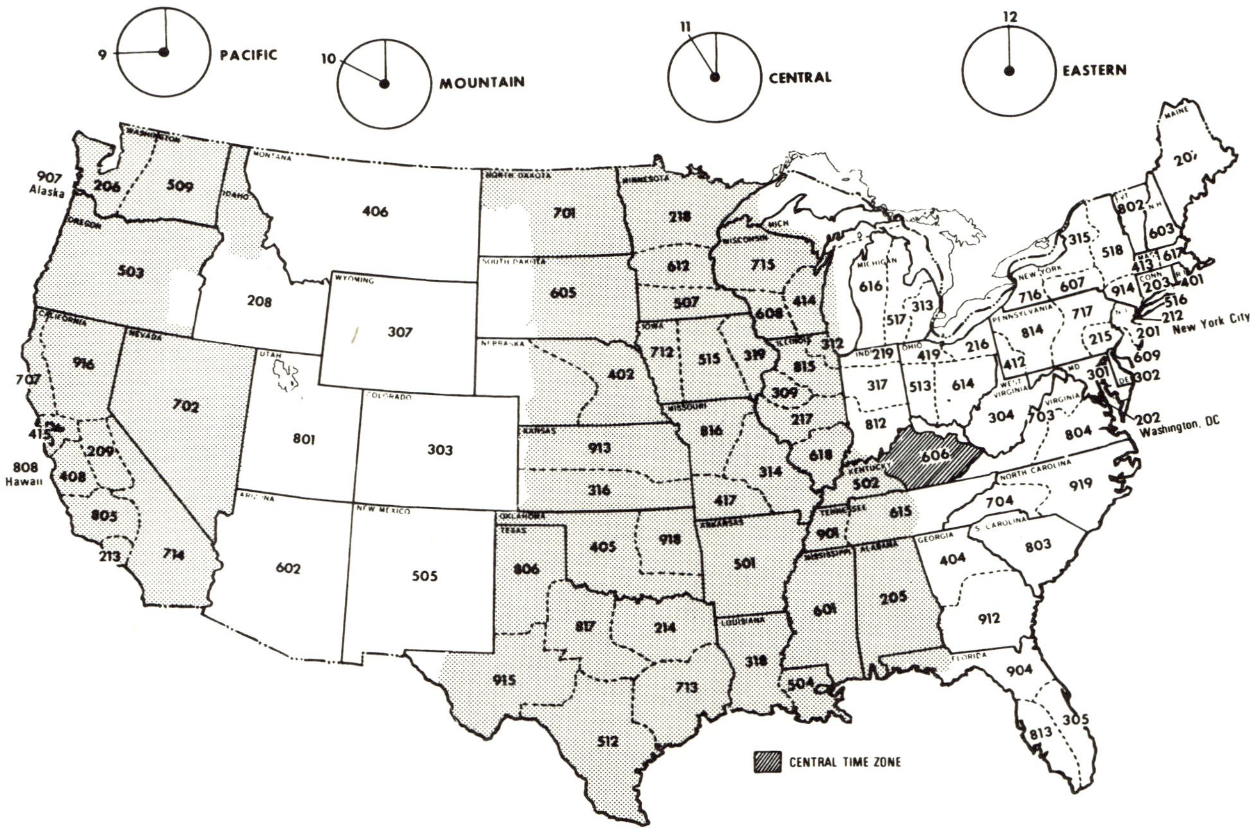

PACIFIC
9
MOUNTAIN
10
CENTRAL
11
EASTERN
12
907 Alaska
808 Hawaii
WASHINGTON
206
509
OREGON
503
CALIFORNIA
916
707
415
209
408
805
213
714
NEVADA
702
IDAHO
208
MONTANA
406
WYOMING
307
UTAH
801
ARIZONA
602
COLORADO
303
NEW MEXICO
505
NORTH DAKOTA
701
SOUTH DAKOTA
605
NEBRASKA
402
KANSAS
913
316
OKLAHOMA
405
918
TEXAS
806
817
214
915
713
512
MINNESOTA
218
612
507
IOWA
712
515
319
MISSOURI
816
314
417
ARKANSAS
501
LOUISIANA
318
504
WISCONSIN
715
414
608
ILLINOIS
312
815
309
217
618
MICH
MICHIGAN
616
517
313
IND
219
317
812
OHIO
419
216
513
614
KENTUCKY
502
606
TENNESSEE
901
615
MISSISSIPPI
601
ALABAMA
205
GEORGIA
404
912
FLORIDA
904
305
813
S CAROLINA
803
NORTH CAROLINA
704
919
VIRGINIA
703
804
WEST VIRGINIA
304
PENNSYLVANIA
814
717
412
215
NEW YORK
716
607
315
518
914
516
212
201 New York City
609
302
MD
301
DE
202 Washington, DC
VT
802
N H
603
MAINE
207
413
617
CONN
203
401
CENTRAL TIME ZONE

32 GENERAL OFFICE PRACTICE
Other Useful Telephone Numbers

Area codes

Area Codes Listed by Number

Area Code	State	Area Code	State	Area Code	State
201	New Jersey	403	Alberta, Canada	606	Kentucky
202	District of Columbia	404	Georgia	607	New York
203	Connecticut	405	Oklahoma	608	Wisconsin
204	Manitoba, Canada	406	Montana	609	New Jersey
205	Alabama	408	California	612	Minnesota
206	Washington	412	Pennsylvania	613	Ontario, Canada
207	Maine	413	Massachusetts	614	Ohio
208	Idaho	414	Wisconsin	615	Tennessee
209	California	415	California	616	Michigan
212	New York City	416	Ontario, Canada	617	Massachusetts
213	California	417	Missouri	618	Illinois
214	Texas	418	Quebec, Canada	701	North Dakota
215	Pennsylvania	419	Ohio	702	Nevada
216	Ohio	501	Arkansas	703	Virginia
217	Illinois	502	Kentucky	704	North Carolina
218	Minnesota	503	Oregon	705	Ontario, Canada
219	Indiana	504	Louisiana	707	California
301	Maryland	505	New Mexico	709	Newfoundland
302	Delaware	506	New Brunswick, Canada	712	Iowa
303	Colorado			713	Texas
304	West Virginia	507	Minnesota	714	California
		509	Washington	715	Wisconsin
305	Florida	512	Texas	716	New York
306	Saskatchewan, Canada	513	Ohio	717	Pennsylvania
		514	Quebec, Canada	801	Utah
307	Wyoming	515	Iowa	802	Vermont
308	Nebraska	516	New York	803	South Carolina
309	Illinois	517	Michigan	804	Virginia
312	Illinois			805	California
313	Michigan	518	New York	806	Texas
314	Missouri	519	Ontario, Canada	807	Ontario, Canada
315	New York			808	Hawaii
316	Kansas	601	Mississippi	809	Bahamas, Puerto Rico, Virgin Islands
317	Indiana	602	Arizona		
318	Louisiana	603	New Hampshire		
319	Iowa	604	British Columbia, Canada	812	Indiana
401	Rhode Island			813	Florida
402	Nebraska	605	South Dakota	814	Pennsylvania

The Telephone

815	Illinois	903	Mexico	914	New York
816	Missouri	904	Florida	915	Texas
817	Texas	906	Michigan	916	California
819	Quebec, Canada	907	Alaska	918	Oklahoma
901	Tennessee	912	Georgia	919	North Carolina
902	Nova Scotia	913	Kansas		

Area Codes Listed by State

UNITED STATES

State	Area Code	State	Area Code
Alabama	205	Minnesota	218, 507, 612
Alaska	907	Mississippi	601
Arizona	602	Missouri	314, 417, 816
Arkansas	501	Montana	406
Bahamas	809	Nebraska	308, 402
California	209, 213, 408, 415	Nevada	702
	707, 714, 805, 916,	New Hampshire	603
Canada	204, 306, 403, 416,	New Jersey	201, 609
	418, 506, 514, 519,	New Mexico	505
	604, 613, 705, 709,	New York	212, 315, 516, 518,
	807, 819, 902		607, 716, 914
Colorado	303	North Carolina	704, 919
Connecticut	203	North Dakota	701
Delaware	302	Ohio	216, 419, 513, 614
District of	202	Oklahoma	405, 918
Columbia	305, 813, 904	Oregon	503
Florida	404, 912	Pennsylvania	215, 412, 711, 814
Georgia	808	Rhode Island	401
Hawaii	208	South Carolina	803
Idaho	217, 309, 312,	South Dakota	605
Illinois	618, 815	Tennessee	615, 901
	219, 317, 812	Texas	214, 512, 713,
Indiana	319, 515, 712		806, 817, 915
Iowa	316, 913	Utah	801
Kansas	502, 606	Vermont	802
Kentucky	318, 504	Virginia	703, 804
Louisiana	207	Washington	206, 509
Maine	301	West Virginia	304
Maryland	413, 617	Wisconsin	414, 608, 715
Massachusetts	903	Wyoming	307
Mexico	313, 517, 616, 906		
Michigan			

34 GENERAL OFFICE PRACTICE

CANADA

Alberta	403
British Columbia	604
Manitoba	204
New Brunswick	506
Newfoundland	709
Nova Scotia	902
Ontario	416, 519, 613, 705, 807
Quebec	418, 514, 819
Saskatchewan	306

5. Telegraph and Other Long-Distance Communication

Domestic Service

Extent of domestic service. Telegrams sent by wire to any point in the continental United States, Canada, and Mexico are considered domestic telegrams. All others are considered overseas cablegrams.

Types of domestic telegrams:

Fast telegram. The fast telegram is also sometimes called a day letter or just plain telegram. It is the fastest service offered: the telegram usually reaches its destination within two hours after being filed with Western Union. A minimum rate is charged, with additional charges for each word in excess of 15. You are not charged for the address and signature.

Night letter. This is the least expensive message service. The night letter is delivered to its destination early the next morning. It may be filed with Western Union at any time up to 2 a.m. A minimum rate is charged, with additional charges for each group of five words in excess of 100. The cost of a 100-word night letter is less than that of a 15-word fast telegram.

Mailgram. The mailgram is cheaper than a fast telegram but more expensive than a night letter. It is delivered in the next mail after being received at its destination. The message may be telephoned in to Western Union, as with a telegram or night letter, or it may be dispatched from your own telex, TWX, computer, or tape.

DOMESTIC MESSAGES

Class	Type of service
Fast Telegram	Fast but expensive. Same-day delivery.
Night Letter	Inexpensive. Delivery next morning.
Mailgram	Delivered in next mail after receipt at post office.

How charges are determined. Word count is all-important in telegrams because you are charged for everything you write. The address and signature are free, but other words are counted as follows:

1. Abbreviations of less than five letters are counted as one word—FOB, USA, NYC, COD.
2. Initials are counted as separate words if they are separated by a space. Thus, T J is considered to be two words, but TJ is one word.
3. Personal names are counted according to the way they are normally written. Thus, McDonald is one word; Van Arsdale is two words.
4. Punctuation marks are not counted, but signs and symbols are counted—$, &, #, ", etc. Up to five characters is counted as one word. Thus, #567 is counted as one word; 600/NL is counted as two words (more than five characters); $99.50 is one word (the decimal point is not counted).

International Service

How to send an international telegram (cablegram). Phone your message in to Western Union. Western Union (which is a *domestic* operator only) will then route your telegram to its destination via one of the international carriers:

ITT World Communications, Inc.
RCA Global Communications, Inc.
Western Union International, Inc. (WUI)
French Telegraph Cable Company

If you want your telegram to go by any specific international carrier, you should instruct Western Union to that effect. If Western Union receives no instructions regarding routing, it will place your telegram into the "unrouted pool" and it will be transmitted by any of the international carriers according to a revolving system.

In certain cities, you can phone your international telegram directly to ITT, RCA, or WUI, without having to contact Western Union.

Types of international telegrams:

Full-rate message (FR). This is the fastest overseas service. A minimum rate is charged, with additional charges (depending on the destination) for each word in excess of seven.

Letter telegram (LT). This is also called an international night letter. The letter telegram is delivered to its destination the next morning. A minimum rate is charged, with additional charges (depending on the destination) for each word in excess of 22. Each word in a letter telegram is charged at half the rate of a word in a full-rate telegram.

Ship-to-Shore. Both full-rate messages and letter telegrams may be sent to and from ships at sea. They are sent in exactly the same way as messages to other foreign destinations.

How charges are determined.

1. There is a charge for both address and signature (unlike do-

38 GENERAL OFFICE PRACTICE

mestic telegrams). In the address, proper names and street names may be run together, up to 15 letters. Thus, RIO DE JANEIRO is counted as three words, while RIODEJANEIRO is counted as one. A run-together name with up to 15 letters counts as one word; up to 30 letters, as two words; etc. Since there is a charge for the signature, the signature is often omitted or signed with a short code name.
2. Punctuation marks are counted in the charges. Each punctuation mark counts as one word when used alone and as one letter when used with a group of letters. Punctuation marks will be omitted from the telegram unless you specifically request that they be included.
3. Abbreviations such as FOB and COD are counted as one word for every five characters.

Other Forms of Long-Distance Communication

Telex. Telex is a low-cost communication system that uses teletypewriters to send messages between terminals. You can send a message from your Telex teletypewriter to any other Telex teletypewriter, domestic or foreign. Telex service is available in manual or automatic; the automatic service uses perforated prepunched tape to send messages at a maximum speed of 66 words per minute. Telex can also be used for two-way written "conversations" to provide instant communication. Telex teletypewriters are automatically activated when an incoming message is signaled: the message is printed out automatically. Telex charges are calculated on the basis of distance and time used. There is no minimum charge. Telex equipment can also send messages to TWX equipment by means of a computer interface. Telex teletypewriters can be leased through Western Union or purchased from Western Union, ITT, RCA, or any of the other telex communication companies.

TWX. Pronounced Twix, TWX is a companion service to Telex. TWX is faster than Telex (up to 100 words per minute), and TWX charges are based on a one-minute minimum. If you are trying to decide between a TWX system and a Telex system, consult a Western Union, ITT, or RCA representative; they will help you

Telegraph and Other Long-Distance Communication 39

determine which system will more economically fulfill your needs.

INFOCOM. This is a private domestic system that may in some instances be more economical than Telex or TWX. Members of the INFOCOM system may send and receive telegrams and exchange messages with Telex and TWX teletypewriters.

Datagram. This is a special voice answering service: call in your message by telephone and Datagram will transmit it to its destination via TWX or Telex. Datagram is very useful for salespeople who are frequently on the road.

Telepost. Telepost is a Western Union service that stores frequently used letters and addresses in a computer. When activated, Telepost will send these letters automatically via Mailgram (within the United States) or by cablegram (overseas). Next-morning delivery is guaranteed.

International leased channels. Private telegraph channels between two points can be leased from international carriers like ITT or RCA. A leased channel is useful when there is a large volume of data to transmit, as between the home office of a company and a branch office. These private channels are leased by the day or by the month; the charges remain the same no matter how much data is transmitted over the channel. Leased channels are available in speed ranging from 16½ words per minute to 100 words per minute.

Standard Time Overseas by Country

Add or subtract from Eastern Standard Time as follows:

	E.S.T.		
Afghanistan	+9½	Aruba	+½
Albania	+6	Australia	+15(1)*
Algeria	+6	Austria	+6
Argentina	+2	Azores	+3

40 GENERAL OFFICE PRACTICE

Bahrain	+8	Libya	+7
Belgium	+6	Luxembourg	+6
Bermuda	+1	Malaysia	+12½
Bolivia	+1	Mexico	−1
Brazil	+2(2)*	Morocco	+5
Bulgaria	+7	Netherlands	+6
Burma	+11½	Netherlands Antilles	+½
Canal Zone	0	New Zealand	+17
Chile	+1	Nicaragua	−1
China	+13	Norway	+6
Colombia	0	Pakistan	+10
Costa Rica	−1	Panama	0
Cuba	0	Paraguay	+1
Curacao	+½	Peru	0
Czechoslovakia	+6	Philippines	+13
Denmark	+6	Poland	+6
Dominican Republic	0	Portugal	+5
Ecuador	0	Puerto Rico	+1
Egypt	+7	Rhodesia	+7
Ethiopia	+8	Romania	+7
Finland	+7	Salvador (El)	−1
France	+6	Saudi Arabia	+8
Germany	+6	Singapore	+12½
Ghana	+5	South Africa	+7
Great Britain	+5	Spain	+6
Greece	+7	Sri Lanka	+10½
Guatemala	−1	Surinam	+1½
Haiti	0	Sweden	+6
Hawaii	−5	Switzerland	+6
Hong Kong	+13	Syria	+7
Hungary	+6	Taiwan	+13
Iceland	+4	Thailand	+12
India	+10½	Tunisia	+6
Iran	+8½	Turkey	+7
Iraq	+8	USSR (Moscow)	+8
Ireland	+5	Uruguay	+2
Israel	+7	Venezuela	+½
Italy	+6	Vietnam	+12
Japan	+14	Virgin Islands	+1
Korea	+13½	Yugoslavia	+6
Lebanon	+7	Zaire	+6

(1)*Except Perth +13
(2)* Except Brasilia +1

Telegraph and Other Long-Distance Communication

Time zones of selected foreign cities

At 12 noon Eastern Standard Time, the standard time in foreign cities is as follows:

City	Time	City	Time
Alexandria	7 p.m.	London	5 p.m.
Amsterdam	6 p.m.	Madrid	6 p.m.
Athens	7 p.m.	Manila	1 a.m.*
Auckland	5 a.m.*	Marseille	6 p.m.
Baghdad	8 p.m.	Melbourne	3 a.m.*
Bangkok	12 midnight	Mexico City	11 a.m.
Barcelona	6 p.m.	Milan	6 p.m.
Beirut	7 p.m.	Montevideo	2 p.m.
Belfast	5 p.m.	Montreal	12 noon
Berlin	6 p.m.	Moscow	8 p.m.
Bogota	12 noon	Munich	6 p.m.
Bombay	10:30 p.m.	New Delhi	10:30 p.m.
Bonn	6 p.m.	Oslo	6 p.m.
Bremen	6 p.m.	Paris	6 p.m.
Brussels	6 p.m.	Rio de Janeiro	2 p.m.
Bucharest	7 p.m.	Rome	6 p.m.
Budapest	7 p.m.	Rotterdam	6 p.m.
Buenos Aires	1 p.m.	Santiago	1 p.m.
Cairo	7 p.m.	São Paulo	2 p.m.
Calcutta	10:30 p.m.	Seoul	2 a.m.*
Cape Town	7 p.m.	Shanghai	1 a.m.*
Caracas	1 p.m.	Singapore	12:30 a.m.*
Casablanca	5 p.m.	Stockholm	6 p.m.
Copenhagen	6 p.m.	Sydney	3 a.m.*
Danzig	6 p.m.	Taipei	1 a.m.*
Djakarta	12 midnight	Teheran	8:30 p.m.
Dublin	5 p.m.	Tel Aviv	7 p.m.
Düsseldorf	6 p.m.	Tokyo	2 a.m.*
Frankfurt	6 p.m.	Valparaiso	1 p.m.
Geneva	6 p.m.	Vancouver	9 a.m.
Halifax	1 p.m.	Vienna	6 p.m.
Havana	12 noon	Warsaw	6 p.m.
Hong Kong	1 a.m.*	Yokohama	2 a.m.*
Istanbul	7 p.m.	Zurich	6 p.m.
Jerusalem	7 p.m.		
Johannesburg	7 p.m.		
Le Havre	6 p.m.		
Leningrad	8 p.m.		
Lima	12 noon		
Lisbon	6 p.m.		
Liverpool	5 p.m.		

6. Mail and Postal Information

Incoming Mail

Letters marked PERSONAL or CONFIDENTIAL. PERSONAL means that the letter is for the attention of the addressee only. CONFIDENTIAL means that it is for the attention of the addressee and other authorized people only. You will often see the notation PERSONAL AND CONFIDENTIAL, although, strictly speaking, this is a contradiction in terms: a letter may be personal or confidential but not both.

You will have to work out an agreement with your employer concerning the opening of letters marked PERSONAL or CONFIDENTIAL. Some employers routinely expect their secretaries to open letters so marked, but this practice is to be discouraged. In the first place, it may openly violate the wishes of the letter writer: if he or she marked the letter PERSONAL, he or she presumably had a good reason for doing so. Secondly, it may expose the secretary to material or information that the secretary would prefer to avoid: classified information that the secretary for his or her own good should not know, personal information that the secretary may find embarrassing, etc.

Annotating the mail. It may often be convenient for the employer if the secretary annotates the mail. That is, the secretary indicates the key points of the letter by underlining them or otherwise flagging them. This is especially useful in the case of lengthy letters, when annotated letters can save the employer much time.

A useful trick in annotating mail (or other material) is to use a yellow felt marking pen for the annotations or underlinings. Yellow pens do not leave marks that will show if the letter is photocopied.

Letters that require attention by others. Some letters may require the attention of other persons in addition to the addressee. Printed forms are useful for this purpose; attach them to the letter and send to the indicated person. The "action requested" form indicates the action to be taken, and the "routing" slip indicates which person or persons are to see the letter.

Handling mail when the employer is away.

1. Acknowledge all correspondence if the manager is to be away for more than five days or a week.
2. Telephone or wire the employer about urgent letters that require his or her immediate attention.
3. If you forward mail to your employer while he or she is away, copy the letters and forward the copies. This is safer than sending the originals through the mail.
4. If you are forwarding material to your employer, number consecutively the packets of mail that you send. The employer will then know whether he or she has received all the packets which you have sent. This practice is especially important when the employer is traveling from place to place.

Outgoing Mail

Addressing Letters. Your mail will be delivered faster if it is addressed in accordance with post office standards. Automated post office mail-sorting equipment processes all mail. If your mail is addressed in a format that is not compatible with the processing machine, then your mail must be processed by hand, thus delaying its delivery.

44 GENERAL OFFICE PRACTICE

The address format preferred by the post office is not the traditional one. If you or your employer find this disturbing, use the traditional address format on the letter itself, but use the approved post office format on the envelope.

The following rules of addressing are those approved by the Postal Service:

(1) All addresses should be typewritten, not handwritten.

(2) If a station name is included along with a post office box number, the station name may either be on the same line as the box number or on the line below it.

(3) Rural route box numbers should be on the same line as the rural route number.

(4) The number of an apartment, room, or suite should preferably be included on the same line as the street address. If there is not enough room on this line, it should be placed on the line immediately above the street address.

(5) Use numerals rather than letters to designate streets whose names are numbers, e.g., "5th Avenue" rather than "Fifth Avenue."

(6) Use abbreviations that will shorten addresses, such as "St.," "Ave.," or "Apt." The post office has published a list of approved abbreviations for street names and other words commonly found in addresses. (See pp. 45–47.)

(7) Use the proper zip code abbreviations for all states and Canadian provinces. (See list, page 45.)

(8) Use no punctuation (no periods and no commas) in the last line of the address.

(9) If possible, limit the last line of the address to 22 positions—13 for the city name, 2 for the state abbreviation, and 5 for the zip code (plus two spaces). The post office has prepared a list of 13-letter abbreviations for cities with long names; this listing is available from the U.S. Postal Service, Washington, D.C. 20260.

Mail and Postal Information 45

U.S. Zip Code Abbreviations

Alabama	AL	Montana	MT
Alaska	AK	Nebraska	NE
Arizona	AZ	Nevada	NV
Arkansas	AR	New Hampshire	NH
California	CA	New Jersey	NJ
Canal Zone	CZ	New Mexico	NM
Colorado	CO	New York	NY
Connecticut	CT	North Carolina	NC
Delaware	DE	North Dakota	ND
District of Columbia	DC	Ohio	OH
Florida	FL	Oklahoma	OK
Georgia	GA	Oregon	OR
Guam	GU	Pennsylvania	PA
Hawaii	HI	Puerto Rico	PR
Idaho	ID	Rhode Island	RI
Illinois	IL	South Carolina	SC
Indiana	IN	South Dakota	SD
Iowa	IA	Tennessee	TN
Kansas	KS	Texas	TX
Kentucky	KY	Trust Territories	TT
Louisiana	LA	Utah	UT
Maine	ME	Vermont	VT
Maryland	MD	Virginia	VA
Massachusetts	MA	Virgin Islands	VI
Michigan	MI	Washington	WA
Minnesota	MN	West Virginia	WV
Mississippi	MS	Wisconsin	WI
Missouri	MO	Wyoming	WY

Canadian Zip Code Abbreviations

Alberta	AB	Nova Scotia	NS
British Columbia	BC	Ontario	ON
Labrador	LB	Prince Edward Island	PE
Manitoba	MB	Quebec	PQ
New Brunswick	NB	Saskatchewan	SK
Newfoundland	NF	Yukon Territory	YT
Northwest Territories	NT		

Official Postal Abbreviations

Academy	ACAD	Annex	ANX
Agency	AGNCY	Arcade	ARC
Airport	ARPRT	Arsenal	ARSL
Alley	ALY	Avenue	AVE

46 GENERAL OFFICE PRACTICE

Bayou	BYU	Ferry	FRY
Beach	BCH	Field	FLD
Bend	BND	Fields	FLDS
Big	BG	Flats	FLT
Black	BLK	Ford	FRD
Bluff	BLF	Forest	FRST
Bottom	BTM	Forge	FRG
Boulevard	BLVD	Fork	FRK
Branch	BR	Forks	FRKS
Bridge	BRG	Fort	FT
Brook	BRK	Fountain	FTN
Burg	BG	Freeway	FWY
Bypass	BYP	Furnace	FURN
Camp	CP	Gardens	GDNS
Canyon	CYN	Gateway	GTWY
Cape	CPE	Glen	GLN
Causeway	CWSY	Grand	GRND
Center	CTR	Great	GR
Central	CTL	Green	GRN
Church	CHR	Ground	GRD
Churches	CHRS	Grove	GRV
Circle	CIR	Harbor	HBR
City	CY	Haven	HVN
Clear	CLR	Heights	HTS
Cliffs	CLFS	High	HI
Club	CLB	Highlands	HGLDS
College	CLG	Highway	HWY
Corner	COR	Hill	HL
Corners	CORS	Hills	HLS
Court	CT	Hollow	HOLW
Courts	CTS	Hospital	HOSP
Cove	CV	Hot	H
Creek	CRK	House	HSE
Crescent	CRES	Inlet	INLT
Crossing	XING	Institute	INST
Dale	DL	Island	IS
Dam	DM	Islands	IS
Depot	DPO	Isle	IS
Divide	DIV	Junction	JCT
Drive	DR	Key	KY
East	E	Knolls	KNLS
Estates	EST	Lake	LK
Expressway	EXPY	Lakes	LKS
Extended	EXT	Landing	LNDG
Extension	EXT	Lane	LN
Fall	FL	Light	LGT
Falls	FLS	Little	LTL
Farms	FRMS	Loaf	LF

Mail and Postal Information 47

Locks	LCKS	Santo	SN
Lodge	LDG	School	SCH
Lower	LWR	Seminary	SMNRY
Manor	MNR	Shoal	SHL
Meadows	MDWS	Shoals	SHLS
Meeting	MTG	Shode	SHD
Memorial	MEM	Shore	SHR
Middle	MDL	Shores	SHRS
Mile	MLE	Siding	SDG
Mill	ML	South	S
Mills	MLS	Space Flight Center	SFC
Mines	MNS	Spring	SPG
Mission	MSN	Springs	SPGS
Mound	MND	Square	SQ
Mount	MT	State	ST
Mountain	MTN	Station	STA
National	NAT	Stream	STRM
Neck	NCK	Street	ST
New	NW	Sulphur	SLPHR
North	N	Summit	SMT
Orchard	ORCH	Switch	SWCH
Palms	PLMS	Tannery	TNRY
Park	PK	Tavern	TVRN
Parkway	PKY	Terminal	TERM
Pillar	PLR	Terrace	TER
Pines	PNES	Ton	TN
Place	PL	Tower	TWR
Plain	PLN	Town	TWN
Plains	PLNS	Trail	TRL
Plaza	PLZ	Trailer	TRLR
Point	PT	Tunnel	TUNL
Port	PRT	Turnpike	TPKE
Prairie	PR	Union	UN
Ranch	RNCH	University	UNIV
Ranches	RNCHS	Upper	UPR
Rapids	RPDS	Valley	VLY
Resort	RESRT	Viaduct	VIA
Rest	RST	View	VW
Ridge	RDG	Village	VLG
River	RIV	Ville	VL
Road	RD	Vista	VIS
Rock	RK	Water	WTR
Rural	R	Wells	WLS
Saint	ST	West	W
Sainte	ST	White	WHT
San	SN	Works	WKS
Santa	SN	Yards	YDS

48 GENERAL OFFICE PRACTICE

Examples of acceptable address formats for envelopes:

Mr. Harold E. Brown
121 Highland Ave.
Middletown NY 11343

Mr. & Mrs. Arthur Jonas
R.R. 3 Box 87
Wheeling WV 33675

Mrs. M. F. James
Box 302
Casper WY 78206

Fourth National Bank
265 E. 66th St.
Coral Gables FL 23905

Smith, Wells Associates
P.O. Box 4423
Grand Central Station
New York NY 10017

M. Cartwright
Suite 1302
1170 Avenue of the Americas
New York NY 10019

Mr. Alfred P. Jones
Box 32 Main St. Station
Peoria IL 52321

Miss Katharine Smith
260 75th Ave. Apt. 32
Cincinnati OH 45202

If you include both a post office box number and a street address in the printed address on the envelope, be aware that the letter will be delivered to the address on the *lower* line.

	Wheeler Printing, Inc.
	P.O. Box 123
Mail will be delivered here	1222 Montgomery St.
	Detroit MI 48227
	Wheeler Printing, Inc.
	1222 Montgomery St.
Mail will be delivered here	P.O. Box 123
	Detroit MI 48230

Note that the zip code must correspond to the address where you actually wish the letter to be delivered.

Domestic Mail

Sources of Information. In any office that does not have a mail room, the secretary is responsible for the handling of all outgoing

Mail and Postal Information 49

mail. Since postal rates and regulations change frequently, the secretary should always have on hand up-to-date mailing information from the post office. Domestic postage rates may be found in Notice 59, Poster 73, or Poster 103, all available free from the local postmaster or post office customer-service representative. International postage rates are available in Publication 51, which is also free.

More detailed information may be found in several other Postal Service publications, all available from the Superintendent of Documents, Government Printing Office, Washington, D.C. 20402. There is a charge for these publications.

The *Postal Service Manual* offers exhaustive information on all phases of post office services, rates, and regulations and procedures relating to post office personnel, transport, and facilities.

Chapter 1 of the *Postal Service Manual* is available separately. It pertains specifically to domestic mailing rates and services; in many cases, it provides all the information that the secretary will need and is usually a better value than the complete manual. Chapter 1 contains complete sections on: first/class mail; second/class mail; third/class mail; fourth/class mail; air mail and priority mail; postage meters; permit imprints; registered mail; insured mail; collect on delivery (C.O.D.); certificates of mailing, return receipts, and restricted delivery; special delivery; special handling; certified mail; and post office lockboxes.

The *Postal Bulletin* provides information on all current and proposed changes in post office rates and services. It is useful mainly for mailers who require advance information regarding any changes that the post office is planning.

International Mail (Publication 42) contains complete information on overseas mail, including rates and fees, services available, prohibitions and regulations, import restrictions, customs requirements, and all other conditions governing international mail.

The *Directory of Post Offices* lists all post offices in the United States, arranged alphabetically by state.

The *Zip Code Directory* gives zip codes for all locales in the United States.

Classes of mail. There are four classes of mail. First-class mail consists of regular letters and correspondence, as well as certain

50 GENERAL OFFICE PRACTICE

other types of sealed material. Second-class mail, also called publication mail, consists of newspapers and periodicals. Third-class, sometimes called advertising mail, relates to most kinds of printed material such as circulars, form letters, catalogs, and advertisements. Fourth-class mail, or parcel post, consists of packages or other material weighing in excess of 16 ounces.

Special services are available from the post office on certain types of mail; these include registered mail, certified mail, special delivery, and insured mail.

These classes and special services are each considered individually in the following section.

How to mail specific items. Certain types of mail are best sent by one particular class. The following list gives the safest and/or most economical way to send these items. Many third- and fourth-class items *may* be sent first class, but the expense will be much higher; only in cases where relatively speedy delivery is required should third- and fourth-class material be sent first class.

Type of Item	*Mailing Class*
Advertisements	Third class

(Many different rates apply to advertisements, particularly to bulk mailings. Consult the post office for particulars.)

Bills	First class
Bonds	
Negotiable	Registered first class
Non-negotiable	First class or Certified
Booklets	Third class
Books	Fourth class

(Special rates apply to books. The package should be marked "Special Fourth-Class Rate—Books.")

Catalogs	Third or Fourth class

(Various postal rates apply to catalogs, depending on size and weight. Consult the post office for particulars.)

Mail and Postal Information 51

Checks	
Endorsed and filled out	First class
Endorsed in blank	Registered first class
Canceled	First class
Certified	Registered first class
Circulars	Third class
Currency	Registered first class
Documents	
Valuable signed originals	Registered first class
Originals without intrinsic value	Certified
Copies	First class
Films	Fourth class

(Special rates apply to films of 16 mm and lesser widths. The package should be marked "Special Fourth-Class Rate—Film.")

Form letters (see also Advertisements)	Third class
Jewels or jewelry	Registered first class
Journals	Second class
Keys	Third class
Magazines	Second class
Manuscripts	Fourth class

(Special rates apply to manuscripts. The package should be marked: "Special Fourth-Class Rate—Manuscript.")

Merchandise, Small	Third class (fourth class if over 16 ounces)
Money	Registered first class
Money Orders	First class
Newspapers	Second class
Packages	
Up to 16 ounces	Third class
Over 16 ounces	Fourth class
Periodicals	Second class
Photographs	Third class (fourth class if over 16 ounces)

(The envelope should be stiffened with cardboard and marked "Photograph—Do Not Bend.")

52 GENERAL OFFICE PRACTICE

Plants and bulbs	Third class (fourth class if over 16 ounces)
Postcards	First class
Price lists	Third class
Printed matter, Miscellaneous	Third class (fourth class if over 16 ounces)
Samples of merchandise	Third class (fourth class if over 16 ounces)
Sheet music	Fourth class

(Special rates apply to printed sheet music. The package should be marked "Special Fourth-Class Rate—Printed Music.")

Stock certificates	
Negotiable	Registered first class
Non-negotiable	First class or Certified
Subscription offers	Third class
Tapes and casettes	Fourth class

(Special rates apply to commercial tape recordings. Mark the package "Special Fourth-Class Rate—Sound Recording.")

First-class mail. All ordinary personal and business correspondence falls into the category of first-class mail. All first-class mail should be sealed, and any oversize or odd-shaped envelopes should be clearly marked "First Class."

It is unnecessary to mark "Air Mail" on a first-class letter if you wish it to travel by air. As of 1976, all first-class mail automatically is sent by air mail; no additional postage is required.

All sealed matter is assumed by the post office to be first-class material unless otherwise indicated on the envelope. If you wish to send a particular item third class or fourth class, make sure you mark it appropriately; otherwise you will be charged the first-class rate.

Second-class mail (publication mail). Second-class mail consists of newspapers and magazines. Bulk rates are available to publishers; rates vary with weight, frequency of publication, amount of advertising contained in the publication, and distance mailed.

Individual copies of newspapers or magazines may also be sent at second-class rates by the general public. To do so, put the newspaper or magazine in a tight-fitting envelope and slit both ends; the envelope must not be sealed. Mark "Second-Class Matter" above the address. Letters cannot be included with the newspaper or periodical unless first-class postage is paid on the letter.

Note also that the *entire* publication must be mailed. Single sections or torn-out articles do not qualify for second-class rates. They are treated as "Printed Matter" and must be sent third class (which rates are somewhat *higher* than the comparable second-class rates).

Third-class mail (advertising mail). Third class is used for most circulars, form letters, and other advertisements. Only printed matter is acceptable; personal or business letters—even stationery—are not acceptable.

Third-class mail has a weight limit of 16 ounces. Above 16 ounces, the same material automatically becomes fourth class.

Third-class mail may be inspected by the post office. It is permissible to seal the envelope, provided that it is clearly labeled "Third Class." It is also advisable to indicate the contents on the face of the wrapper, such as "Printed Matter" or "Advertisement."

There are two subcategories of third-class mail: single-piece rate and bulk rate. The bulk rate requires a post office permit and is applicable to mailings of at least 200 pieces and not less than 50 pounds. Bulk rate mail must be presorted and bundled by the mailer.

Fourth-class mail (parcel post). All parcels or packages that weigh 16 ounces or more are sent fourth class. (Packages of less than 16 ounces must go third class.)

Various weight and size limitations apply to fourth class, depending on the package's destination. Generally, parcels up to 70 pounds may be mailed anywhere in the United States. Such parcels should not exceed 100 inches in girth and length combined (girth is defined as a parcel's circumference at its thickest point). As an example, a package 24 inches long, 12 inches wide, and 10 inches thick has a combined length and girth of 68 inches (24 + 12 + 12 + 10 + 10).

Letters may not be included in packages mailed parcel post unless first-class postage is paid on the letter itself. In this case, the package should be marked above the address "First-Class Mail Enclosed." Invoices and copies of customer orders may be included in fourth-class parcels without paying additional rates.

Parcels inevitably receive rough treatment in the mails; they should be packed carefully to protect the contents (see p. 64). Additional insurance against rough handling may be obtained by using Special Handling (see p. 57).

Fourth-class mail is sent by ground transportation. For faster delivery of these items, they may be sent by priority mail or Express Mail.

Special fourth-class mail. Various items qualify for special rates in the fourth-class category. These include: books, tape recordings, films (only up to 16 mm), printed music, test materials, scripts of plays, manuscripts, material for the blind, and printed medical information. Mark each such parcel "Special Fourth-Class Rate" and list the enclosed material, such as "Books" or "Sheet Music."

Priority mail. Priority mail is an air-mail service for heavy items. All first-class mail over 13 ounces is classified as priority mail; and any other class or item of mail weighing over 9 ounces may be sent by priority mail if the proper rates are paid. (Second-, third-, and fourth-class mail does not normally go via air transport. Priority mail is the way to send such items by air mail.)

The same weight and size limits that govern fourth-class mail (parcel post) also apply to priority mail.

Express Mail. Express Mail guarantees overnight delivery of letters or parcels to most cities in the United States. It is used for fast and reliable delivery of important documents and objects. Mail deposited by 5 P.M. at a designated post office is guaranteed by the Postal Service to be ready for pickup by the addressee at the destination post office at 10 A.M. on the next business day. An alternative arrangement is to have the post office deliver the item to the addressee; in this case, the Postal Service guarantees delivery by 3 P.M. on the day after mailing.

The Postal Service has established a 95 percent reliability record on Express Mail service. If a shipment is late for any reason, postage is refunded to the mailer.

Large mailers can arrange specially tailored Express Mail

service agreements with the Postal Service. Such service options include: door-to-door pickup and delivery; door-to-destination airport delivery; delivery from originating airport to addressee's home or office address; and airport-to-airport delivery.

International Express Mail offers fast delivery to overseas countries. It is currently available to Great Britain, Australia, Hong Kong, and the Netherlands. Programmed Express Mail service contracts also offer deliveries to several additional European countries.

A complete list of Express Mail post offices in the United States is found in the Zip Code Directory. Further information on various types of Express Mail may be obtained in these post office publications:

Publication 163—*Express Mail Programmed Service*
Publication 45—*International Express Mail Service*
Notice 43—*Express Mail, Regular Service*

Registered mail. Registered mail is the safest way to send valuable items such as jewelry, original documents, stock and bond certificates. It is a high-security service that includes proof of mailing and proof of delivery. This service is available on all first-class and priority-mail items. Registered mail is carried under lock by the Postal Service and is segregated from other mail.

If a registered letter is lost or damaged in transit, the post office will indemnify the sender for up to $10,000. If a registered letter is lost, report it as soon as possible at the nearest post office. Your employer's signature will probably be necessary on the postal claim forms.

Registered mail should be mailed directly from the post office; do not deposit registered letters in mailboxes.

Whenever you send a letter by registered mail, be sure to write the name of the recipient on the receipt given to you by the post office; this will enable you to identify that particular receipt at a later date.

Several additional services are available to users of registered mail. A return receipt showing delivery details may be requested in cases where the sender wants positive proof of delivery; in this case, the post office will stamp the letter "Registered, Return Receipt Requested." Restricted delivery service is also available for senders who want to ensure that a registered letter is delivered to one particular person and to no other; in this case, the letter is marked "Registered, Deliver to Addressee Only." Additional fees over and above the regular fee for registered mail are charged for these services.

Certified mail. Certified mail provides proof of mailing and delivery. Unlike registered mail, however, it does *not* provide indemnity in case of loss or damage. Use certified mail only when the item you are mailing does not have monetary value in itself. Certification is available on all first-class and priority mail.

A special return receipt showing delivery information may be requested for an additional fee. Restricted delivery service is also available at an extra charge; use this service when the letter should be delivered directly into the hands of the addressee.

The sender of a certified letter receives a receipt stating that the letter was mailed, and the post office at the destination keeps a record of delivery. In addition, the carrier receives a signature from the addressee at the point of destination; this signature is kept on file at the post office for two years.

Certificate of mailing. The post office will provide a certificate of mailing in cases when the sender needs proof that a particular item was mailed. The certificate does not provide indemnity if the item is lost, nor does it provide evidence of delivery. The post office does not keep records of such certificates.

Insured mail. Insurance protection of up to $200 may be obtained on all third- and fourth-class mail. Insurance is not available on first- and second-class material; for these items, use registered mail. Insurance is, however, available on priority mail (air parcel post).

The fee charged by the post office for insurance on a particular item depends on the declared value of the material being mailed. Even if the item is worth more than $200, the post office will not indemnify the sender for more than this amount if the item is lost or damaged.

Insurance must be obtained at a post office; do not deposit such mail in a mailbox.

A return receipt is available for an additional fee; this provides the sender with proof of delivery. Restricted delivery service is also available when the item must be delivered to the addressee in person.

Special delivery. Special-delivery mail is given preferential treatment in processing and handling by the Postal Service. The destination post office delivers such mail even on Sundays and holidays.

Special delivery ensures that a letter will be delivered to the addressee on the day it arrives at the post office of destination; the letter is delivered by a special-delivery messenger. This service, however, does not speed delivery between the post office of origin and the post office of destination; it merely ensures prompt delivery once the letter is received at the destination post office. If a particular letter must reach an addressee within a very short period of time, it is safer to use Express Mail rather than special delivery.

Special delivery is available on all classes of mail. Certain post offices are not equipped to handle special delivery mail. Before sending a letter by special delivery, make sure that the originating post office and the destination post office both offer special-delivery service.

Special-delivery fees vary according to the class of mail being posted and the weight of the item.

Special-delivery mail may be deposited in mailboxes, but quicker service is obtained by posting it directly at a post office. Special-delivery sticker labels are available free from the post office and should be affixed to all special-delivery mail.

Special handling. Special handling is available on all third- and fourth-class mail. It entitles such material to the same handling as that given to first-class material. Unlike special delivery, however, it does not ensure immediate delivery at the post office of destination.

C.O.D. An article sent C.O.D. (collect on delivery) is paid for by the addressee. The post office collects this price and remits it to the sender in the form of a postal money order.

All first-, third-, and fourth-class mail may be sent C.O.D. Registered mail and priority mail may also be sent C.O.D. Special delivery and special handling are both available on C.O.D. mail.

The maximum amount collectible by the post office on any one C.O.D. item is $300. The sender must guarantee return postage and forwarding, in case such handling is needed.

C.O.D. fees are based upon a graduated scale depending on the amount to be collected from the addressee. The fee also includes indemnity up to $300 if the article is lost or damaged by the post office in transit. For an additional fee, the post office will also notify the sender of non-delivery of articles.

Mailgram. A mailgram is a special letter-telegram that ensures overnight delivery of messages virtually anywhere in the United States. It is a mail-via-satellite service offered jointly by the U.S. Postal Service and Western Union. The message is sent by Western Union to the destination post office, where it is placed in a special mailgram envelope and delivered to the addressee on the next business day.

Mailgrams are less expensive than telegrams. Mailgram rates are based on 100-word units in the message to be transmitted. In addition, special rates are available to high-volume users who have access to Western Union's terminals via their own TWX terminals, Telex terminals, or computers.

Because of time zone differences, send mailgrams before 7 P.M. (*destination* time) to ensure next-day delivery.

Prohibited items. In general, any articles that may cause injury to postal workers or in any way damage the mail are prohibited in domestic and international mail. Severe penalties may result from mailing such materials.

Prohibited articles include: explosives; flammable, corrosive, or toxic materials; radioactive substances; intoxicating liquors; poisons (except those specifically for scientific use); small firearms and loaded guns; and foul-smelling items.

Meat and meat products cannot be sent through the mail without a certificate of inspection. Plants and plant products must in certain cases be accompanied by special certificates.

Convenient Services Available from the Post Office

Money Orders. Postal money orders are a safe way to send money through the mail. They are available in amounts up to $300 and may be redeemed by the addressee at all post offices and at many banks, stores, and businesses. Money orders are insured by the Postal Service; if they are lost or stolen, the Postal Service will replace them.

Stamps by mail. At certain post offices, stamps may be ordered by mail. Order blanks are available at the post office; orders for stamps are mailed postage-free by the sender, and the stamps are returned through the mail. A small fee is charged for handling. This service makes it possible to avoid time-consuming trips to the post office.

Self-service postal centers. Customer-operated vending and mailing equipment is located at certain post offices and shopping centers. These centers provide 24-hour-a-day, 7-day-a-week mailing services for both letters and parcels. In addition, they dispense stamps (either individually or by the book), postcards, envelopes, and parcel insurance. All items are sold at face value; no additional fees are charged.

On-site meter setting. For a small fee, the post office will send a representative to your place of business to set your postage meter. This service is usually offered on a regularly scheduled basis, by agreement with the post office. This service eliminates time-consuming trips to the post office; it also ensures that the postage meter will always be available for use, with sufficient postage.

International Mail

Rates and regulations on international mail change constantly. For up-to-date information, obtain a copy of Publication 51, *International Postage Rates and Fees*. It is available free from the post office. More exhaustive information is included in Publication 42, *International Mail*, available for a fee from the Superintendent of Documents, Government Printing Office, Washington, D.C. 20402.

Addressing international mail. The complete address should be printed *in English* on all foreign correspondence. Capitalize the name of the foreign country to which the letter is going, and place it alone on the bottom line of the address block. When the letter is being sent to a foreign country in which a different alphabet is used (as Saudi Arabia or the U.S.S.R.), it is desirable also to include the address written in the proper characters of the particular language.

Stamps for international mail. Use regular-denomination U.S. stamps or metered mail for overseas correspondence. Note that air-mail stamps may be used only on articles being delivered by air; and special stamps are good only toward payment of the special delivery fee, not toward regular postage.

Labeling. All air-mail articles must be marked "Air Mail" or have an air mail sticker affixed. In addition, if the letter or parcel is going to a non-English-speaking country, the item should also be marked "Par Avion."

Articles and letters being delivered by special delivery should be marked both "Special Delivery" and "Exprès" or should have an international "Exprès" sticker affixed.

Classes of International Mail

Letters and letter packages. All personal letters, as well as typewritten business correspondence, is classified in this category; typewritten letters may not be sent by the cheaper "Printed Matter" rate. Packets of correspondence of up to four pounds are termed "letter packages" and also qualify for this category.

If the letter or letter package is bulky and might be confused with parcel post (see below), mark the words "Letter (lettre)" clearly on the letter or letter package.

Small items of dutiable merchandise may be sent in letter packages, provided that such items are accepted for importation in the country of destination. Certain countries accept *no* merchandise mailed in letter packages. Before mailing any merchandise, consult the post office or check Publication 42 *(International Mail)* to make sure that the items will be accepted.

Whenever merchandise is mailed in letter packages, customs forms must be attached to the outside of the parcel. The proper form to use is the green Form 2976. (If the value of the contents of the letter package exceeds $120, use Form 2976-A instead; the upper portion of the green label is attached to the outside of the letter package and the remainder of the form is enclosed inside.) These customs forms are available free from the post office.

Mail and Postal Information 61

Registration, return receipt, special delivery, special handling, and air mail are available to almost all countries. Insurance, certified mail, and C.O.D. are not available.

Aerogrammes are available from the post office and from private suppliers and may be sent to all countries at a uniform rate. They consist of a sheet of paper which can be folded into the shape of an envelope; the letter is written on the inside of the sheet.

Letter rates vary according to country of destination. Both air and surface transportation is available. Air mail is considerably quicker, though much more expensive. Surface mail may take a matter of weeks or months to reach its destination.

Postcards. Only single cards may be sent to other countries; reply-paid cards or folded (double) cards are not acceptable in international mail. All international postcards must be at least 5½ by 3½ inches. Maximum allowable size is 6 by 4¼ inches. Rates are the same to all countries except Canada and Mexico, to which lower rates apply.

Printed matter. Printed matter consists of items which do not have the character of actual personal or business correspondence. Handwritten or typewritten letters or papers do not qualify as printed matter.

Printed matter includes: newspapers and magazines, books, pamphlets and circulars, sheet music, manuscripts, drawings and blueprints, maps, catalogs, advertisements, notices and solicitations, prospectuses, printing proofs, unframed photographs, albums of photographs, engravings, and patterns.

Material not considered "Printed Matter" includes: stationery, stamps (canceled or uncanceled), framed photographs, photographic negatives and slides, films, and playing cards.

Reproductions of handwritten or typewritten material obtained by the use of a printing press *is* acceptable as "Printed Matter."

Printed matter is subject to various weight limits according to country of destination. Consult Publication 51, *International Postage Rates and Fees,* for information.

"Printed Matter" should be clearly written on the wrapper of all material sent in this class.

Special low rates apply to books and sheet music. Mark "Books" or "Sheet Music" on the face of the parcel.

Air mail is available on all printed matter. Other available services are: registration, special delivery (to most countries), special handling, and return receipt. Insurance, certified mail, and C.O.D. are not available.

Dutiable printed material must have a green customs Form 2976 attached to the wrapper (or Form 2976-A if the material exceeds $120 in value). To find out whether printed matter is dutiable, consult the United States Customs Service.

Matter for the blind. The Postal Service has issued no published regulation regarding exactly what materials qualify as matter for the blind. Consult the post office before you mail any articles in this class.

Matter for the blind may be sent *free* via surface transportation. Air mail is also available, but regular rates are charged.

A weight limit of 15 pounds applies to each parcel sent in this class. Matter should be marked "Matter for the Blind" on the wrapper. Matter for the blind should be wrapped securely but not sealed; the post office reserves the right to inspect materials sent in this class.

Small packets. Small items of merchandise may be sent in this class. Rates are lower than for letter packages, which may also contain merchandise. Depending on country of destination, a 1- or 2-pound limit applies to small packets.

Some countries will not accept small packets. Check Publication 42, *International Mail,* or consult the post office, before mailing an item in this class.

Small packets may not include personal or business correspondence, although invoices may be included. The following items also may not be sent in small packets: money, stamps, precious metals and precious stones, and jewelry.

All matter in this class must be marked "Small Packet." If the destination is a non-English-speaking country, also include the foreign-language equivalent, e.g., "Petit Paquet" (French), "Packchen" (German), or "Pequeño Paquete" (Spanish).

All small packets, regardless of whether they contain dutiable material, must bear the green customs Form 2976 (or Form 2976-A if the packet's value is over $120).

Air mail is available on small packets to all countries that accept these items. Other special services available are: registration, special delivery (to most countries), special handling, and return receipt. Insurance, certified mail, and C.O.D. are not available.

Parcel post. Parcel post is available to most countries. Various customs restrictions and regulations apply, depending on the country of destination. Refer to Publication 42, *International Mail*, or consult the post office before mailing an item in this class.

Various size and weight limits apply to parcel post. In general, parcels should not exceed 3½ feet in length, or 6 feet in length and girth combined. Maximum weight for parcel post is either 22 or 44 pounds, depending on country. See Publication 51, *International Postage Rates and Fees*, for particulars.

Parcels should be carefully packed. Containers of 275-pound test, such as fiberboard or double-faced corrugated cardboard, are preferred.

At least one customs declaration form must be attached to all packages sent via parcel post. Some countries require more than one. Any of these forms may be required: 2966-A, 2966, or 2972. All are available free from the post office. Publication 51, *International Postage Fees and Rates*, contains a listing of the various customs forms required for each foreign country.

Air mail is available to most countries. Insurance is available on parcels sent to many countries (consult Publication 51). Registration is available to only a few countries (consult the post office). Special handling is available only between the U.S. mailing point and the U.S. point of dispatch. The following services are not available: special delivery, C.O.D., and certified mail.

It is also possible to employ *customhouse brokers* to prepare material for overseas parcel post. These are commercial U.S. firms that prepare customs documents, provide expert crating or packaging, and expedite delivery in the country of destination.

International Express Mail. Special high-speed delivery services are available to certain foreign countries. See p. 55 for details. Publication 45, *International Express Mail Service*, available from the post office, contains complete information on rules and regulations that apply to this service.

International money orders. Money orders to be sent to overseas countries may be purchased in exactly the same way as are do-

64 GENERAL OFFICE PRACTICE

mestic money orders. (See p. 58.) Most large post offices issue international money orders, as well as selected smaller post offices.

Prohibited items. In general, all articles prohibited in domestic U.S. mail are also prohibited in international mail. (See p. 58 for a list of articles prohibited in domestic mail.) These include any articles that may damage the mail or cause injury to postal workers, such as firearms, poisons, explosives, and radioactive substances. Also forbidden in international mail are matches and most live or dead creatures. Consult the post office or Publication 42, *International Mail,* before mailing questionable articles; failure to do so may result in seizure of these articles in the country of destination.

Packing

Fragile items should be packed in cushioning material such as polystyrene, excelsior, or plastic foam. Rolled-up newspaper may be wrapped around mirrors and framed pictures for good protection.

The post office prefers that boxes not be wrapped in wrapping paper. Simply tape the packages shut, making sure that the ends of flaps of cardboard boxes are completely taped; otherwise the flaps may come loose in transit. Masking tape is acceptable for sealing boxes, but reinforced tape is preferable.

Before sealing any parcel, place a list of the contents inside the package along with the names and addresses of both the addressee and the sender; this is necessary in case the address label on the outside of the package is damaged in transit.

The Postal Service may refuse to accept inadequately packed parcels for mailing.

Complete information on packing can be found in Postal Service Publication 2, *Packaging for Mailing,* available free from the post office.

Recall of Mail

If you mail a letter which, for some reason, you wish to recall—i.e., to stop before it is delivered—you may be able to do so by contacting the post office promptly.

Mail and Postal Information 65

Call the post office and give the name and address on the envelope you wish recalled. Also send a written notice to the post office containing the same information. Once the post office has received this written authorization from you, it will release the letter. You must present a similarly addressed envelope to the post office for identification.

If the letter has already left your local post office, the destination post office will be telegraphed, at your expense, to hold the letter for return.

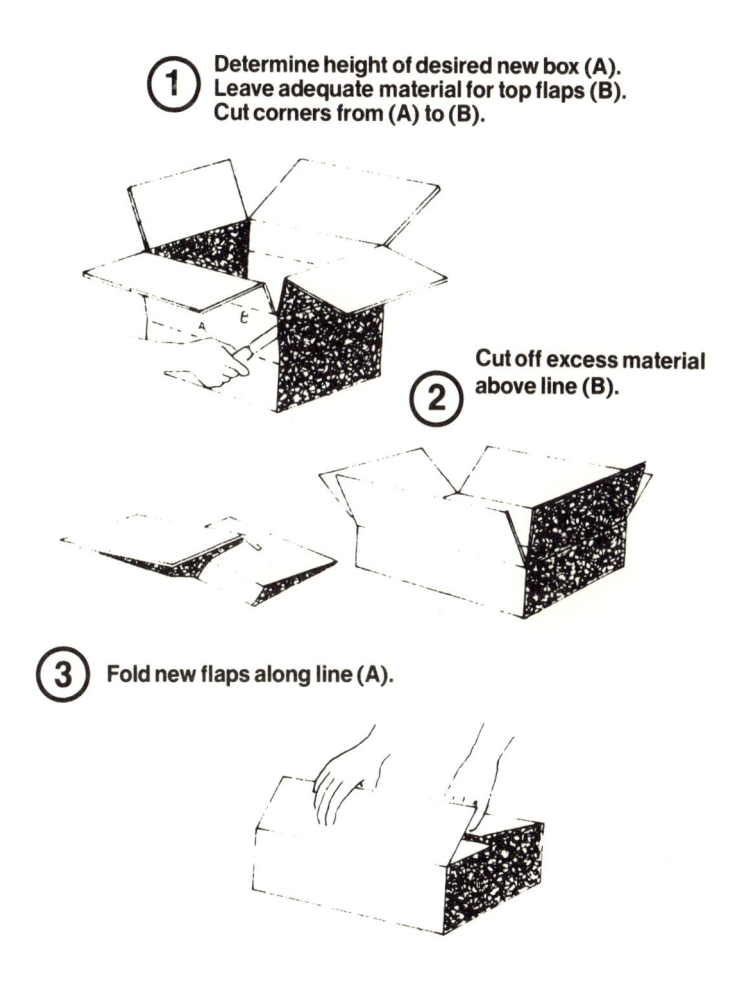

① Determine height of desired new box (A).
Leave adequate material for top flaps (B).
Cut corners from (A) to (B).

② Cut off excess material above line (B).

③ Fold new flaps along line (A).

66 GENERAL OFFICE PRACTICE

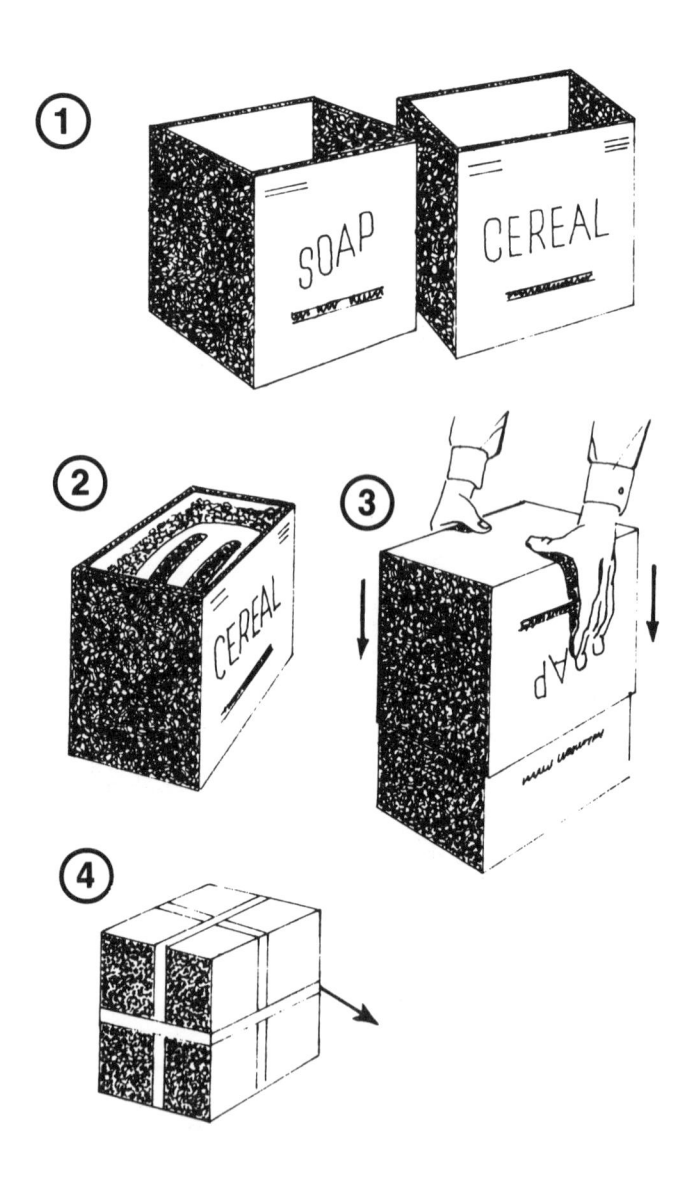

Mail and Postal Information 67

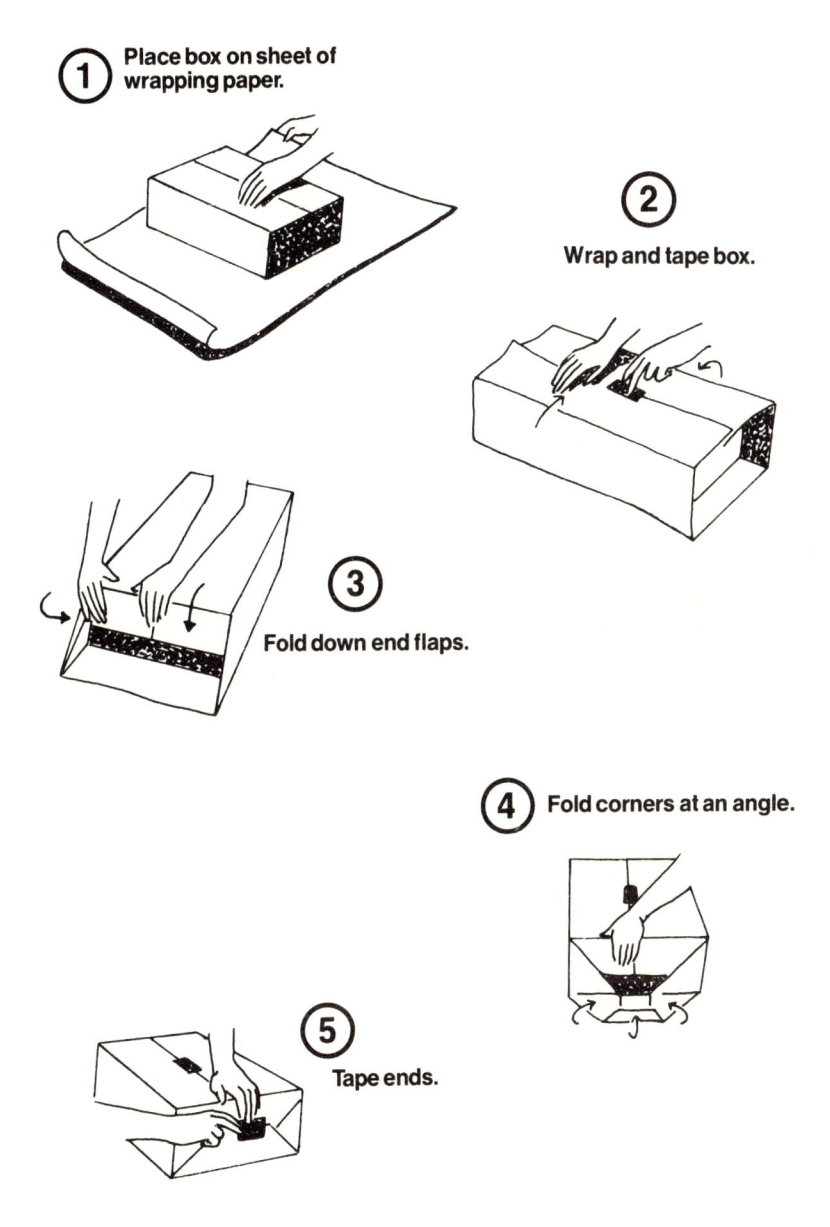

① Place box on sheet of wrapping paper.

② Wrap and tape box.

③ Fold down end flaps.

④ Fold corners at an angle.

⑤ Tape ends.

68 GENERAL OFFICE PRACTICE

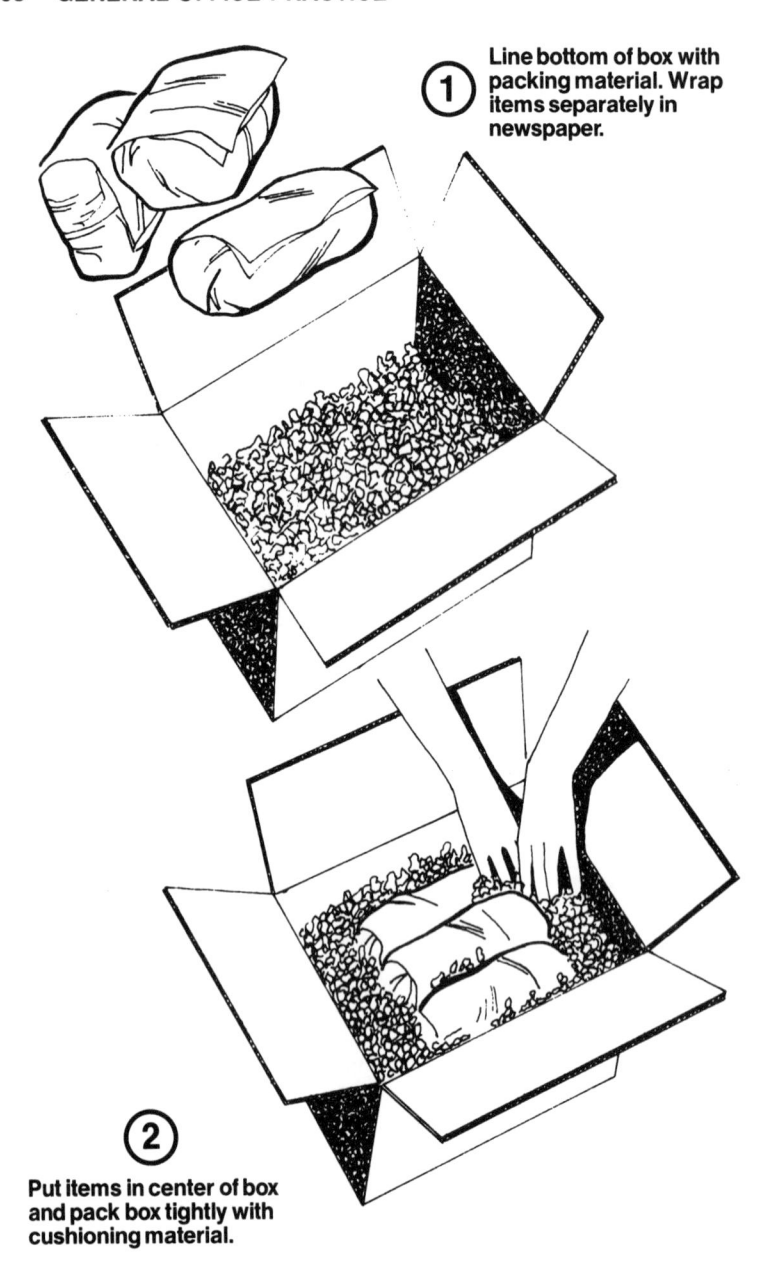

① Line bottom of box with packing material. Wrap items separately in newspaper.

② Put items in center of box and pack box tightly with cushioning material.

Mail and Postal Information 69

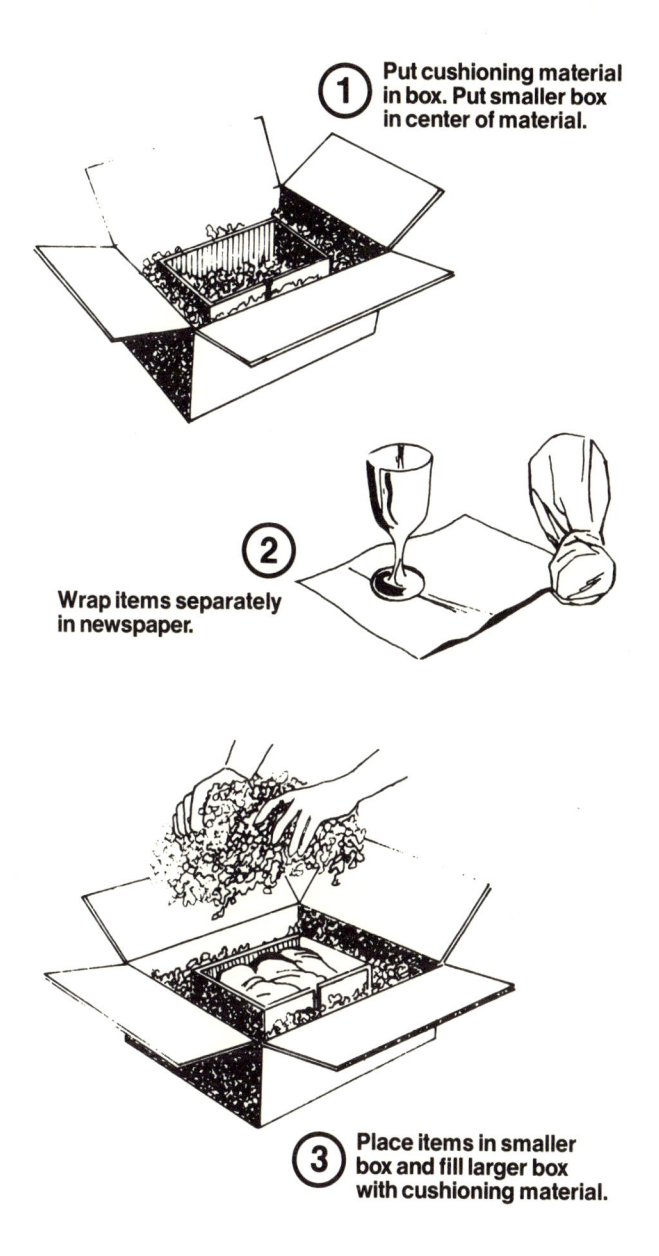

① Put cushioning material in box. Put smaller box in center of material.

② Wrap items separately in newspaper.

③ Place items in smaller box and fill larger box with cushioning material.

70 GENERAL OFFICE PRACTICE

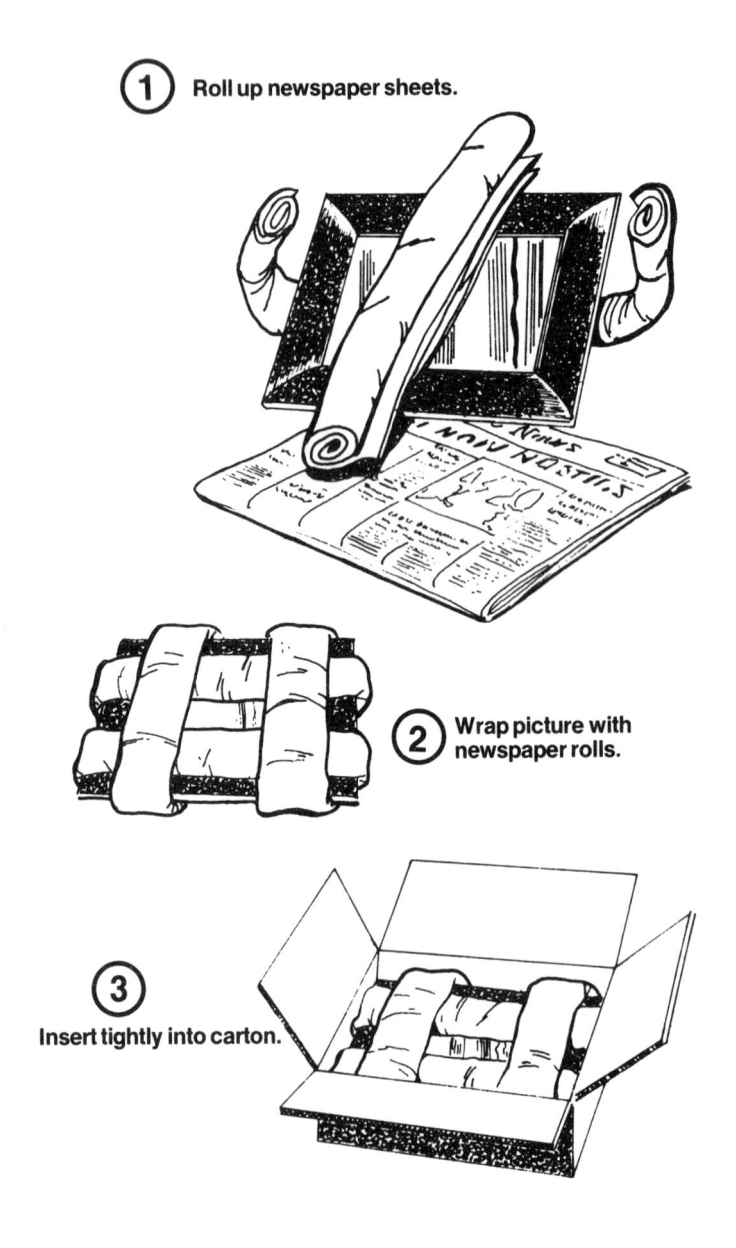

① Roll up newspaper sheets.

② Wrap picture with newspaper rolls.

③ Insert tightly into carton.

Mail and Postal Information 71

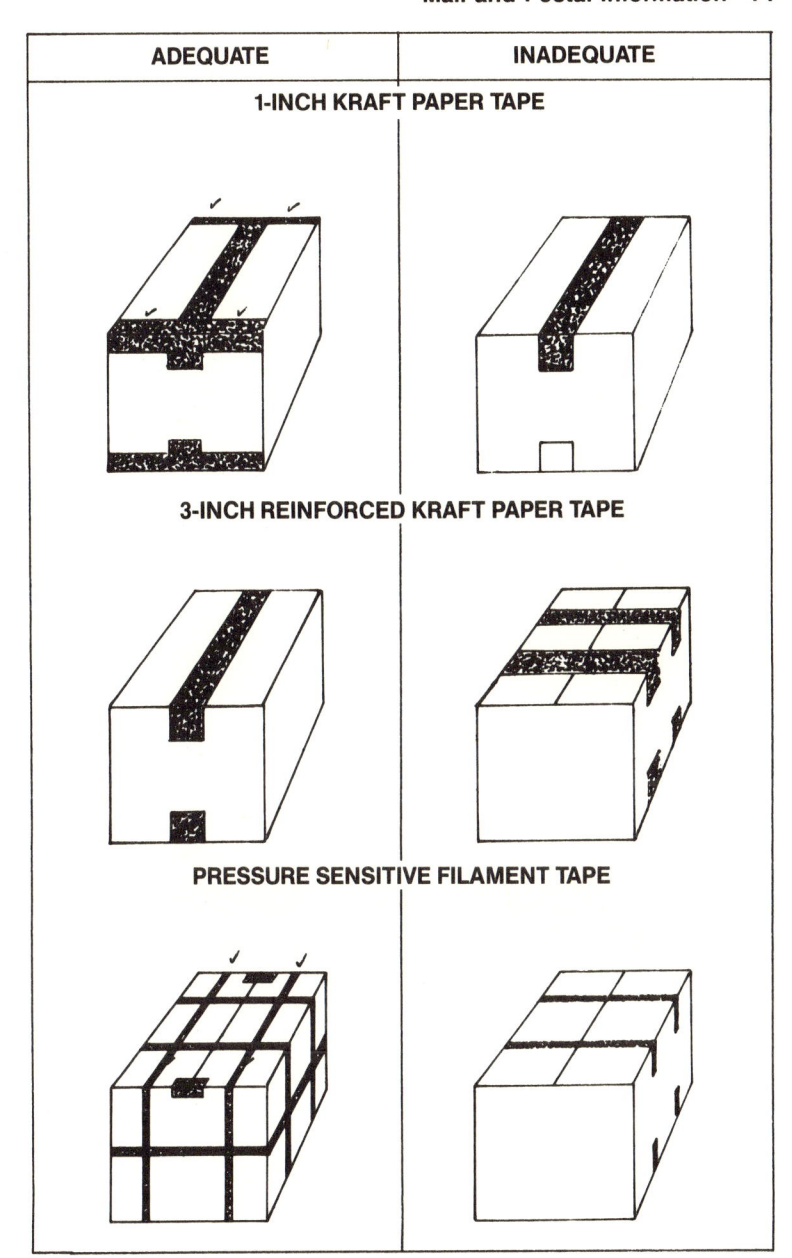

ADEQUATE	INADEQUATE
1-INCH KRAFT PAPER TAPE	
3-INCH REINFORCED KRAFT PAPER TAPE	
PRESSURE SENSITIVE FILAMENT TAPE	

7.
Travel Arrangements and International Business

Planning a Business Trip

When to use a travel agent. Travel agents are particularly useful in planning foreign trips and in organizing lengthy or complex domestic trips. Routine domestic trips do not require a travel agent's services, although an agent may nevertheless be useful.

A travel agent will make all necessary plane and hotel reservations, arrange for rented cars, advise on passport and visa requirements, submit a complete printed itinerary, and perform many other useful services.

A company or an individual may open an account with a travel agency and be billed periodically, thus avoiding the necessity of paying for all tickets and reservations individually. This service is very convenient for any company whose managers do a lot of traveling.

Plane travel. Airline reservations can usually be made over the telephone via a toll-free 800 number. You can either ask the airline to hold the tickets at the airport for your employer's arrival or request that the tickets be sent to you ahead of time. If you have the tickets sent to you, be sure to check them carefully for errors. Airline tickets should contain the following information:

Travel Arrangements and International Business

1. Flight numbers
2. Departure time
3. Name of the airport the flight leaves from
4. City of destination
5. Airline letter code.

It is important that you check this last item, the airline letter code. The *name* of the airline does not appear on the ticket; only the letter code is on the ticket. You must make sure that the tickets are for the correct airline. This is especially important when the trip contains several laps and more than one airline is being used.

Airline Letter Codes

AC	Air Canada	LH	Lufthansa German Airlines
AF	Air France		
JM	Air Jamaica	MI	Mackey International Airlines
NE	Air New England		
FJ	Air Pacific	NA	National Airlines
AS	Alaska Airlines	NY	New York Airways
AZ	Alitalia	NW	Northwest Orient Airlines
TS	Aloha Airlines	OA	Olympic Airways
AA	American Airlines	OZ	Ozark Airlines
BN	Braniff International Airways	PW	Pacific Western
		PA	Pan American World Airways
BA	British Airways		
CO	Continental Airlines	PI	Piedmont Airlines
DL	Delta Air Lines	QF	Qantas Airways, Ltd.
EA	Eastern Airlines	SN	Sabena World Airlines
AY	Finnair	SK	Scandinavian Airlines
FL	Frontier Airlines	SR	Swissair
HA	Hawaiian Air	TP	TAP Air Portugal
RW	Hughes Air West	TI	Texas International Airlines
IB	Iberia Airlines		
LL	Icelandic Airlines	TW	Trans World Airlines
EI	Aer Lingus	UA	United Airlines
JL	Japan Air Lines	AL	USAIR
KL	KLM	RG	Varig Airlines
GK	Laker Airways	WA	Western Airlines

74   GENERAL OFFICE PRACTICE

Official Airline Guide. This is a complete guide to all air travel in the United States and Canada. It lists the airlines servicing each city; plane schedules; availability of car rental services at each airport; and general information on international flight connections. It is available in single copies or yearly subscriptions from Reuben H. Donnelley, 2000 Clearwater Drive, Oak Brook, Illinois 60521.

Train travel. Train travel is much more common in Europe and Japan than in the United States. However, company officials do occasionally travel by rail, and of course the railroads are often used for personal trips. Sleeping accommodations on American rail lines are as follows:

> Compartment. Private room with upper and lower berth. Toilet facilities but no sofa.
> Bedroom. Private room with upper and lower berth; the lower berth may be used as a sofa. Toilet facilities.
> Roomette. Private room with one bed which folds against the wall. Sofa for daytime use. Toilet facilities.

Complete information on all trains and train schedules in the United States, Canada, and Mexico is to be found in *The Official Guide of the Railways,* issued monthly by the National Railway Publications Company, 424 West 33 Street, New York, New York 10001. Information on trains and train schedules in Europe, the U.S.S.R., the Middle East, and North Africa is contained in Cook's *Continental Timetable,* available from travel agents or through regional offices of Thomas Cook Travel.

Automobile travel. If your employer uses an automobile extensively on his or her business trips, he or she may find it useful to become a member of the AAA.

American Automobile Association. The nearest branch of the AAA will be found in the telephone directory. The AAA provides services to its members as follows:

1. Advises which roads and highways to use for either speed or scenic beauty.
2. Provides a "Triptik." This consists of complete detailed maps of the entire journey; the route is outlined in color.

Travel Arrangements and International Business 75

Also included are lists of recommended hotels and AAA-approved service stations.
3. Provides up-to-the-minute information on highway conditions.
4. Provides breakdown services. If your car breaks down on the road, call the AAA and they will help arrange for pick-up and repair and for a new rented car if needed.

Hotel reservations. Information on hotels is available from a wide variety of sources. Relatively complete information on hotels and motels in the United States is contained in two guides. *Hotel Guide and Travel Index* is published by Ziff-Davis Publishing Company, Inc., One Park Avenue, New York, New York 10016. *The Official Hotel Red Book and Directory* is available from the American Hotel Association Directory Corporation.

Hotel reservations may be made by telephone, telegraph, or mail. Large hotels and hotel chains, such as Hilton and Holiday Inn, have toll-free 800 numbers for making reservations. Always get confirmations of hotel reservations in writing or by wire. The employer should carry these confirmations with him or her on the trip.

Itineraries. An itinerary is necessary for every business trip with several laps. If you are working with a travel agent, he will provide the itinerary; if not, you will have to prepare it yourself. The itinerary should contain the following:

1. Points of departure and arrival
2. Airline (or railroad)
3. Date and time of departure and arrival
4. Flight number
5. Car rental at point of arrival
6. Hotel

ITINERARY

From	To	Via	Depart	Arrive	Car Rental	Hotel
Atlanta	Denver	American #704	2/7 — 10:30am	2/7 — 12:30pm	Hertz	Brown Palace
Denver	S.F.	Western #111	2/8 — 12:00N	2/8 — 2:25pm	Hertz	Fairmont
S.F.	L.A.	PSA #789	2/9 — 7:20pm	2/9 — 9:05pm	Avis	Beverly Hills
L.A.	Honolulu	American #575	2/11 — 8:15am	2/11 — 1:36pm	National	Royal Hawaiian
Honolulu	Hong Kong	TWA #499	2/20 — 11:56am	2/20 — 10:05am	—	Kowloon Hilton
Hong Kong	Singapore	JAL #570	2/21 — 3:45pm	2/21 — 4:35pm	—	Raffles
Singapore	Tokyo	JAL #680	2/25 — 10:05am	2/25 — 11:02am	—	Imperial
Tokyo	Atlanta	Pan Am #645	2/27 — 6:30am	2/27 — 11:46pm	—	—

Appointment schedule. Provide your employer with a complete schedule of all appointments on the trip. Include the city and state, date and time, name and address of the person with whom your employer has the appointment, phone number, and any clarifying remarks.

APPOINTMENT SCHEDULE

City	Date & Time	Appointment	Tel. No.	Remarks
Denver	2/8 — 3:45pm	Mr. Ford—Ideal Toy Co., 320 Main St.	345-7788	
	2/8 — 7:30pm	Wilson—445 Plainview Crescent	785-9340	Dinner
S.F.	2/9 —10:30am	Ms. Grady—Western Union, 45 Market St.	555-9000	
	2/9 — 3:30pm	Mr. Kingsley—S.F. Stock Exchange, 500 California St.	576-3948	
L.A.	2/10—12:30N	Forsythe—Beverly Hills Hotel	875-0030	Lunch
Honolulu	2/13—11:30am	Mr. Roan-Kahala Fruit Works, 3 Pali Ave.	476-0394	
	2/13— 1:00pm	U. of Hawaii, 7200 Moana Blvd.	987-3444	Board Mtg.

Foreign Travel

What a travel agent can do for you. Here are some of the things a good travel agent will do:

1. Prepare itineraries. If the traveler is not sure of his or her schedule, itineraries will be treated as tentative and can be changed at will.
2. Make all arrangements for plane tickets, hotel reservations, car rentals, sightseeing, etc.
3. Indicate whether passports, visas, health certificates, vaccinations, etc. are required. The travel agent will procure all necessary documents except those where the traveler's personal appearance is necessary.
4. Procure foreign money (bills and coins) in exchange for dollars.
5. Advise or assist in getting traveler's checks or letters of credit from banks.
6. Advise on any currency restrictions or customs requirements.
7. Have the traveler met on arrival; a foreign representative will be on hand to take care of the traveler's baggage and see him or her through customs.
8. Arrange for a rental car at the airport (or a private car or limousine, if that is desired).
9. Procure flight insurance and baggage insurance.
10. Make recommendations for sightseeing.
11. Bill the traveler (or the traveler's company) in a single accounting, thus avoiding the need to pay for all reservations and accommodations singly.

Rain insurance. If your employer is going on a pleasure trip, he or she can procure "rain insurance," thus gaining some solace if the trip is ruined by bad weather. Several variations of rain insurance are available, as snow insurance (to protect against lack of snow on skiing trips) or cold insurance (in case Florida has a cold wave during the trip).

Passports. All United States citizens need passports to depart from and reenter the United States and to enter most foreign countries. Passport information is available from the nearest passport office: look in the telephone directory under "United States Government, Passports, U.S." Ordinarily, three or four weeks are required to obtain a passport, so be sure to apply for the passport as early as possible.

To obtain a passport, you must present:

1. Evidence of U.S. citizenship, such as a previously issued (expired) passport, a birth certificate, or other evidence of citizenship, such as a baptismal certificate, if no birth certificate is available.
2. Two passport photos taken within the last six months. Photos should be 2-by-2 inches. They may be in either black-and-white or color and must be full-faced front views.
3. Identification, such as a driver's license, a certificate of naturalization, a certificate of citizenship, or a government (federal, state, or local) card or pass. Credit cards and social security cards are not acceptable.

A passport is good for five years after which a new passport must be applied for. New passport applications may be made by mail if the applicant has held a passport for not more then eight years prior to the date of application.

Lost or stolen passports should be reported immediately to the Passport Office, Department of State, Washington, DC 20524 or to the nearest American consulate.

Visas. Visas are required in order to enter certain foreign countries. Visas are granted for a specific length of time and are usually stamped in the traveler's U.S. passport. The traveler must obtain the necessary visas *before* going abroad. Visas are obtainable from the embassies or consulates of the countries in question; these embassies or consulates may be located by consulting the telephone directory.

Luggage limitations. In international travel, the free baggage allowance is 66 pounds for first-class passengers and 44 pounds for economy passengers. Excess weight is charged at the rate of one percent of the one-way *first-class* fare per kilogram (2.2 pounds). There is no limit on the number of bags each passenger may carry. If carry-on luggage is to be placed under the seats, it must be smaller than 9-by-13-by-23 inches.

Customs. Articles acquired abroad are subject to duties and taxes when they are brought into the United States. Articles totaling $100 may be brought in duty-free, except for liquor and cigars. Questions regarding dutiable items should be submitted to the District Director of Customs in the following cities:

Anchorage AK 99501	New York NY 10004
Baltimore MD 21202	–(Write: Area Director of Customs)
Boston MA 02109	Nogales AZ 85621
Bridgeport CT 06609	Norfolk VA 23510
Buffalo NY 14202	Ogdensburg NY 13669
Charleston SC 29402	Pembina ND 58271
Chicago IL 60607	Philadelphia PA 19106
Cleveland OH 44199	Port Arthur TX 77640
Detroit MI 48226	Portland ME 04111
Duluth MN 55802	Portland OR 97209
El Paso TX 79985	Providence RI 02903
Galveston TX 77550	St. Albans VT 05478
Great Falls MT 49403	St. Louis MO 63101
Honolulu HI 96806	St. Thomas VI 00801
Houston TX 77052	San Diego CA 92101
Laredo TX 78040	San Francisco CA 94126
Los Angeles–San Pedro CA 90731	San Juan PR 00903
Miami FL 33132	Savannah GA 31401
Milwaukee WI 53202	Seattle WA 98104
Minneapolis MN 55401	Tampa FL 33601
Mobile AL 36602	Washington DC 20018
New Orleans LA 70130	Wilmington NC 28401

Sending home "unsolicited gifts." When you are abroad, you may send gift packages to addressees in the United States. The value of the package should be under $10. Mark the package "Unsolicited Gift—Value under $10." The package will not be subject to customs and will not be opened by postal officials.

Vaccinations and immunizations. The traveler needs no health certificates in order to *leave* the United States (although he or she may need them to enter certain foreign countries). However, a smallpox vaccination certificate is needed to *reenter* the United States if during his trip the traveler has visited a country in which smallpox was present. Most travelers consider it wise to receive

Travel Arrangements and International Business

a smallpox vaccination before leaving the United States so that they will have no problems upon returning.

The traveler may also need various health or immunization certificates in order to enter certain foreign countries. Up-to-date information is available from a travel agent or from any local, county, or state health department.

Certain immunizations may be desirable but not mandatory. The traveler should consult his physician before leaving the United States if he is to visit any countries where dangerous or debilitating diseases are present.

Further checklist for business travelers. Business travelers abroad are faced by certain problems and conditions that the ordinary pleasure traveler does not face. The secretary should take account of the following:

1. Some foreign countries impose special requirements on business travelers but not on pleasure travelers. It is very important that a businessman traveling in one of these countries be aware of these regulations. Consult the country's consulate or your travel agent for this information.
2. If you so desire, the Department of Commerce will announce the traveler's visit to all Foreign Offices. This may be very useful to businessmen traveling for the purpose of making contacts or for those who are traveling in obscure territory. The traveler should write to the Department of Commerce six to eight weeks before his or her trip, stating the purpose of the trip and the itinerary. Send the letter to:

    Travel Officer, International Trade Service Divisions
    Special Services and Intelligence Branch
    Department of Commerce
    Office of International Trade
    Washington DC 20230

3. Trade papers and publications in the cities or countries that the business traveler will be visiting are usually happy to carry announcements of the visit. The secretary should write to these publications several weeks before the trip, giving the dates of the visit as well as the address where the employer may be reached while there.

4. Your employer may be subject to lengthy or complicated customs or immigration inspections in connection with company business, especially importing, when he returns to the United States. It will be advantageous for him or her to carry a letter of authority, addressed "To Whom It May Concern," signed by the president of the firm, authorizing the employer to represent the firm.
5. Credit information on foreign companies is available abroad from foreign offices of Dun & Bradstreet. If your employer will need such information on his or her trip, it may be wise to subscribe to the Dun & Bradstreet credit service.

Letters of Introduction. Your employer can request letters of introduction from his or her bank(s), business associates, personal friends, etc. The bank or individual will give the employer a letter which can be presented abroad to the bank's correspondents, the individual's business contacts, etc. They in turn will be able to help your employer with introductions and contacts in foreign cities where he is a stranger. Here is an example of a request for a letter of introduction:

Mr. Franklin N. Jones
Vice-President
First Central Bank
414 Main Street
Erie, PA 56464

Dear Mr. Jones:

I am planning a three-month business tour of Japan and the Far East in which I will collect information on the importation of transistorized television sets. I expect to call on television manufacturers in Tokyo, Yokohama, Seoul, Taiwan, Hong Kong, Singapore, and Macao.

I believe that a letter to your correspondents in each of these cities would prove helpful to me. I would appreciate it very much if you would supply me with a letter of introduction.

Of course, I will be happy to provide you upon my return with any information that may interest you.

Yours truly,

United States foreign service. American embassies and consulates are located in most foreign countries. Embassies are staffed by ambassadorial representatives, while consulates are primarily concerned with commercial representation. Both embassies and consulates can provide American businessmen and travelers with information on local trade; provide contacts for business representatives; and set up appointments with national government officials.

United States Embassies and Consulates

Afghanistan
Kabul

Algeria
Algiers
Oran

Arab Republic of Egypt
Cairo
Alexandria

Argentina
Buenos Aires

Australia
Canberra
Brisbane
Melbourne
Perth
Sydney

Austria
Vienna
Salzburg

Bahamas
Nassau

Bahrain
Manama

Bangladesh
Dacca

Barbados
Bridgetown

Belgium
Brussels
Antwerp

Belize
Belize City

Benin
Cotonou

Bermuda
Hamilton

Bolivia
La Paz

Botswana
Gaborone

Brazil
Brasilia
Belém
Pôrto Alegre
Recife
Rio de Janeiro
Salvador
São Paulo

Bulgaria
Sofia

Burma
Rangoon
Mandalay

Burundi
Bujumbura

Cameroon
Yaounde
Douala

Canada
Ottawa
Calgary
Halifax
Montreal
Quebec
St. John's
Toronto
Vancouver
Winnipeg

Central African Republic
Bangui

Ceylon—*see* SRI LANKA

Chad
Ndjamena

Chile
Santiago

China, Republic of
Taipei

Colombia
Bogota
Cali
Medellin

Costa Rica
San Jose

GENERAL OFFICE PRACTICE

Cyprus
Nicosia

Czechoslovakia
Prague

Dahomey—see BENIN

Denmark
Copenhagen

Dominican Republic
Santo Domingo

Ecuador
Quito
Guayaquil

Egypt—see ARAB
REPUBLIC
OF EGYPT

El Salvador
San Salvador

England—see UNITED
KINGDOM

Equatorial Guinea
Malabo

Fiji
Suva

Finland
Helsinki

France
Paris
Bordeaux
Lyon
Marseilles
Nice
Strasbourg

French West Indies
Martinique

Gabon
Libreville

Gambia
Banjul

Germany, West
Berlin (West)
Bonn
Bremen
Dusseldorf
Frankfurt am Main
Hamburg
Munich
Stuttgart

Germany, East
Berlin (East)

Ghana
Accra

Greece
Athens
Thessaloniki

Guatemala
Guatemala City

Guinea
Conakry

Guyana
Georgetown

Haiti
Port-au-Prince

Honduras
Tegucigalpa

Hong Kong
Hong Kong

Hungary
Budapest

Iceland
Reykjavik

India
New Delhi
Bombay
Calcutta
Madras

Indonesia
Jakarta
Medan
Surabaya

Iran
Teheran
Isfahan
Shiraz
Tabriz

Ireland
Dublin

Ireland, Northern
—see UNITED
KINGDOM

Israel
Jerusalem
Tel Aviv

Italy
Rome
Florence
Genoa
Milan
Naples
Palermo
Trieste
Turin

Ivory Coast
Abidjan

Jamaica
Kingston

Japan
Tokyo
Naha, Okinawa
Osaka-Kobe
Sapporo
Fukuoka

Travel Arrangements and International Business

Jordan
Amman

Kenya
Nairobi

Korea, South
Seoul

Kuwait
Kuwait

Laos
Vientiane

Lebanon
Beirut

Lesotho
Maseru

Liberia
Monrovia

Libya
Tripoli

Luxembourg
Luxembourg

Malagasy Republic
Tananarive

Malawi
Blantyre
Lilongwe

Malaysia
Kuala Lumpur

Mali
Bamako

Malta
Valletta

Mauritania
Nouakchott

Mauritius
Port Louis

Mexico
Mexico, D.F.
Ciudad Juarez
Guadalajara
Hermosillo
Matamoros
Mazatlan
Merida
Monterrey
Nuevo Laredo
Tijuana

Morocco
Rabat
Casablanca
Tangier

Nepal
Katmandu

Netherlands
The Hague
Amsterdam
Rotterdam

Netherlands Antilles
Curaçao

New Zealand
Wellington
Auckland

Nicaragua
Managua

Niger
Niamey

Nigeria
Lagos
Ibadan
Kaduna

Norway
Oslo

Oman
Muscat

Pakistan
Islamabad
Karachi
Lahore
Peshawar

Panama
Panama

Papua New Guinea
Port Moresby

Paraguay
Asunción

Peru
Lima

Philippines
Manila
Cebu

Poland
Warsaw
Poznan
Krakow

Portugal
Lisbon
Oporto
Ponta Delgada,
  São Miguel, Azores

Qatar
Doha

Rumania (*or*
  Romania)
Bucharest

Russia—*see* UNION OF
  SOVIET
  SOCIALIST REPUBLICS

Rwanda
Kigali

Saudi Arabia
Jidda
Dharan

Scotland—*see*
UNITED KINGDOM

Senegal
Dakar

Sierra Leone
Freetown

Singapore
Singapore

Somalia
Mogadiscio

South Africa
Pretoria
Cape Town
Durban
Johannesburg

South Korea—*see*
KOREA, SOUTH

Spain
Madrid
Barcelona
Bilbao
Seville

Sri Lanka
Colombo

Sudan
Khartoum

Surinam
Paramaribo

Swaziland
Mbabane

Sweden
Stockholm

Switzerland
Bern
Zurich
Geneva

Syria
Damascus

Tanzania
Dar Es Salaam
Zanzibar

Thailand
Bangkok
Chiang Mai
Songkhla
Udorn

Togo
Lome

Trinidad and Tobago
Port-of-Spain

Tunisia
Tunis

Turkey
Ankara
Adana
Istanbul
Izmir

Union of Soviet Socialist Republics
Moscow
Leningrad

United Arab Emirates
Abu Dhabi

United Kingdom
London
Liverpool
Belfast, Northern Ireland
Edinburgh, Scotland

Upper Volta
Ouagadougou

Uruguay
Montevideo

Venezuela
Caracas
Maracaibo

Yemen Arab Republic
Sana

Yugoslavia
Belgrade
Zagreb

Zaire
Kinshasa
Bukavu
Lubumbashi

Zambia
Lusaka

Travel Arrangements and International Business

Variant spellings. Foreign spellings of city and country names occasionally differ from the American spellings. Here are the most commonly encountered forms:

Foreign	American
Anvers	Antwerp
Athenai	Athens
Belgique	Belgium
Bruxelles	Brussels
Chili	Chile
Cordoba	Cordova
Deutschland	Germany
Ellas	Greece
España	Spain
Firenze	Florence
Genf	Geneva
Göteborg	Gothenburg (Sweden)
's Gravenhage	The Hague
Habana	Havana
Italia	Italy
Köbenhavn	Copenhagen
Köln	Cologne
Lisboa	Lisbon
Moskva	Moscow
München	Munich
Praha	Prague
Torino	Turin
Venezia	Venice
Wien	Vienna
Warszawa	Warsaw

Information for international business travelers. The following pages contain information that will be useful to businessmen abroad.

FOREIGN COUNTRIES, CAPITALS, AND NATIONALITIES

Country	Capital	The People	Official Language(s)	Adjective
Afghanistan	Kabul	Afghan(s)	Persian, Pushto	Afghan
Albania	Tirana	Albanian(s)	Albanian	Albanian
Algeria	Algiers	Algerian(s)	Arabic, French	Algerian
Andorra	Andorra la Vella	Andorran(s)	Catalan	Andorran
Angola	Luanda	Angolan(s)	Portuguese	Angolan
Argentina	Buenos Aires	Argentine(s)	Spanish	Argentine
Australia	Canberra	Australian(s)	English	Australian
Austria	Vienna	Austrian(s)	German	Austrian
Azores	Ponta Delgada	Azorean(s)	Portuguese	Azorean
Bahamas	Nassau	Bahamian(s)	English	Bahamian
Bahrain	Manama	Bahraini(s)	Arabic	Bahraini
Bangladesh	Dacca	Bengali(s)	Bengali	Bangladesh
Barbados	Bridgetown	Barbadian(s)	English	Barbadian
Belgium	Brussels	Belgian(s)	Flemish, French	Belgian
Belize	Belmopan	Belizean(s)	English	Belizean
Benin *(formerly Dahomey)*	Porto-Novo	Beninese	French	Beninese
Bermuda	Hamilton	Bermudan(s)	English	Bermudan
Bhutan	Thimbu	Bhutanese	Bhutanese	Bhutanese
Bolivia	La Paz	Bolivian(s)	Spanish	Bolivian
Botswana	Gaborone	Botswana	English	Botswana
Brazil	Brasilia	Brazilian(s)	Portuguese	Brazilian
Brunei	Brunei	Bruneian(s)	English	Brunei
Bulgaria	Sofia	Bulgarian(s)	Bulgarian	Bulgarian
Burma	Rangoon	Burman(s)	Burmese	Burmese
Burundi	Bujumbura	Burundian(s)	French, Rundi	Burundian
Cambodia —*see* KAMPUCHEA				

Travel Arrangements and International Business 89

Cameroon	Yaoundé	Cameroonian(s)	English, French	Cameroonian
Canada	Ottawa	Canadian(s)	English, French	Canadian
Canary Islands	Las Palmas	Canarian(s)	Spanish	Canarian
Cape Verde	Praia	Cape Verdean	Portuguese	Cape Verdian
Central African Republic	Bangui	Central African(s)	French	Central African
Ceylon—*see* SRI LANKA				
Chad	Ndjamena	Chadian(s)	French	Chadian
Chile	Santiago	Chilean(s)	Spanish	Chilean
China, People's Republic of	Peking	Chinese	Chinese	Chinese
China, Republic of	Taipei	Chinese	Chinese	Chinese
Colombia	Bogotá	Colombian(s)	Spanish	Colombian
Comoro Islands	Moroni	Comoran(s)	French	Comoran
Congo	Brazzaville	Congolese	French	Congolese *or* Congo
Costa Rica	San José	Costa Rican(s)	Spanish	Costa Rican
Cuba	Havana	Cuban(s)	Spanish	Cuban
Cyprus	Nicosia	Cypriot(s)	Greek, Turkish	Cypriot
Czechoslovakia	Prague	Czechoslovak(s)	Czech, Slovak	Czechoslovak
Dahomey—*see* BENIN				
Denmark	Copenhagen	Dane(s)	Danish	Danish
Dominican Republic	Santo Domingo	Dominican(s)	Spanish	Dominican
Ecuador	Quito	Ecuadorean(s)	Spanish	Ecuadorean
Egypt, Arab Republic of	Cairo	Egyptian(s)	Arabic	Egyptian
El Salvador	San Salvador	Salvadoran(s)	Spanish	Salvadoran
England—*see* UNITED KINGDOM				

Equatorial Guinea	Malabo	Equatorial Guinean(s)	Spanish	Equatorial Guinean
Ethiopia	Addis Ababa	Ethiopian(s)	Amharic	Ethiopian
Finland	Helsinki	Finn(s)	Finnish	Finnish
France	Paris	Frenchman(men)	French	French
Gabon	Libreville	Gabonese	French	Gabonese
Gambia	Banjul	Gambian(s)	English	Gambian
Germany, East (German Democratic Republic)	East Berlin	East German(s)	German	German
Germany, West (Federal Republic of Germany)	Bonn	West German(s)	German	German
Ghana	Accra	Ghanaian(s)	English	Ghanaian
Gibraltar	Gibraltar	Gibraltarian(s)	English	Gibraltar
Great Britain—see UNITED KINGDOM				
Greece	Athens	Greek(s)	Greek	Greek
Grenada	St. George's	Grenadian(s)	English	Grenadian
Guatemala	Guatemala City	Guatemalan(s)	Spanish	Guatemalan
Guinea	Conakry	Guinean(s)	French	Guinea
Guinea-Bissau	Bissau		Portuese	
Guinea, Equatorial—see EQUATORIAL GUINEA				
Guyana	Georgetown	Guyanese	English	Guyanese
Haiti	Port-au-Prince	Haitian(s)	French	Haitian
Honduras	Tegucigalpa	Honduran(s)	Spanish	Honduran
Hong Kong	Victoria	English	Chinese	Hong Kong
Hungary	Budapest	Hungarian(s)	Hungarian	Hungarian

Iceland	Reykjavik	Icelander(s)	Icelandic
India	New Delhi	Indian(s)	Indian
Indonesia	Jakarta	Indonesian(s)	Indonesian
Iran	Teheran	Iranian(s)	Iranian
Iraq	Baghdad	Iraqi(s)	Iraqi
Ireland (*or* Irish Republic)	Dublin	Irishman (men)	Irish
Israel	Jerusalem	Israeli(s)	Israel
Italy	Rome	Italian(s)	Italian
Ivory Coast	Abidjan	Ivory Coaster(s)	Ivoirain
Jamaica	Kingston	Jamaican(s)	Jamaican
Japan	Tokyo	Japanese	Japanese
Jordan	Amman	Jordanian(s)	Jordanian
Kampuchea	Phnom Penh	Kampuchean	Kampuchean
Kenya	Nairobi	Kenyan(s)	Kenyan
Khmer Republic—*see* CAMBODIA			
Korea, North	Pyongyang	North Korean(s)	Korean
Korea, South	Seoul	South Korean(s)	Korean
Kuwait	Kuwait	Kuwaiti(s)	Kuwaiti
Laos	Vientiane	Lao	Lao *or* Laotian
Lebanon	Beirut	Lebanese	Lebanese
Lesotho	Maseru	Basotho	Basotho
Liberia	Monrovia	Liberian(s)	Liberian
Libya	Tripoli	Libyan(s)	Libyan
Liechtenstein	Vaduz	Liechtensteiner(s)	Liechtenstein
Luxembourg	Luxembourg	Luxembourger(s)	Luxembourg
Malagasy Republic (Madagascar)	Tananarive	Malagasy	Malagasy
Malawi	Lilongwe	Malawian(s)	Malawian

Icelandic	
English, Hindi	
Bahasa Indonesia	
Persian	
Arabic	
English, Irish	
Arabic, Hebrew	
Italian	
French	
English	
Japanese	
Arabic	
Khmer	
English, Swahili	
Korean	
Korean	
Arabic	
Lao	
Arabic	
English	
English	
Arabic	
German	
French, German	
French, Malagasy	
English, Nyanja (*or* Chewa)	

Country	Capital	Citizen	Language(s)	Adjective
Malaysia	Kuala Lumpur	Malaysian(s)	Malay	Malaysian
Maldives	Male	Maldivian(s)	Maldivian	Maldivian
Mali	Bamako	Malian(s)	French	Malian
Malta	Valletta	Maltese	English, Maltese	Maltese
Mauritania	Nouakchott	Mauritanian(s)	Arabic, French	Mauritanian
Mauritius	Port Louis	Mauritian(s)	English	Mauritian
Mexico	Mexico City	Mexican(s)	Spanish	Mexican
Monaco	Monaco	Monacan (or Mongol	French	Monacan
Mongolia	Ulan Bator	Mongol	Mongolian (Khalkha)	Mongolian
Morocco	Rabat	Moroccan(s)	Arabic	Moroccan
Mozambique	Maputo	Mozambican(s)	Portuguese	Mozambique
Nauru		Nauruan(s)	English	Nauruan
Nepal	Katmandu	Nepalese	Nepali	Nepalese
Netherlands	Amsterdam (*official*) The Hague (*de facto*)	Netherlander(s)	Dutch	Dutch
New Zealand	Wellington	New Zealander(s)	English	New Zealand
Nicaragua	Managua	Nicaraguan(s)	Spanish	Nicaraguan
Niger	Niamey	Nigerois	French	Niger
Nigeria	Lagos	Nigerian(s)	English	Nigerian
North Korea—*see* KOREA, NORTH				
North Vietnam—*see* VIETNAM, NORTH				
Norway	Oslo	Norwegian(s)	Norwegian	Norwegian
Oman	Muscat	Omani(s)	Arabic	Omani
Pakistan	Islamabad	Pakistani(s)	Bengali, English, Urdu	Pakistani
Panama	Panama	Panamanian(s)	Spanish	Panamanian
Papua New Guinea	Port Moresby	Papua New Guinean(s)	English	Papua New Guinean
Paraguay	Asunción	Paraguayan(s)	Spanish	Paraguayan

Country	Capital	Noun	Language	Adjective
Peru	Lima	Peruvian(s)	Spanish	Peruvian
Philippines	Quezon City	Filipino(s)	English, Philippino	Philippine
Poland	Warsaw	Pole(s)	Polish	Polish
Portugal	Lisbon	Portuguese	Portuguese	Portuguese
Puerto Rico	San Juan	Puerto Rican(s)	English, Spanish	Puerto Rican
Qatar	Doha	Qatari(s)	Arabic	Qatari
Rhodesia	Salisbury	Rhodesian(s)	English	
Rumania (*or* Romania)	Bucharest	Rumanian (*or* Romanian)	Rumanian (*or* Romanian)	
Russia—*see* UNION OF SOVIET SOCIALIST REPUBLICS				
Rwanda	Kigali	Rwandan(s)	French, Ruanda	Rwandan
Samoa, Western—*see* WESTERN SAMOA				
San Marino	San Marino	Sanmarinese	Italian	Sanmarinese
São Tomé and Principe	São Tomé		Portuguese	
Saudi Arabia	Riyadh	Saudi	Arabic	Saudi Arabian
Senegal	Dakar	Senegalese	French	Senegalese
Seychelles	Victoria	Seychellois	English	Seychelles
Sierra Leone	Freetown	Sierra Leonean(s)	English	Sierra Leonean
Singapore	Singapore	Singaporean(s)	Chinese, English, Malay, Tamil	Singapore
Somalia	Mogadishu	Somali	Somali	Somali
South Africa	Pretoria *(administrative capital)*, Capetown *(legislative capital)*, Bloemfontein *(judicial capital)*	South African(s)	Afrikaans, English	South African

94 GENERAL OFFICE PRACTICE

South Korea—see KOREA, SOUTH			
South Yemen	Aden	Arabic	South Yemeni
Spain	Madrid	Spanish	Spanish
Sri Lanka (formerly Ceylon)	Colombo	Sinhalese	Sri Lankan
Sudan	Khartoum	Arabic	Sudanese
Surinam	Paramaribo	Dutch	Surinam
Swaziland	Mbabane	English	Swazi
Sweden	Stockholm	Swedish	Swedish
Switzerland	Bern	French, German, Italian, Romansh	Swiss
Syria	Damascus	Arabic	Syrian
Tanzania	Dar es Salaam	English, Swahili	Tanzanian
Thailand	Bangkok	Thai	Thai
Togo	Lomé	French	Togolese
Tonga	Nukualofa	English, Tongan	Tongan
Trinidad and Tobago	Trinidad and Tobago	English	Trinidadian and Tobagan
Tunisia	Tunis	Arabic	Tunisian
Turkey	Ankara	Turkish	Turkish
Uganda	Kampala	English	Ugandan
Union of Soviet Socialist Republics (U.S.S.R.)	Moscow	Russian	Soviet
United Arab Emirates	Abu Dhabi	Arabic	Arabic
United Kingdom	London	English	British
Upper Volta	Ouagadougou	French	Upper Voltan

Note: nationality (singular) forms shown in source between language and adjective columns: South Yemeni, Spaniard(s), Sri Lankan(s), Sudanese, Surinamer(s), Swazi, Swede(s), Swiss, Syrian(s), Tanzanian(s), Thai, Togolese, Tongan(s), Trinidadian(s) and Tobagan(s), Tunisian(s), Turk(s), Ugandan(s), Russian(s), Arabic, Briton, British, Upper Voltan(s).

Uruguay	Montevideo	Uruguayan(s)	Spanish	Uruguayan
Vatican City State			Italian	
Venezuela	Caracas	Venezuelan(s)	Spanish	Venezuelan
Vietnam, Socialist Republic of (North and South)	Hanoi	Vietnamese	Vietnamese	Vietnamese
Western Samoa	Apia	Western Samoan(s)	English, Samoan	Western Samoan
Yemen	San'a	Yemeni	Arabic	Yemeni
Yugoslavia	Belgrade	Yugoslav(s)	Macedonian, Serbo-Croatian, Slovenian	Yugoslav
Zaire	Kinshasa	Zairian(s)	French	Zairian
Zambia	Lusaka	Zambian(s)	English	Zambian

GENERAL OFFICE PRACTICE
FOREIGN MONEY

COUNTRY	MONEY	SYMBOL	SUBDIVISIONS
Afghanistan	afghani	Af	100 puls
Albania	lek	L	100 qintar
Algeria	dinar	DA	100 centimes
Andorra	French franc	Fr or F	100 centimes
	Spanish peseta	Pta or P	100 centimos
Angola	escudo	A. Esc	100 centavos
Argentina	peso	$	100 centavos
Australia	dollar	$	100 cents
Austria	schilling	S or Sch	100 groschen
Bahamas	dollar	B$	100 cents
Bahrain	dinar	BD	1000 fils
Bangladesh	taka	—	100 paisa
Barbados	dollar	$	100 cents
Belgium	franc	Fr or F	100 centimes
Bermuda	dollar	$	100 cents
Bhutan	rupee	Re (pl Rs)	100 paise
Bolivia	peso	$B	100 centavos
Botswana	rand	R	100 cents
Brazil	cruzeiro	$ or Cr$	100 centavos
Brunei	dollar	—	100 sen
Bulgaria	lev	Lv	100 stotinki
Burma	kyat	K	100 pyas
Burundi	franc	FBu	100 centimes
Cameroon	franc	Fr or F	100 centimes
Canada	dollar	$	100 cents
Cape Verde	escudo	Esc	100 centavos
Central African Republic	franc	Fr or F	100 centimes
Chad	franc	Fr or F	100 centimes
Chile	escudo	E or E°	100 centesimos
China, People's Republic of	yuan	$	10 chiao 100 fen
China (Taiwan)	yuan or dollar	NT$	10 chiao
Colombia	peso	$ or P	100 centavos
Congo (Brazzaville)	franc	Fr or F	100 centimes
Costa Rica	colon	¢ or ¢	100 centimos
Cuba	peso	$	100 centavos
Cyprus	pound	£	1000 mils
Czechoslovakia	koruna	Kčs	100 halers
Denmark	krone	DKr	100 öre

Travel Arrangements and International Business

Dominican Republic	peso	RD$	100 centavos
Ecuador	sucre	S/	100 centavos
Egypt, Arab Republic of	pound	£ E	100 piasters
El Salvador	colon	₡ or ¢	100 centavos
Equatorial Guinea	peseta	Pta or P	100 centimos
Ethiopia	dollar	Eth$ or E$	100 cents
Finland	markka	M or Mk	100 pennia
France	franc	Fr or F	100 centimes
Gabon	franc	Fr or F	100 centimes
Gambia	pound	£G	—
Germany, East	mark	M or OM	100 pfennigs
Germany, West	deutsche mark	DM	100 pfennigs
Ghana	cedi	¢	100 pesewas
Greece	drachma	Dr	100 lepta
Guatemala	quetzal	⌀ or Q	100 centavos
Guinea	franc	Fr or F	100 centimes
Guyana	dollar	G$	100 cents
Haiti	gourde	G or G or Gde	100 centimes
Honduras	lempira	L	100 centavos
Hong Kong	dollar	HK$	100 cents
Hungary	forint	F or Ft	100 filler
Iceland	krona	Kr	100 aurar
India	rupee	Re (pl Rs)	100 paise
Indonesia	rupiah	Rp	100 sen
Iran	rial	R or Rl	100 dinars
Iraq	dinar	ID	5 riyals
Ireland	pound	£	100 pence
Israel	shekel		100 agorot
Italy	lira	L or Lit	100 centesimi
Ivory Coast	franc	F or Fr	100 centimes
Jamaica	dollar	$	100 cents
Japan	yen	¥ or Y	100 sen
Jordan	dinar	JD	1000 fils
Kenya	shilling	Sh	100 cents
Korea, North	won	W	100 jun
Korea, South	won	W	100 chon
Kuwait	dinar	KD	1000 fils
Laos	kip	K	100 at
Lebanon	pound	L£ or LL	100 piasters
Lesotho	rand	R	100 cents
Liberia	dollar	$	100 cents

98 GENERAL OFFICE PRACTICE

Libya	dinar	LD	1000 dirhams
Liechtenstein	franc	F	100 centimes
Luxembourg	franc	Fr or F	100 centimes
Macao	pataca	P or $	100 avos
Malagasy Republic	franc	Fr or FMG	100 centimes
Malawi	kwacha	K	100 tambala
Malaysia	dollar	M$	100 cents
Maldives	rupee	MRe	100 lari
Mali	franc	Ff or F	100 centimes
Malta	pound	£	100 pence
Mauritania	franc	Fr or F	100 centimes
Mauritius	rupee	Re (pl Rs)	100 cents
Mexico	peso	$	100 centavos
Monaco	franc	Fr or F	100 centimes
Mongolia, Outer	tugrik	—	100 mongo
Morocco	dirham	DH	100 francs
Mozambique	escudo	M. Esc	100 centavos
Nauru	dollar	$A	100 cents
Nepal	rupee	Re (pl Rs)	100 paise
Netherlands	gulden or guilder or florin	F or Fl or G	100 cents
New Zealand	dollar	NZ$	100 cents
Nicaragua	cordoba	C$	100 centavos
Niger	franc	Fr or F	100 centimes
Nigeria	naira	₦	100 kobo
Norway	krone	Dr	100 öre
Oman	rial	R	1000 baizas
Pakistan	rupee	Re (pl Rs)	100 paisa
Panama	balboa	B/	100 centesimos
Paraguay	guarani	G/ or G	100 centimos
Peru	sol	S/ or $	100 centavos
Philippines	peso	₱ or P	100 sentimos
Poland	zloty	Zl or Z	100 groszy
Portugal	escudo	$ or Esc	100 centavos
Rhodesia	pound	£	20 shillings 240 pence
Rumania	leu	L	100 bani
Rwanda	franc	Fr or F	100 centimes
San Marino	lira	L	100 centesimi
Saudi Arabia	riyal	R or SR	20 qursh 100 halala
Senegal	franc	Fr or F	100 centimes
Seychelles	rupee	Re (pl Rs)	100 cents

Country	Currency	Symbol	Subunit
Sierra Leone	leone	Le	100 cents
Singapore	dollar	S$	100 cents
Somalia	shilling	Sh or So Sh	100 cents
South Africa	rand	R	100 cents
South Yemen	dinar	£SY	1000 fils
Spain	peseta	Pta or P	100 centimos
Sri Lanka	rupee	Re (pl Rs)	100 cents
Sudan	pound	£S or LSd	100 piasters
Surinam	guilder	Sur. f.	100 cents
Swaziland	rand	R	100 cents
Sweden	krona	Kr	100 öre
Switzerland	franc	Fr or F	100 centimes
Syria	pound	£S or LS	
Tanzania	shilingi	Sh	100 senti
Thailand	baht or tical	Bht or B	100 satang
Togo	franc	Fr or F	100 centimes
Tonga	pa'anga	T$	100 seniti
Trinidad and Tobago	dollar	TT$	100 cents
Tunisia	dinar	D	1000 millimes
Turkey	lira or pound	£T or LT or TL	100 kurus
Uganda	shilling	Sh	100 cents
USSR	ruble	R or Rub	100 kopecks
United Kingdom	pound		100 pence
Upper Volta	franc	Fr or F	100 centimes
Uruguay	peso	$	100 centesimos
Venezuela	bolivar	B	100 centimos
Vietnam, North	dong	D	100 xu
Vietnam, South	piaster	Vn$ or Pr	100 cents
Western Samoa	dollar	$	100 cents
Yemen	rial	YR	40 buqshas
Yugoslavia	dinar	Din	100 paras
Zaire	zaire	Z	100 makuta (sing: lakuta)
Zambia	kwacha	K	100 ngwee

Holidays and Business Hours of Frequently Visited Countries.

Brazil
   New Year's Day, 1 January
   Carnival, 4 days before Ash Wednesday
   Good Friday

100 GENERAL OFFICE PRACTICE

    Tiradentes, 21 April
    Labor Day, 1 May
    Independence Day, 7 September
    All Souls Day, 2 November
    Proclamation of the Republic, 14 November
    Christmas Day, 25 December

    Normal business hours: 9 to 5 weekdays

Canada
    New Year's Day, 1 January
    Epiphany (Quebec only), 6 January
    Good Friday
    Easter Monday
    Ascension Day (Quebec only)
    Victoria Day, 20 May
    St. John the Baptist (Quebec only), 24 June
    Canada Day, 1 July
    Labor Day, 2 September
    Thanksgiving, 14 October
    Remembrance Day, 11 November
    Immaculate Conception (Quebec only), 8 December
    Christmas, 25 December
    Boxing Day, 26 December

    Normal business hours: 9 to 5 weekdays

France
    New Year's Day, 1 January
    Easter Monday
    Labor Day, 1 May
    Ascension Day
    Whit Monday
    Bastille Day, 14 July
    Assumption, 15 August
    All Saints' Day, 1 November
    Armistice Day, 11 November
    Christmas, 25 December

    Normal business hours: 9 to 12 and 2 to 6 weekdays

Great Britain
    New Year's Day, 1 January
    St. Patrick's Day (Northern Ireland only), 17 March
    Good Friday

Easter Monday
Spring Bank Holiday, last Monday in May
Bank Holiday (Northern Ireland only), 12 July
Summer Bank Holiday, last Monday in August
Christmas, 25 December
Boxing Day, 26 December

Normal business hours: 9:30–12:30 and 2:30–5 or 6 weekdays

Hong Kong
New Year's Day, 1 January
Chinese New Year, 3 days January or February
Ching Ming Festival, April
Good Friday
Easter Monday
Queen's Birthday, April
Tuen Ng Festival, June
First weekday in July
First Monday in August
Liberation Day, last Monday in August
Chung Yeung Festival, October
Christmas, 25 December
Boxing Day, 26 December

Normal business hours: 9 to 1 and 2 to 5 weekdays
9 to 1 Saturday

Italy
New Year's Day, 1 January
Epiphany, 6 January
St. Giuseppe, 19 March
Easter Monday
Liberation Day, 25 April
Labor Day, 1 May
Ascension Day
Anniversary of the Republic, 2 June
Corpus Domini, June
St. Peter and St. Paul, 29 June
Assumption (Ferragosto), 15 August
All Saints' Day, 1 November
National Unification, 4 November
Immaculate Conception, 8 December
Christmas, 25 December

102 GENERAL OFFICE PRACTICE

    St. Stephen's Day, 26 December
    Normal business hours: 9 to 1, 4 to 7 weekdays

Japan
    New Year, 28 December through 3 January
    Adults' Day, 15 January
    Commemoration Day, 11 February
    Vernal Equinox Day, 21 March
    Emperor's Birthday, 29 April
    Constitution Memorial Day, 3 May
    Children's Day, 5 May
    Respect for the Aged Day, 15 September
    Autumnal Equinox Day, September (variable)
    Physical Culture Day, 10 October
    Culture Day, 3 November
    Labor Thanksgiving Day, 23 November
    Normal business hours: 9 to 5 weekdays
                            9 to 12 Saturday

Mexico
    New Year's Day, 1 January
    Holy Week
    Labor Day, 1 May
    Treaty Abrogation Day, 14 July
    Anniversary of Battle of San Jacinto, 14 September
    Independence Day, 15 September
    Columbus Day, 12 October
    Immaculate Conception, 8 December
    Christmas, 25 December
    Normal business hours: 9 to 5 weekdays

South Korea
    New Year, 1 and 2 January
    Lunar New Year, late January or early February
    Independence Movement Day, 1 March
    Memorial Day, 6 June
    Constitution Day, 17 July
    Liberation Day, 15 August
    Moon Festival, late September or early October
    Armed Forces Day, 1 October

National Foundation Day, 3 October
Hangul (Alphabet) Day, 9 October
United Nations Day, 24 October
Christmas, 25 December

Normal business hours: 9 to 5 weekdays
                       9 to 1 Saturday

Taiwan
Founding of the Republic, 1 January
Chinese New Year, January or February
Youth Day, 29 March
Tomb-sweeping Day and death of Chiang Kai-shek, 5 April
Birthday of Confucius, 28 September
Double Tenth National Day, 10 October
Taiwan Retrocession Day, 25 October
Chiang Kai-shek's birthday, 31 October
Dr. Sun Yat-Sen's birthday, 12 November
Constitution Day, 25 December

Normal business hours: 8 to 12 and 2 to 6 weekdays

West Germany
New Year's Day, 1 January
Good Friday
Easter Monday
Ascension Day
Whit Monday
Unity Day, 17 June
Repentance Day, 21 November
Christmas, 25 December
Boxing Day, 26 December

Normal business hours: 8 to 5 weekdays

Letter Writing

8. Guidelines for Good Letters

Stationery and Letterheads

Stationery size. The standard sizes of stationery are as follows. The Standard style is used for ordinary business correspondence. Executive (Monarch) size is used for personal letterhead stationery. The Baronial style is used for half-sheets.

Standard	8½ × 11
Executive (Monarch)	7¼ × 10½
	or
	7½ × 10
Baronial (Half-sheet)	5½ × 8½

Envelope size. The widely available envelope sizes are as follows. Standard size business letters are usually mailed in No. 10 or No. 9 envelopes. Window envelopes are often No. 6-¾.

No. 6-¾	3⅝ × 6½
Monarch	3⅞ × 7½
No. 9	3⅞ × 8⅞
No. 10	4⅛ × 9½

Kinds of paper. Business and personal letterhead stationery is printed on bond paper. The other types of paper are used for brochures, news releases, manuscripts, etc.

- Bond. Bond is the paper most often used for letters and business forms. It takes ink well and can be erased easily.
- Coated. Coated papers have smooth glossy coatings. They are used for high printing quality. There are many varieties: coated on one or both sides, dull coated, etc.
- Text. Text papers have attractive textures and colors. They are used for booklets, announcements, and special purposes.
- Book. Less expensive than text papers, book papers are used mostly for books.
- Offset. Offset is similar to book paper, but it is treated to resist the moisture present in offset printing.
- Cover. Cover papers are heavier weights of coated and text papers. They are often used as covers for booklets. In addition, some papers are made exclusively for covers.
- Index. Index paper is stiff and receptive to ink.
- Newsprint. Newsprint paper is used for newspapers.
- Tag. Often used for printing tags, tag paper may be printed on one or both sides. It bends and folds well.

Weight. Most printing papers are identified by "basis weight." This is the weight of 500 sheets—one ream—of the paper in its basic size. (The basic size differs for different grades. The basic size of a sheet of bond paper is 17" × 22"; the basic size of a sheet of newsprint is 24" × 36".)

The greater the weight of the paper, the heavier each individual sheet. Business and personal letterhead stationery is preferably printed on 24-pound paper, although 20-pound paper may also be used. Airmail stationery is printed on 13-pound paper.

Content. Cotton content and rag content signify a very high quality paper. Most ordinary commercial paper is made from wood pulp, which is manufactured in many grades and qualities. Business and personal letterhead paper is usually made from one of the better grades of wood pulp.

Grain. The "grain" of a paper is the direction in which the fibers run. In letterhead paper, the grain should be parallel to the lines of writing, i.e., it should run across the paper, not up-and-down. This makes for easier typing, easier erasing, and easier folding.

Paper also has a "felt" side and a "wire" side. The "felt" side is the side from which the watermark can be read. The letterhead should be printed on the felt side.

Kinds of envelopes. The basic envelope styles and their uses are as follows.

> Commercial. Commercial envelopes are used for most business and for statements.
> Window. Window envelopes are used mainly for invoices and statements. They save time in addressing and eliminate the possibility of typing the wrong address on the envelope.
> Self-sealing. Self-sealing envelopes have upper and lower flaps which have adhesive that seals without water, thus saving time.
> Open-side. Open-side envelopes are good for direct mail and periodicals. Absence of seams permits good-looking front and back printing.
> Baronial. Baronial envelopes are similar to open-side envelopes. They are used for announcements, invitations, etc.
> Bankers flap. Bankers flap envelopes are for very bulky material. The paper is much stronger than ordinary commercial envelopes.
> Wallet flap. Wallet flap envelopes are like bankers flap envelopes; they hold a great deal and are made of strong paper.
> Clasp. Clasp envelopes are used for carrying bulky correspondence safely. They are strong, and they can be opened and closed many times.
> String-and-button. String-and-button envelopes are similar to clasp envelopes.
> Open-end. Open-end envelopes have wide seams and gummed flaps to protect their contents under rough handling. Widely used for mailing reports, catalogs, magazines, booklets, etc.
> Expansion. Expansion envelopes have pleated sides, which enable them to expand as more material is inserted in them.

Kinds of printing. You can select one of several kinds of printing for your letterhead. The most expensive is engraving, which produces a raised design on the paper. The raised portion may be printed, or it may be left unprinted. It's the most expensive method of printing, and it also looks the most luxurious.

Another kind of printing, called thermographic or electrostatic printing, creates a raised type. It is similar to engraving but less expensive. You can usually have it with a shiny finish or a dull one: check with the printer to see if you can get what you like.

Letterpress is a type of printing frequently used by commercial job printers. Letterpress produces a sharp, clear impression.

Offset printing is usually the least expensive. A good offset letterhead can be nearly as crisp and sharp as a good letterpress job. A poor one can be abominable. Usually, you get what you pay for in printing, so be sure to see samples of other work the printer has done before you commit your job.

How to Order Stationery

Ask the printer for a written quotation that specifies the weight and content of paper and the type of printing that will be on it.

In placing your order, specify:

1. The quantity in sheets
2. The printing or engraving style
3. The weight
4. The grain
5. That the letterhead should be printed on the felt side of the paper
6. The size
7. The color

The printer will usually submit a price that includes printing both stationery and envelopes. One word of caution may prevent dissatisfaction: to cut corners, a printer may use the same type on the envelope as on the stationery. If the print size is appropriate, there may be nothing wrong with it. But you may need a different type size on the envelope—often an envelope's type should be smaller because the printing surface is smaller. Find out in advance exactly what the printer plans to put on the envelope.

LETTER WRITING

Selecting a Letterhead

Your printer or stationer will be able to show you books of sample letterheads, which you can adapt to your business.

One of the first things to think about is the information you want to put on your letterhead. Certainly, the name of your company, your address, and your telephone number are essential. But then consider: might you want to put on more than one address; more than one telephone number? Also, what about the names of any individuals: if you're the president, do you want your name on it? Or if you're selecting letterheads for a committee, do you want their names to appear?

Also, you might want to have your letterheads match your business cards. If your cards are distinctive or have special artwork, your printer may be able to transfer the design to your letterhead.

When you're in doubt, select a simpler rather than a more elaborate design. For example, some letterheads place the company's address on the bottom of the sheet. It often looks quite good, but it requires an alert typist. If you write long letters, you're apt to run the typed lines too close to the address, ruining the appearance of the page.

If you prefer an original letterhead design, retain the services of a commercial artist who's had considerable experience in lettering. A local advertising agency or commercial artist can often do the job for you; check the **Yellow Pages** of your telephone book if you don't know any artists. Tell them what you're interested in, find out the price for (a) four or five sketches from which you can select what you want, and (b) finished artwork, ready for printer. If possible, get estimates from two or three sources.

Sample Letterheads

RANDOLPH P. JENNERS
4250 PARK AVENUE
NEW YORK, NEW YORK 10016

Page, Arbitrio & Resen

Designers
595 Madison Avenue
New York, New York 10022
212-421-8190

The Lehman Corporation
ONE SOUTH WILLIAM STREET
New York, N.Y. 10004

BETTY OWEN

SECRETARIAL SYSTEMS, INC.
630 THIRD AVENUE AT 41st STREET
NEW YORK, NEW YORK 10017
212/867-7667
TYPING
STENOSCRIPT

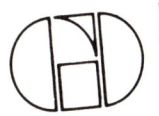

GROSSET & DUNLAP, INC.
PUBLISHERS

51 MADISON AVENUE, NEW YORK, N.Y. 10010 · 212 MURRAY HILL 9-9200
Cable Address: GROSLAP, NEW YORK   Telex: 12-7748

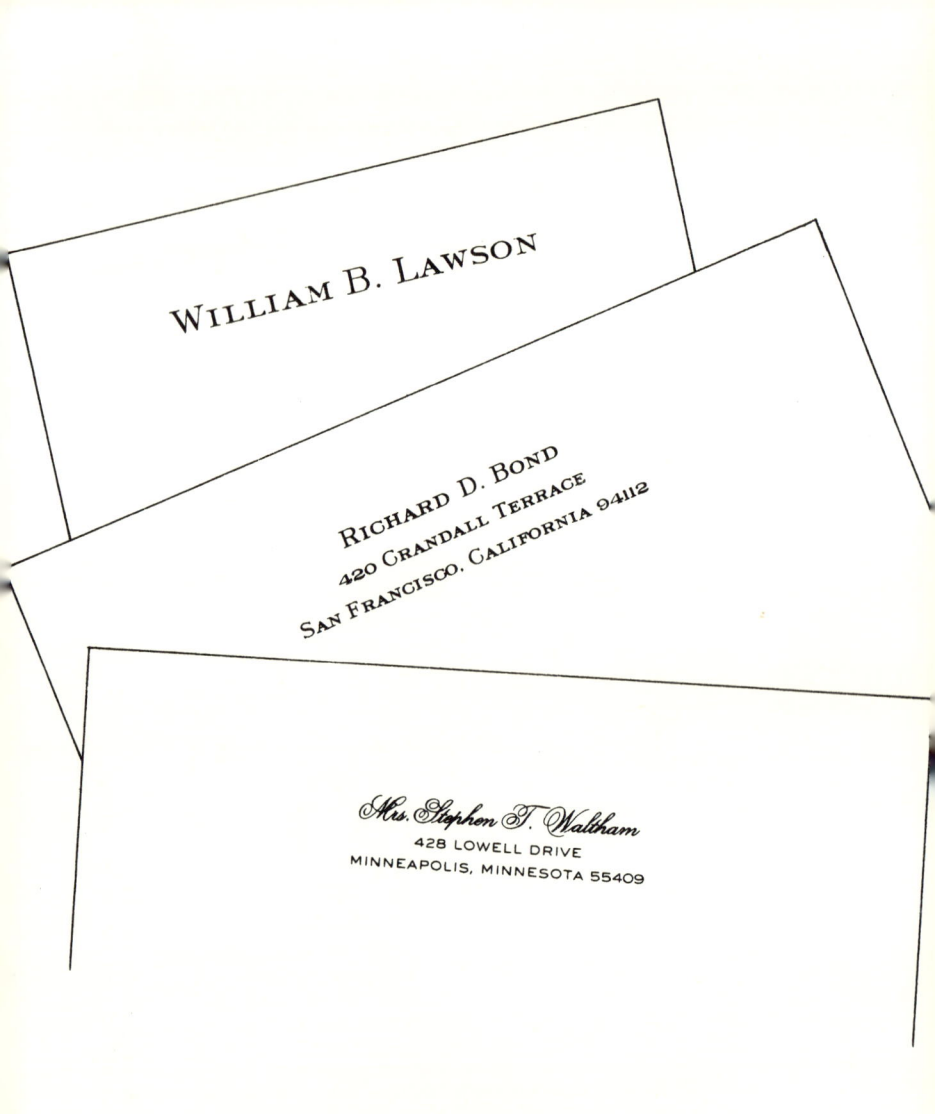

How to Cut Correspondence Costs

Letters are expensive to write. Dictating, drafting, transcribing, and typing all consume valuable time. It can take 59 minutes to prepare a handwritten draft of a 175-word letter. A printed form letter can be completed in 3½ minutes, while a half hour may be needed for a letter dictated to a stenographer. There are several ways to reduce writing time.

Time Factors in Writing a Typical Letter[1]

MINUTES REQUIRED

Action	Individually Composed Letter			Predrafted Letter		
	hand-drafted	dictated to stenographer	machine dictated	manually typed	automatically typed	printed form
Planning, drafting[2]	22½	5	5	0	0	0
Dictating	0	5	5	0	0	0
Taking dictation	0	5	0	0	0	0
Selecting letters[3]	0	0	0	2	2	1
Transcribing, typing	9	10	9½	7	1½	1½
Proofreading	2	2	2	1½	½	½
Reviewing, signing	2	3	3	1½	½	½
TOTAL MINUTES	35½	30	24½	12	4½	3½

[2] Get-ready time excluding that required for research.
[3] Time required to select predrafted letter and instruct typist.

LETTER WRITING

Typical Writing, Dictating, and Typing Rates

For a standard page of 30–40 lines:
- —Dictating time per page .... 15 min.
- —Transcribing time per page .... 25 min.
- —Dictating and transcribing time .... 1½ pages/hr.
- —Type from copy .... 3 pages/hr.

(Average ratio of dictating and transcribing time to typing from copy is one to three.)

	Per Hour
Address envelopes, longhand	100 envelopes
Address envelopes, typewriter	140 envelopes
Address envelopes, addressing machine	1,000 envelopes
Write longhand drafts (175-word letter)	2 letters
Type letters from longhand drafts	1.5 letters
Type letters from steno notes	2 letters
Type letters from dictating machine	2.4 letters
Type guide letters (Correspondex)	6.7 letters
Type form letters	20 letters
Type speed letters from longhand draft	4 letters

	Words/Min.
Typing, average for straight copy	42
Typing, forms and letters	20
Typing, automatic typewriter	110
Write longhand	18
Dictate to machine	80
Take shorthand	24
Type dictated longhand notes	15
Transcribe shorthand notes	15
Transcribe machine dictation	30

Dictate Letters. An executive who dictates can cut the cost of his letters in half. Too many letters that could be dictated are still handwritten. The time gained for more urgent projects makes the goal of becoming adept at dictating letters worthwhile.

Use the Telephone. A telephone call can replace several letters. It also adds a more personal note and may prevent confusion of important messages. Make your calls brief, be courteous but to the point.

Use Informal Replies. Replying right on the original correspondence and returning it to the sender can be a quick way to answer inquiries. Requests for publications are usually returned this way along with the publication. A photocopy of the letter and reply can serve as a file record, if one is needed. An abbreviated reply can be used with outgoing letters. It is common practice on a form letter to tell the addressee to respond on the front or back of the letter. With both inquiry and answer on the same letter, action has been taken in an economical and time-saving fashion.

Use Semi-Automatic Typewriters. Electric typewriters with unitized magnetic recording cards can cut a third off typing time. A typist does the initial typing at a fast rate but does not have to be extra careful. The final typing is done at speeds of 150–175 words per minute.

More use of form letters and guide letters. Form letters are preprinted letters; guide letters (or guide paragraphs) are stored in computers and printed out on automatic typewriters as desired.

Form letters should be used not only for transmittals and other routine matters, but also as a substitute for longer replies. They are used in legal, medical, and engineering correspondence. They apply wherever there is a need to tell the same story over and over again in correspondence. Each time a guide letter is used, even a small office saves at least $1.75. Form letters save even more.

A form letter is appropriate and economical if:
1. It is about a routine business or informational matter.
2. It is not a personal letter.
3. The letter will be used often. A form letter will be economical when:

Number of lines in letter	Number of letters used per month
5	30 or more
10	20 or more
15	15 or more
20 or more	10 or more

114 LETTER WRITING

Letter Format

Several standard styles for business letters are illustrated in the following pages.

Block style. The distinguishing feature of the block style is that each line of the letter begins flush with the left margin. There are no indentations.

Modified block style. This is identical to the block style except that the date line, the reference line, and the complimentary close and signature are not typed at the left margin. They may be typed starting in the dead center of the page, slightly to the right of dead center, or flush with the right margin.

Semi-block style. Identical to the modified block style except that the first line of each paragraph of the body of the letter is indented.

Official style. In this format the inside address is placed below the signature, flush with the left margin. The typist's initials and enclosure notations are typed two spaces below the inside address. The official style may be used for personal letters in business, when the writer and the addressee are on a first name basis.

Simplified style. The simplified letter omits the salutation and complimentary close. The subject line takes the place of the salutation. This is a somewhat impersonal style used in general correspondence and in government correspondence.

NOTE: See page 137 for an illustration of the special format used in letters to the U.S. Government, Department of Defense.

Continuation pages. When the entire letter will not fit onto one sheet of paper, it must be continued onto a second sheet. At least three lines of the body of the letter must be carried over onto the second sheet. The complimentary close and/or typed signature line should never stand alone on the second sheet.

The second sheet has no letterhead; it is a blank sheet of paper. At least six blank lines should be left at the top of the continuation sheet. The continuation sheet should have a heading containing the page number, the addressee's name, and the date. Either of the two following formats may be used, whichever accords better with the style of the letterhead sheet.

GROSSET & DUNLAP, INC.
PUBLISHERS

51 MADISON AVENUE, NEW YORK, N.Y. 10010 • 212-689-9200
Cable Address: GROSLAP, NEW YORK #Telex: 12-7748

June 28, 19--

Your letter 5/31/--

CERTIFIED MAIL
PERSONAL

Mr. Franklin N. Ross
Jones & Jones, Inc.
200 Tenth Street
New York NY 10011

Dear Mr. Ross:

SUBJECT: INTERNAL SECURITY

We appreciate the problem you are in with your manuscript and want to do everything we can to help you. We assure you that the manuscript will be seen by only our three senior editors.

We have recommended that the manuscript be published under a pseudonym and have your assurances that you will comply. Since your name does not currently appear on any part of the manuscript, there is no way it can be definitely attributed to you.

Should you have any trouble with the officers of your company, please get in touch with us by telephone before taking any action. We need hardly tell you that any adverse publicity at this time would jeopardize the publication of your book.

Sincerely,

Thomas J. Josephson, President

TJJ/rt

Enc. 2

GROSSET & DUNLAP, INC.
PUBLISHERS

51 MADISON AVENUE, NEW YORK, N.Y. 10010 • 212-689-9200
Cable Address: GROSLAP, NEW YORK #Telex: 12-7748

March 13, 19--

File DCB-447
Contract No. 356001

SPECIAL DELIVERY

First Women's Bank
Stanfield Building
320 Fortune Avenue
Netherford CA 99665

Attention Ms. Nancy J. Holmes

Ladies:

SUBJECT: PRINTED CHECKS

This letter will confirm our telephone conversation of this morning, in which you requested certain changes in Contract No. 356001 for printed checks.

We will be happy to have the checks printed in green rather than in blue. We have notified our printer of this change and have been assured that the delivery date of the checks will not be affected.

If you wish to make any further changes in the specifications of this contract, I suggest that you do so promptly, as any further delays beyond March 31 will entail an additional charge.

We expect that the checks will be delivered to you during the last week in April.

Yours truly,

(Mrs.) Suzanne Wilson
Director of Sales

gh

Enclosure

Copy to Ms. Fiona Willis
        Women's Bank of Lanford
        Lanford WA 56748

GROSSET & DUNLAP, INC.
PUBLISHERS

51 MADISON AVENUE, NEW YORK, N.Y. 10010 • 212-689-9200
Cable Address: GROSLAP, NEW YORK #Telex: 12-7748

October 22, 19--

File KGB-22-XY

REGISTERED MAIL

Foremost Publications, Inc.
Reprint Department
One Harmon Plaza
Northford TX 49983

Att: Mr. Jonas T. Donnelly

Gentlemen:

<u>Paperback Reprint Rights</u>

  This letter will constitute a preliminary agreement whereby we confirm our intention to purchase your paperback reprint rights to the Nature & Science series.

  The terms of this agreement have been discussed by our respective purchasing departments and are considered in detail in the enclosed contract.

  Any further changes in this contract will be subject to the approval of our legal department and Mr. Donnelly.

  We have enclosed our check for the stated amount.

         Very truly yours,

         GROSSET & DUNLAP, INC.

         James Davis, Counsel
         Legal Department

JD:lm

Enc: 1. Contract 555-KL-01
   2. Cert. ck. $20,000

cc: Mr. Grey
  Ms. Duncan
  Mrs. Burbank

GROSSET & DUNLAP, INC.
PUBLISHERS

51 MADISON AVENUE, NEW YORK, N.Y. 10010 • 212-689-9200
Cable Address: GROSLAP, NEW YORK #Telex: 12-7748

September 25, 19--

Dear Alice:

    We have run into a slight problem with the specifications for the Babcock construction project. I knew that you would want to be advised promptly, since your department will probably be considerably affected.

    The basic problem is that the architect's plans were drawn up before the modifications were received from Babcock. Therefore, they were predicated on the assumption that pre-stressed concrete, rather than cast steel I-beams, would be used in the internal support mechanism of the cantilevered arches of the plaza building.

    We now have two choices: either we reject Babcock's modifications and stick with the pre-stressed concrete, or we go back to the drawing board and redesign the arches using the cast steel I-beams. Whatever we do, there will be a delay in the final composition of the blueprints for the project.

    Which alternative do you prefer? I know it will be a difficult choice, but I'd appreciate it if you could think about it soon and give me an answer as soon as you are able.

                                      Sincerely,

Ms. Alice Pierce
International Blueprints, Inc.
220 Fortune Road
Burghley TX 44576

GROSSET & DUNLAP, INC.

PUBLISHERS

51 MADISON AVENUE, NEW YORK, N.Y. 10010 • 212-689-9200
Cable Address: GROSLAP, NEW YORK #Telex: 12-7748

November 3, 19--

Order 33-456-1003-1

Ms. Sadie Wilson
Chief Purchasing Agent
Norbert & Weiner Co.
37 Cold Spring Road
Nyack NY 30045

ERROR IN YOUR ACCOUNT

Thank you for letting us know that there was an error in last month's statement of your account. Please accept our apologies. We have rectified the error and have credited your account with the full purchase price of the refrigerator.

We have also made a note of the correct spelling of your street address and have entered this address in our computer. We are sorry that you had to send us three notices before the computer picked up the error. We have been having a little trouble with the computer lately, but the problem has been solved and you should have no further difficulties.

We have redeposited your check in our account at First City Bank, as you asked us to do.

JOAN D. BURNS - CLAIMS ADJUSTOR

qlo

cc: Mr. Jason Pollock
    Accounts Supervisor
    First City Bank
    Mellon NJ 34567

GROSSET & DUNLAP, INC.
PUBLISHERS

51 MADISON AVENUE, NEW YORK, N.Y. 10010 • 212 MURRAY HILL 9-9200

April 15, 19--

Mr. Kirk R. Bliss
444 Renwick Row
Charleston SC 77654

Dear Mr. Bliss:

    This will confirm our telephone conversation of this morning in which I told you that the board meeting is scheduled for May 4.

    We will meet at 10:00 a.m. Enter through the unmarked south gate. We will talk to the reporters at noon after the meeting is adjourned.

                      Sincerely,

                      Martin Q. Hubbell

tj

```
                                    six lines
    Mr. Joseph J. Lee        -2-     January 27, 19--
                                     four lines
    and we anticipate that your order will be shipped during the first
    week in April, depending...
```

```
                                    six lines
    Page 2
    Mr. Joseph J. Lee
    January 27, 19--
                                     four lines
    and we anticipate that your order will be shipped during the first
    week in April, depending...
```

Positioning the letter on the page. You will first have to estimate the number of words in the letter. Count the number of lines in the rough draft or in your shorthand notes and multiply by the approximate number of words in a line. Then use the following table.

LENGTH OF LETTER	NUMBER OF WORDS	SPACING	PICA MARGINS	ELITE MARGINS	DATE LINE FROM TOP OF PAGE
Short	up to 75	Double	20,64	25,77	15 spaces
Medium	75—150	Single	15,69	18,84	15 spaces
Long	150 and up	Single	12,72	15,90	14 spaces

This table uses what is called the 6-6-6 system; that is, 6 spaces down to the letterhead, 6 more spaces to the date line, and 6 to the inside address. These spacings can of course be adjusted slightly depending on the length and arrangement of the letter.

The Parts of a Business Letter

Date. The date line is usually typed two to four spaces below the letterhead; up to six spaces if the letter is very short. For clarity's sake, it should be positioned flush with either the right- or left-hand margin, depending on the style of the letter.

Date the letter the day it was dictated, not the day it was transcribed.

In United States Government correspondence and in British correspondence, the usual order of the month and day in the date line is reversed:

28 June 19—

File references. File, correspondence, control, order, invoice, or policy numbers are typed two to four lines below the date. Any of the following styles are suitable for the reference line:

    Your letter 3/13/—   Order X-333
    Your File R456   Our Job PX-9
    Policy 47856   File No. 345

Special mailing notations. If SPECIAL DELIVERY or CERTIFIED MAIL (or any other special notation) appears on the envelope, it must also appear on the letter. The notation is typed in full capitals two or three lines above the inside address.

Personal and Confidential. If PERSONAL or CONFIDENTIAL appears on the envelope, it must also appear on the letter. The two words should not be used together. PERSONAL means that the letter may be opened and read only by the addressee. CONFIDENTIAL indicates that the letter may be opened and read by the addressee and any other person authorized to view such material.

PERSONAL or CONFIDENTIAL is typed in full capitals two or three lines above the inside address. When a special mailing notation is also included in the letter, PERSONAL or CONFIDENTIAL immediately follows the special mailing notation.

Inside Address. The inside address is typed two to twelve lines below the date line, depending on the length of the letter.

The addressee's name should always be preceded by a title such as *Mr., Mrs., Ms., Miss,* or *Dr.,* even if the name is followed by a business title.

If the addressee's business title is short, place it directly after the name; if it is long, place it on the next line:

Mr. Lawrence Ellis, Editor
Channing & Sons, Inc.
37 Madison Avenue
New York NY 10010

Ms. Jan Simon
Administrative Manager
Cooper & Higgins
One Beckford Boulevard
Cincinnati OH 43902

Mr. William Jasper
Vice President and Director
  of Research and Development
Ogilvy and Mather, Inc.
230 Park Avenue
New York NY 10017

It is unnecessary to use both a post office box number and a street address. Use the post office box number in preference to the street address, if you know it.

Spell out numbered street names from *one* to *twelve.* Numbered street names over twelve may be written with the endings *st, rd,* or *th* or as numerals only. Use figures for all house numbers except *One.* Separate the house number from a numerical name of a street with a hyphen.

5 Second Street, Room 10 (*not* Room 10, 5 Second Street)
587 Eleventh Street (*not* 11th)
One Bankers Plaza (*not* 1 Bankers Plaza)
7 Bankers Plaza
47 West 13 Street, *or* 47 West 13th Street
1435—25 Avenue, *or* 1435—25th Avenue

If the letter is addressed to a particular department in a company, place the name of the department on the line following the name of the company.

Titles in inside address. (See chapter 9, pp. 145–75, for the correct forms of address to those in official or honorary positions.)

Complementary titles—Always precede a name by a complementary title unless the initials of a degree (see below) or *Esquire* (see below) are used.

Ms. E. W. Dickson
Miss Mary Jones
Professor J. D. Blackwell
Mr. Harry Smith, Jr.
Dean Sarah Frank

Degrees—The initials of a degree following a name take the place of a complementary title preceding a name.

Ralph T. Holmes, LL.D.
  not Mr. Ralph T. Holmes, LL.D.

Use only the initials of the highest degree, unless the degrees are of equal importance, when they may both be used.

John Cane, Ph.D.
  not John Cane, A.B., A.M., Ph.D.
Harold J. Herkimer, LL.D., Ph.D.

Do not use initials in combination with a title if they both refer to the same degree.

Dr. Raymond Sears
Raymond Sears, M.D.
  not Dr. Raymond Sears, M.D.
Professor May James
  not Professor May James, Ph.D.

In the case of the doctor's degree, the preferred usage is *Dr.* rather than *Ph.D.*

Dr. P. D. Smith
  rather than P. D. Smith, Ph.D.

Esquire—The title Esq. is commonly used in England and the English colonies to address the heads of firms, bankers, doctors, lawyers, and other professional people. In the United States, it is used primarily in addressing attorneys and other high-ranking professional men who do not have other titles. No other titles are ever used with Esquire. There is no female form; do not use Esquire in addressing a woman.

>Joseph Jones, Jr., Esq.
>   *not* Mr. Joseph Jones, Jr., Esq.
>Honorable J. Dawes
>   *not* Honorable J. Dawes, Esq.

Messrs.—This title (abbreviation of *Messieurs*) is most often used in addressing professional partnerships, such as lawyers or architects. *Messrs.* should not be used when Company (Co.), Corporation (Corp.), or Incorporated (Inc.) are part of the firm's name.

>Messrs. Smith and Jones
>   *not* Messrs. Smith and Jones, Inc.
>John Crane & Sons
>   *not* Messrs. John Crane & Sons

Business titles—A business title may be included after the addressee's name or on the line below, whichever gives the better balance. If the inclusion of the title makes the inside address too long (five lines or more), it may be omitted. The business title always comes after, never before, the name.

>>Mr. L. L. Dean, President
>>International Factors, Inc.
>>
>>Mr. Horatio R. Fayerweather
>>Treasurer, Roth & Company
>>
>>Dr. J. P. Gonzales
>>Superintendent of Schools
>>   *Incorrect:*   Chairman Joseph Madero
>>   Director Marjorie Jamison
>>   Secretary L. D. Kearns

Professional titles—Professional titles such as Professor, Dean, or President may be used if desired. Professional titles, as opposed to business titles, precede the addressee's name.

> President Quentin Stout
> Queensland University

> Dean Janet Baker
> School of Music

When the addressee has a doctor's degree and also holds the rank of professor, the address may read:

> Dr. Beverly Sutherland
> Professor of Fine Arts
>   *or* Professor Beverly Sutherland

Titles for women—Socially, a married woman or a widow is addressed by her husband's name preceded by Mrs. In business, she may be addressed by either her husband's name or by her given name preceded by Mrs. Use Miss or Ms. when you do not know whether a woman is married. When addressing a divorcee, use Mrs. or Miss, according to her preference; when in doubt, use Mrs.

In addressing a firm, such as a law firm, composed entirely of women, use Mesdames or Mmes.

Do not address married women by their husbands' titles; simply use Mrs. If a woman is addressed jointly with her titled husband, use Dr. and Mrs. Franklin T. Adams, Judge and Mrs. F. R. Leavis.

Men and Women—When addressing a man and woman in their individual capacities, use their respective titles and place one name under the other.

> Mrs. Russell May
> Mr. Hitchcock Smith
> Universal Globes, Inc.

> Dr. Simon Fairfax
> Miss Janice Rule
> Department of the Budget

Guidelines for Good Letters 127

Traditionally, when addressing a husband and wife, the woman's title is dropped. In modern usage, the woman's title is often retained.

Dr. and Mrs. Frank Smith (traditional)
Dr. Frank Smith and Dr. Elizabeth Smith
Dr. Elizabeth Smith and Dr. Frank Smith
Drs. Frank and Elizabeth Smith
Drs. Elizabeth and Frank Smith
Dr. Elizabeth Smith and Mr. Frank Smith (when only the woman is titled)
Dr. Elizabeth and Mr. Frank Smith

When you do not know whether the addressee is a man or a woman, use the form of address appropriate to a man.

Foreign addresses.

Foreign Titles Corresponding to "Mr.," "Mrs.," and "Miss"

American	French Title	Abbr.	German Title	Abbr.
Mr.	Monsieur	M.*	Herrn	
Messrs.	Messieurs	MM.*	Herren	
Mrs.	Madame	Mme*	Frau	Fr.*
Miss	Mademoiselle	Mlle*	Fräulein	Frl.*
Ladies	Mesdames	Mmes*		
Misses	Mesdemoiselles	Mlles*	Fräulein	Frl.*

Spanish Title	Abbr.	Italian Title	Abbr.
Señor	Sr.	Signor	Sig.
Señores	Sres.	Signori	Sigg.
Señora	Sra.	Signora	Sig.ra*
Señorita	Srta.	Signorina	Sig.na*
Señoras	Sras.*	Signore	Sig.re*
Señoritas	Srtas.*	Signorine	Sig.ne*

*Abbreviation not used in addresses. Write the title out.

Sir. The British title "Sir" is never followed by a last name only. It must be followed by a forename, initial, or title.

> Sir Thomas Landon *or* Sir Thomas
> *not* Sir Landon

Attention. The attention line, if used, is double spaced between the inside address and the salutation. The word *Attention* may be used with or without a colon or may be omitted altogether. Note that the salutation must agree with the inside address, not with the person mentioned in the attention line.

> Jones & Jones, Inc.
> 25 Main Street
> Springfield MA 01055
>
> Attention Mr. Daniel Ford
>
> Gentlemen:
>
> United Brands Corp.
> U.S. Plaza
> Hartford NJ 22340
>
> Attention: D. D. Ryan
> Overseas Division
>
> Gentlemen:
>
> Department of the Treasury
> Federal Building
> Rapid City ND 44578
>
> Miss Martha Dustin
>
> Gentlemen:

Salutations. The following are the preferred salutations in modern usage (see chapter 9, pp. 145–75, for salutations in letters addressed to persons with specialized titles):

> Dear Sir:
> Dear Madam:

Gentlemen:
Ladies:
Ladies and Gentlemen:
Dear Mr. Howard: (informal in United States, formal in England)
My dear Mrs. Howard: (formal in United States, informal in England)
Dear Mr. and Mrs. Howard:
Dear Barbara, (personal)
To Whom It May Concern, (for very general or legal letters)

Subject line. Wherever possible, business letters should contain a subject line. The subject line briefly states the topic of the letter and facilitates reading, routing, and filing the letter. Since the subject line is part of the body of the letter, not the address, it is typed below the salutation, not above it. Keep the subject line as brief as possible. It may be typed in full capitals, or it may be underlined with only the important words capitalized.

General Insurance, Inc.
312 Main Street
Foxboro CA 90090

Gentlemen:

    Policy XJT-444-01

Mr. R. J. Fox
P.O. Box 493
New York NY 10017

Dear Sir:

    FILING SYSTEMS

In the Simplified Letter style, the subject line takes the place of the salutation.

Complimentary close. The complimentary close is typed two lines below the last line of the letter. It may be positioned flush with the left margin or the right margin or positioned in the center, depending on the style of the letter. There is no complimentary close in the Simplified Letter style.

130 LETTER WRITING

Capitalize only the first word of the complimentary close. The complimentary close should not be preceded by such phrases as "Hoping to hear from you" or "As ever, I am."

If the letter is taken from dictation and no complimentary close is indicated, use a complimentary close that reflects the tone of the letter. If in doubt, use "Very truly yours."

Highly formal—for official correspondence

  Respectfully yours,
  Respectfully,
  Very respectfully,

Neutral, polite—for general correspondence

  Very truly yours,
  Yours very truly,
  Yours truly,

Friendly, less formal—for general correspondence

  Sincerely,
  Yours sincerely,
  Very sincerely yours,
  Sincerely yours,

More informal—for general correspondence

  Cordially,
  Cordially yours,
  Yours cordially,

Informal—first-name basis

  As ever,
  Regards,
  Best regards,
  Best wishes,
  Kindest regards,
  Kindest personal regards,

British usage

> Faithfully yours,
> Yours faithfully,
> Yours sincerely,

Signature. Leave at least four spaces for the writer's handwritten signature. The writer's name is usually typed directly below the handwritten signature, although it may be omitted in informal correspondence when the writer's name appears on the letterhead. However, if the writer's handwritten signature is illegible, his name should be typed below the signature even if it appears on the letterhead.

In business correspondence, the writer's title and position should also be typed under the signature if they do not appear on the letterhead.

Henry T. Avery, Director, Research Department	when title and department name do not appear on letterhead
Henry T. Avery, Director	when department name appears on letterhead
Henry T. Avery	when both title and department name appear on letterhead

Titles such as Dr., Prof., or Rev. should not precede signatures. However, the initials of academic degrees may be typed after the writer's name if the writer so wishes. The initials M.D. or Ph.D. are often included when the writer wishes to be addressed as Dr. in return correspondence.

Joseph J. Jones, LL.D.
Jane K. Smith, Ph.D.
Martin Frankel, M.D.

A woman should sign her name as she wishes to be addressed in return correspondence. The courtesy titles Mrs., Miss, or Ms.

are often included as well to facilitate return correspondence, but they may be omitted when the writer feels that her marital status is irrelevant. If a married woman prefers to use her husband's name, she should sign herself Martha K. Hamilton, with her married title typed below it, Mrs. James P. Hamilton. The following are all acceptable for the typed signature line.

Jennifer Rand
(Miss) Jennifer Rand
(Ms.) Jennifer Rand
(Mrs.) Jennifer Rand
Mrs. Gerald Rand

The company name may appear in the signature block if it does not appear in the letterhead. The company name should also be included in the signature block in contractual or legal letters in which the writer acts as a representative of his company. In this case, type the company name in full capitals (two lines below the complimentary close) exactly as it appears in the letterhead.

for legal correspondence:

Very truly yours,
INTERNATIONAL FACTORS, INC.
   handwritten signature
Harold K. Dawson, President

also acceptable in general correspondence:

Very truly yours,
   handwritten signature
Harold K. Dawson, President
INTERNATIONAL FACTORS, INC.

When a secretary signs a letter in her own name, her employer should be mentioned by title and surname *only*.

(Miss) Janet Barnes
Secretary to Mr. Jacobson

Frederick Ashton
Secretary to Ms. Johnson

Norma J. O'Donnell
Assistant to Mr. Keyes

When a secretary signs her employer's name to a letter, the preferred usage is for her to write her employer's name followed immediately by her own initials.

Identification initials. The typist's and the writer's initials are placed two lines below the last line of the signature block. They need not appear on the master copy of the letter but should always appear on the carbon copies; this facilitates record-keeping and filing. The initials of the writer may be omitted from the notation, if desired, provided that the writer's name is typed in the signature block or appears in the letterhead. The following are all acceptable forms for identification initials.

RST:ksl	RST:KSL	RST/KL
RST:kl	RST:KL	RT/kl
ksl	RST:K	Ralph S. Toll/KL
kl	RST:k	Ralph S. Toll/k

If the letter is written and dictated by one person for the signature of a second and typed by a third, the proper order of the initials is (1) signer, (2) author, (3) typist.

  RST:JJB:KL   RST-JB:kl

If the letter is written and signed by one person, transcribed by a second, and typed by a third, the proper order of the initials is (1) writer/signer, (2) transcriber, (3) typist.

  RST:lcj:kl   RST/lj.kl

Enclosures. The enclosure notation is typed one or two lines below the identification initials, if there are any, or one or two lines below the last line of the signature block, if there are no identification initials. If there is more than one enclosure, indicate the number. If the enclosure is of special importance, identify it. If the enclosure is to be returned, make an indication to that effect.

> Enc.   Enc. 2   2 encs.
> Enclosure   Enclosures (3)   encl.
>
> Enc: 1. Cert. ck. $5,660
>   2. Mtge. - Smith to Jones
>
> Enc: Policy XX-100e-33 (to be returned)

Carbon copies. The carbon copy notation is typed one to two lines below the last previous notation. The following are acceptable:

> cc Mr. William H. Hill
>
> Copy to J. J. Randall, Esq.
>
> cc: Mr. Allan Jones
>   Ms. Kate Josephson
>
> Copies to   Mr. Axel
>   Mrs. Jennings
>   Ms. Reed
>
> cc: Dr. Charles Jordan
>
> cc: RST
>   KSL
>   MJJ

Blind carbons. If you do not wish the addressee to know that copies are being sent, use the bcc or bcc: notation. Type the blind carbon notation in the upper left hand corner of the *copies* only.

Postscript. A postscript should be indented five spaces from the left margin to give it prominence. The abbreviation **PS** or **P.S.** may be included or omitted as you wish. The writer's initials should be typed or written after the postscript, and if the postscript bears a different date from that of the letter, include this date with the postscript. If the postscript is handwritten on the master copy of the letter only, it should be typed on all carbon copies.

Envelopes

The figures below illustrate the proper style for addresses on envelopes.

```
┌─────────────────────────────────────────────────────────────┐
│  ⊕    GROSSET & DUNLAP, INC.                                │
│       PUBLISHERS                                            │
│  51 MADISON AVENUE, NEW YORK, NEW YORK 10010                │
│                                                             │
│                                        REGISTERED           │
│                                                             │
│          PERSONAL                                           │
│                                                             │
│                   Mr. John R. Radd                          │
│                   F. P. Bliss & Sons                        │
│                   44 Main Street                            │
│                   Rochester NY 11555                        │
│                                                             │
│                                                             │
└─────────────────────────────────────────────────────────────┘
```

```
┌─────────────────────────────────────────────────────────────┐
│  ⊕    GROSSET & DUNLAP, INC.                                │
│       PUBLISHERS                                            │
│  51 MADISON AVENUE, NEW YORK, NEW YORK 10010                │
│                                                             │
│                                         AIR MAIL            │
│                                                             │
│                                                             │
│               Smythe, French & Windsor                      │
│               10 Downing Street                             │
│               London                                        │
│               ENGLAND                                       │
│                                                             │
│          Attention Mr. F. D. Jackson                        │
│                                                             │
└─────────────────────────────────────────────────────────────┘
```

136 LETTER WRITING

How to Fit a Large Letter into a Small Envelope. Standard 8½ × 11 business letters are normally mailed in No. 10 envelopes (4⅛ × 9½). However, if you wish to mail a letter in the smaller No. 6¾ envelope (3⅝ × 6½), fold it as follows:

Step One—Fold the letter in half.

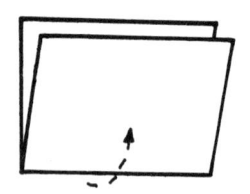

Step Two—Fold the right side of the letter over by one-third.

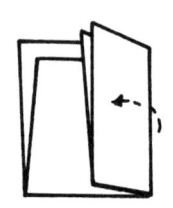

Step Three—Fold the left side of the letter evenly over the right.

Step Four—Insert the creased edge of the letter into the envelope.

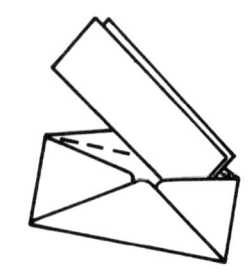

Government Correspondence

Letters to most government agencies may be typed in any of the commonly acceptable business letter styles. Letters to the Department of Defense, however, should follow a special format.

The following principles apply to letters directed to the Department of Defense.

1. Use a Modified Block style, and number each paragraph.
2. The special mailing notation, if there is one, appears in the upper left corner of the letter.
3. The writer's name, the typist's initials, and the writer's telephone number (if it does not appear on the letterhead) may be typed in the upper right corner. Each element should be separated by slashes.
4. If the letter contains classified or secret information, the highest applicable classification category must be stamped at the top and bottom of each page of the letter. In addition, the bottom of the letterhead sheet should be stamped with the CLASSIFIED BY and the NATIONAL SECURITY INFORMATION blocks.
5. Type the date in the inverted style, as 15 March 19—.
6. If your company has been assigned a control number by the Defense Department, type it one line below the date.
7. The SUBJECT block, if there is one, contains:
   line 1: contract number
   line 2: program or project title
   line 3: subject of the letter, followed by the security classification in parentheses, as (C) for Confidential or (TS) for Top Secret.
8. The inside address is replaced by the TO block:
   line 1: name of the office or its initials
   line 2: name of the official to whom the letter is being sent
   line 3: organization name (Department of Defense)
   line 4: address (city, state, and zip code)
9. Use a THROUGH block if the letter must go through designated channels before reaching the addressee. The THROUGH block should be arranged like the TO block, containing the office, individual, agency, and address.

10. Use a REFERENCE if the addressee must consult previous correspondence or other documents before acting on the letter. List the appropriate documents numerically or alphabetically.
11. Omit the salutation and the complimentary close.
12. The signature block should contain the company name (even if it is on the letterhead), the writer's handwritten signature, the writer's typed signature, and the writer's title and department name if they do not appear on the letterhead.
13. Use Enclosure(s), Encl., or Enc. for Navy and Air Force correspondence. Use Inclosure(s) or Inc. for Army correspondence. If the enclosure is classified, list the abbreviation of the classification category in parentheses before the description of the enclosure.
14. If any individuals are to receive carbon copies, list their addresses as well as their names.

Classified information. The classification categories for controlled information are: Unclassified (U), Confidential (C), Secret (S), and Top Secret (TS).

Classified material must be enclosed in two sealed opaque envelopes before mailing. Both envelopes must contain the names and addresses of the sender and the receiver, and the inner envelope must contain the appropriate classification stamp.

Confidential material should be sent by CERTIFIED mail and Secret information by REGISTERED mail. Top Secret information is not sent through the mails.

For further information, consult Department of Defense publication DoD 5200.1-R (Information Security Program Regulation), available from the Superintendent of Documents, U.S. Government Printing Office, Washington, DC 20402.

Characteristics of Good Letters

Good letters capture the reader's attention in the first sentence and hold it to the end of the letter. The best letters are short, simple, and to the point; these are the letters that the recipient is most apt to read and respond to. Here are some guidelines for writing effective business letters:

1. Pinpoint your message. Keep the letter short; short letters produce better results than long ones. Come to the point at once, specify the action desired or taken, and close quickly. Eliminate all extraneous background information.

   If you have several matters to discuss, it may be better to write more than one letter, so that each may be dealt with separately. Recipients tend to respond to short letters first. With only one—or at most two—subjects per letter, there is less chance for confusion and error.
2. Keep your paragraphs short. Short paragraphs are easier to read; readers are put off by overly long paragraphs. As a general rule, try not to make your paragraphs longer than four or five lines. A paragraph may be as short as one sentence.
3. State your business at once. The first sentence should contain, in a kernel, the essential matter of the letter.
4. Use simple sentences. Avoid long, involved sentences. Put only one idea in each sentence. Wherever possible, break up compound sentences containing such words as and, but, or, as, since, because, if, etc.
5. Use short words. Do not use big words which the reader may not understand; substitute small words instead. If you cannot find a substitute for a difficult word, try to reword the sentence so that the word is avoided entirely.
6. Do not use words that may antagonize the reader, such as failure, unfortunately, mistake, trouble, complaint, error, poor, etc. If you are making a complaint, or responding to one, these words may only further annoy the reader. Never accuse the reader: even if you are in the right, you will not get results from an inflammatory letter.
7. Avoid trite and outmoded phrases. See page 140 for a list of such phrases.

Tips for writing difficult letters. Occasionally you will have to write letters that are either so involved or so delicate that you are at a loss as to how to write them. You may find yourself staring at a blank sheet of paper, unable to put pen to paper. There are several remedies for this problem.

First, you can make a list. List each important point you want to make in the letter. Such a list might include, for example, received defective goods, returning them, demand credit, send new invoice, want special shipment, etc. Then take each point in turn and describe it in one or two sentences. You will then have a basic first draft of your letter. Revise it and switch sentences around as you wish. If possible, ask someone else to read and criticize it. Then write the final draft.

If you are no good at making lists, then you will have to follow another procedure. Try this one. Get a sheet of paper and write down the first idea that comes into your head. Once you've written it, don't try to revise it. Don't worry about whether or not it makes sense. Next, write down the second idea that comes into your head. Keep writing until you can think of no more things to say. Now you may revise the letter. You may find that it requires less correction than you expected. Even if you've written too much, you will not find it difficult to revise, since most of what you want to say is already on the paper.

Lastly, if large blank sheets of paper intimidate you, try composing your letter on individual 3-by-5 index cards. You may find it eliminates the fear of having to fill up a huge expanse of empty space.

Trite and Outmoded Phrases

Here is a list of incorrect and aged phrases. They are wrong, clumsy, wordy, or old-fashioned. Become familiar with them so that you can avoid them.

Abovementioned Use "This" or "that."
Accompanied by The preposition *with* is usually better. "I am enclosing a form with this letter," not, "This letter is accompanied by a form."
Acknowledge receipt of Use "We received."
Acquaint Use "tell" or "inform"; "acquaint" is both stiff and dated. "Advise" can also be replaced by "tell" or "inform."
Advise "Tell" and "say" are better.
Aforementioned Use "this" or "that."
Alternative Avoid the phrase "the only other alternative." Instead, write: "the alternative."
Anxious is correct only when anxiety exists. If you really mean "eager," then use it.
Appreciate your informing me is clumsy. Try something simple, such as "please write me," or "please tell me."

Apt Often used incorrectly when the writer means "likely." Apt suggests a predisposition as: "A smart student is apt to get high marks." "Likely" suggests possibility, as: "A few bad apples are likely to spoil the barrel."
At about "He will arrive at about nine o'clock." This is incorrect. Use "at" or "about" but not both.
At all times "Always" is better.
At this time "Now" is better.
At the present time "Now" is better.
At an early date "Soon" is better.
At your earliest convenience "Soon" is usually better.
At the earliest possible moment "Soon" or "immediately" is better.
Attached please find   "Attached" is enough;
Attached herewith   the other words are
Attached hereto   unnecessary
Brought to our notice Use "We note" or "We see."
By means of Simply use "by."
Commence "Begin" and "start" are less stiff and usually preferable.
Communicate, communication Avoid these long words if possible. Be specific: Instead of "communicate," say "write," "wire," or "telephone." Instead of "communication," say "letter," "telegram," or "memo."
Conclude Another stiff word. It's better to "end" or "close" a letter than to "conclude" it.
Contents carefully noted Eliminate.
Demonstrates "Shows" is the simpler, preferable form.
Desire "If you wish" or "if you want" sounds better than "if you desire."
Determine is overworked. Use "decide" or "find out."
Different Often unnecessary; as in: We had six different choices for dinner.
Due to the fact that is a wordy way of saying "because."
Duly Needless and unnecessary.
Earliest practicable date "Practicable" is a hazy word; use "soon" or "immediately."
Effectuate "Effect" means the same thing and is shorter.
Enclosed herewith   "Enclosed" is enough
Enclosed please find   "Enclosed" is enough

142 LETTER WRITING

Equivalent "Equal" is usually better and it is shorter.
Finalize Use "end," "conclude," or "complete."
For your information Usually superfluous, and can be eliminated.
For the month of July Write: "for July"
For the purpose of Use "to."
For the reason that Write: "since," "because," or "as."
For your information Usually superfluous, and can be eliminated.
Forward Often used when "send" would be better.
Fullest possible extent Say simply: "full extent" or "fully."
Furnish "Give" is shorter and more direct.
Implement "Carry out" is more direct.
In addition to Write: "besides."
In compliance with your request Write: "as you requested."
In a position to Use "We can" or "We are able."
In possession of Use "have" or "has."
In a satisfactory manner Write: "satisfactorily"
In the near future Write: "soon."
In the event that Write: "if"
In the amount of Write: "for"
In the meantime Write: "meantime" or "meanwhile."
In order to Write: "to"
In regard to Write: "about"
In view of the fact that Write: "as"
Inasmuch as "As," "since," and "because" are much shorter.
Indicate "Show" is less overworked, shorter, and more direct.
Initiate Usually "begin" is better.
Kindly Don't use it for "please." Write "Please reply," not "Kindly reply."
Liquidate How about "pay off," instead?
Meets with our approval Use "We approve."
None as a subject is usually plural, unless a single subject is indicated. "None of the jobs are open." "None of the work is finished."
Not in a position to "Cannot" is better.
Notwithstanding the fact that A wordy way of saying "although" or "even though."
On Unnecessary in stating dates. "He arrived Monday," not "He arrived on Monday."

Previous to, prior to "Before" usually sounds better.
Quite means "truly," "really," "wholly," or "positively." Avoid the phrases: "quite a few" and "quite some."
Rarely ever, seldom ever "Ever" is unnecessary.
Receipt is acknowledged Try: "We received."
Reside "Live" is preferable.
State Often too formal. Use: "say" or "tell."
Submitted "Sent" is preferable and more direct.
Subsequent to "After" is shorter and more direct.
Take pleasure Trite. Use: "are happy" or "are pleased."
This is to inform you You can usually omit this phrase.
This is to thank you Can you use the shorter "Thank you"?
Under separate cover Be more specific: by third-class mail, etc.
Utilize, utilization Use the shorter word "use."
Wish to apologize Say simply "I [or we] apologize."
Wish to advise Can usually be eliminated.
Wish to state Needless and unnecessary.
With the result that Use "so that."

9. Forms of Address

In the following tables, where the term "Mr." is used, it should be understood that if the official is a woman, she should be addressed as Ms., Miss, Mrs., or Madam. For a formal close to a business letter, use "Very truly yours"; for an informal close, use "Sincerely yours." Be sure to include the correct Zip Code number in your address.

CORRECT FORMS OF ADDRESS

United States Government Officials

Person	Address	Salutation	Oral Reference / Written Reference
The President	The President The White House	Dear Mr. President:	1. Mr. President 2. The President
President-elect of the United States	The Honorable John J. Jones President-elect of the United States (local address)	Dear Mr. Jones:	1. Mr. Jones 2. The President-elect or Mr. Jones
Former President of the United States*	The Honorable John R. Jones (local address)	Dear Mr. Jones:	1. Mr. Jones 2. Former President Jones or Mr. Jones
The Vice-President of the United States	The Vice-President of the United States United States Senate	Dear Mr. Vice-President	1. Mr. Vice-President: or Mr. Jones The Vice-President

*If a former president has a title, such as *General of the Army*, use the title.

LETTER WRITING

Person	Address	Salutation	
			1. Oral Reference
			2. Written Reference
The Chief Justice of the United States Supreme Court	The Chief Justice of the United States The Supreme Court of the United States	Dear Mr. Chief Justice:	1. Mr. Chief Justice 2. The Chief Justice
Associate Justice of the United States Supreme Court	Mr. Justice Jones The Supreme Court of the United States	Dear Mr. Justice:	1. Mr. Justice Jones or Justice Jones 2. Mr. Justice Jones
Retired Justice of the United States Supreme Court	The Honorable John R. Jones (local address)	Dear Justice Jones:	1. Mr. Justice Jones or Justice Jones 2. Mr. Justice Jones
Cabinet Officers addressed as "Secretary"*	The Honorable John R. Jones Secretary of State The Honorable John Jones Secretary of State of the United States of America (if written from abroad)	Dear Mr. Secretary:	1. Mr. Secretary or Secretary Jones or Mr. Jones 2. The Secretary of State, Mr. (Mr. or The Secretary) Jones

Former Cabinet Officer	The Honorable John R. Jones (local address)	Dear Mr. Jones:	1. Mr. Jones 2. Mr. Jones
The Speaker of the House of Representatives	The Honorable John R. Jones Speaker of the House of Representatives	Dear Mr. Speaker: or Dear Mr. Jones	1. Mr. Speaker or Mr. Jones 2. The Speaker, Mr. Jones (The Speaker or Mr. Jones)
Former Speaker of the House of Representatives	The Honorable John R. Jones (local address)	Dear Mr. Jones:	1. Mr. Jones 2. Mr. Jones

---

*Titles for cabinet secretaries are Secretary of State; Secretary of the Treasury; Secretary of Defense; Secretary of the Interior; Secretary of Agriculture; Secretary of Commerce; Secretary of Labor; Secretary of Health, Education, and Welfare; Secretary of Housing and Urban Development; Secretary of Transportation.

148 LETTER WRITING

Person	Address	Salutation	Oral Reference / Written Reference
Postmaster General	The Honorable John R. Jones The Postmaster General	Dear Mr. Postmaster General:	1. Mr. Postmaster General *or* Postmaster General Jones or Mr. Jones 2. The Postmaster General, Mr. Jones (Mr. Jones or The Postmaster General)
The Attorney General	The Honorable John R. Jones The Attorney General	Dear Mr. Attorney General:	1. Mr. Attorney General *or* Attorney General Jones 2. The Attorney General, Mr. Jones (Mr. Jones or The Attorney General)

Forms of Address 149

Under Secretary of a Department	The Honorable John R. Jones Under Secretary of Labor	Dear Mr. Jones:	1. Mr. Jones 2. Mr. Jones
United States Senator	The Honorable John R. Jones United States Senate	Dear Senator Jones:	1. Senator Jones or Senator 2. Senator Jones
Former Senator	The Honorable John R. Jones (local address)	Dear Senator Jones:	1. Senator Jones or Senator 2. Senator Jones
Senator-elect	Honorable John R. Jones Senator-elect United States Senate	Dear Mr. Jones:	1. Mr. Jones 2. Senator-elect Jones or Mr. Jones
Committee Chairman–United States Senate	The Honorable John R. Jones, Chairman Committee on Foreign Affairs United States Senate	Dear Mr. Chairman: or Dear Senator Jones:	1. Mr. Chairman or Senator Jones or Senator 2. The Chairman or Senator Jones

150 LETTER WRITING

Person	Address	Salutation	Oral Reference / Written Reference
Subcommittee Chairman—United States Senate	The Honorable John R. Jones, Chairman, Subcommittee on Foreign Affairs United States Senate	Dear Senator Jones:	1. Senator Jones or Senator 2. Senator Jones
United States Representative or Congressman	The Honorable John R. Jones House of Representatives The Honorable John R. Jones Representative in Congress (local address) (when away from Washington, DC)	Dear Mr. Jones:	1. Mr. Jones 2. Mr. Jones, Representative (Congressman) from New York or Mr. Jones
Former Representative	The Honorable John R. Jones (local address)	Dear Mr. Jones:	1. Mr. Jones 2. Mr. Jones

Forms of Address 151

Resident Commissioner	The Honorable John R. Jones Resident Commissioner of (Territory) House of Representatives	Dear Mr. Jones:	1. Mr. Jones 2. Mr. Jones
Territorial Delegate	The Honorable John R. Jones Delegate of Puerto Rico House of Representatives	Dear Mr. Jones:	1. Mr. Jones 2. Mr. Jones
Directors of Heads of Independent Federal Offices, Agencies, Commissions, and Organizations.	The Honorable John R. Jones Director, Mutual Security Agency	Dear Mr. Jones:	1. Mr. Jones 2. Mr. Jones
Librarian of Congress	The Honorable John R. Jones Librarian of Congress	Dear Mr. Jones:	1. Mr. Jones 2. The Librarian of Congress or Mr. Jones

152 LETTER WRITING

Person	Address	Salutation	1. Oral Reference 2. Written Reference
Other High Officials of the United States: Public Printer, Comptroller General, etc.	The Honorable John R. Jones Public Printer The Honorable John R. Jones Comptroller General of the United States	Dear Mr. Jones:	1. Mr. Jones 2. Mr. Jones
Federal Judge	The Honorable John J. Jones Judge of the United States District Court for the ―― District of ――	Dear Judge Jones:	1. Judge Jones 2. The Judge 　　or 　　Judge Jones
Secretary to the President	The Honorable John R. Jones Secretary to the President The White House	Dear Mr. Jones:	1. Mr. Jones 2. Mr. Jones
Assistant Secretary to the President	The Honorable John R. Jones Assistant Secretary to the President The White House	Dear Mr. Jones:	1. Mr. Jones 2. Mr. Jones

Press Secretary to the President	Mr. John R. Jones Press Secretary to the President The White House	Dear Mr. Jones:	1. Mr. Jones 2. Mr. Jones

State and Local Government Officials

Governor of a State or Territory*	The Honorable John R. Jones Governor of New York	Dear Governor Jones:	1. Governor Jones or Governor 2. a) Governor Jones b) The Governor c) The Governor of New York (used only outside his or her own state)
Acting Governor of a State or Territory	The Honorable John R. Jones Acting Governor of New York	Dear Mr. Jones:	1. Mr. Jones 2. Mr. Jones
Governor-elect	The Honorable John R. Jones Governor-elect of New York	Dear Mr. Jones:	1. Mr. Jones 2. Mr. Jones, the Governor-elect

*The form of address for governors varies from state to state. In Massachusetts by law and in certain other states by courtesy, use His (Her) Excellency, the Governor of Massachusetts.

154 LETTER WRITING

Person	Address	Salutation	
Former Governor	The Honorable John R. Jones	Dear Mr. Jones:	1. Oral Reference: Mr. Jones 2. Written Reference: John R. Jones, former Governor of New York
Lieutenant Governor	The Honorable John R. Jones Lieutenant Governor of New York	Dear Mr. Jones:	1. Mr. Jones 2. The Lieutenant Governor of New York, Mr. Jones or The Lieutenant Governor
Secretary of State	The Honorable John R. Jones Secretary of State of New York	Dear Mr. Secretary:	1. Mr. Jones 2. Mr. Jones
Attorney General	The Honorable John R. Jones Attorney General of New York	Dear Mr. Attorney General:	1. Mr. Jones 2. Mr. Jones

Forms of Address

Chief Justice* of a State Supreme Court	The Honorable John R. Jones Chief Justice of the Supreme Court of Minnesota**	Dear Mr. Chief Justice:	1. Mr. Chief Justice or Judge Jones 2. Mr. Chief Justice Jones or Judge Jones
Associate Justice of a Supreme Court of a State	The Honorable John R. Jones Associate Justice of the Supreme Court of Minnesota	Dear Justice Jones:	1. Mr. Justice Jones 2. Mr. Justice Jones
Presiding Justice	The Honorable John R. Jones Presiding Justice, Appellate Division Supreme Court of New York	Dear Justice Jones:	1. Mr. Justice (or Judge) Jones 2. Mr. Justice (or Judge Jones)
President of the Senate of a State	The Honorable John R. Jones President of the Senate of the State of New York	Dear Mr. Jones:	1. Mr. Jones 2. Mr. Jones

*In some states, the title is Chief Judge. Do not use Mr., Mrs., Miss, or Ms. with Chief Judge.
**In some states, the name of the high court may be different, as Court of Appeals in New York.

156 LETTER WRITING

Person	Address	Salutation	1. Oral Reference 2. Written Reference
Speaker of the Assembly or The House of Representatives ***	The Honorable John R. Jones Speaker of the Assembly of the State of New York	Dear Mr. Jones:	1. Mr. Jones 2. Mr. Jones
Treasurer, Auditor, or Comptroller of a State	The Honorable John R. Jones Treasurer of the State of New York	Dear Mr. Jones	1. Mr. Jones 2. Mr. Jones
State Senator	The Honorable John R. Jones The State Senate	Dear Senator Jones:	1. Senator Jones or Senator 2. Senator Jones
State Representative, Assemblyman, or Delegate	The Honorable John R. Jones House of Delegates	Dear Mr. Jones:	1. Mr. Jones 2. Mr. Jones or Delegate Jones
District Attorney	The Honorable John R. Jones District Attorney, Albany County County Courthouse	Dear Mr. Jones:	1. Mr. Jones 2. Mr. Jones

Forms of Address 157

Mayor of a city	The Honorable John R. Jones Mayor of New York	Dear Mayor Jones:	1. Mayor Jones or Mr. Mayor Jones 2. Mayor Jones
President of a Board of Commissioners	The Honorable John R. Jones, President Board of Commissioners of the City of New York	Dear Mr. Jones:	1. Mr. Jones 2. Mr. Jones
City Attorney, City Counsel, Corporation Counsel	The Honorable John R. Jones, City Attorney (City Counsel, Corporation Counsel)	Dear Mr. Jones:	1. Mr. Jones 2. Mr. Jones
Alderman	Alderman John R. Jones City Hall	Dear Mr. Jones:	1. Mr. Jones 2. Mr. Jones
Clerk of a Court	William R. Jones, Esquire Clerk of the Superior Court of New York	Dear Mr. Jones:	1. Mr. Jones 2. Mr. Jones

***Note: The House of Delegates in Maryland, Virginia, and West Virginia; the House of General Assembly in New Jersey.

158 LETTER WRITING

Person	Address	Salutation	1. Oral Reference 2. Written Reference
Judge of a Court	The Honorable John R. Jones Judge of the United States District Court for the Southern District of California	Dear Judge Jones:	1. Judge Jones 2. Judge Jones

Foreign Heads of State

Person	Address	Salutation	1. Oral Reference 2. Written Reference
Prime Minister	His Excellency, John Jones Prime Minister of India	Dear Mr. Prime Minister:	1. Mr. Jones 2. Mr. Jones or The Prime Minister
British Prime Minister	The Right Honorable John Jones, K.G., M.C., M.P. Prime Minister	Dear Mr. Prime Minister: or Dear Mr. Jones:	1. Mr. Jones 2. Mr. Jones or The Prime Minister
Canadian Prime Minister	The Right Honorable John Jones, C.M.G. Prime Minister of Canada	Dear Mr. Prime Minister: or Dear Mr. Jones:	1. Mr. Jones 2. Mr. Jones or The Prime Minister

Forms of Address

President of a Republic	His Excellency, John Jones President of the Dominican Republic	Dear Mr. President:	1. Your Excellency 2. President Jones
Premier	His Excellency, John Jones Premier of the French Republic	Dear Mr. Premier:	1. Mr. Jones 2. Mr. Jones or The Premier
Queen	Her Gracious Majesty, the Queen	May it please your Majesty:	1. Your Majesty 2. Her Majesty
King	His Gracious Majesty, the King	May it please your Majesty	1. Your Majesty 2. His Majesty
Diplomats			
American Ambassador	The Honorable John R. Jones American Ambassador*	Dear Mr. Ambassador:	1. Mr. Ambassador or Mr. Jones 2. The American Ambassador** (Mr. Jones)

*If an ambassador or minister holds a military title, omit The Honorable, thus General John R. Jones, American Ambassador (or minister). If an ambassador is not resident in the country to which he is accredited, add the name of the country, as The American Ambassador to France.

**Omit American when referring to ambassadors to Central or South American countries; use The Ambassador of the United States.

LETTER WRITING

Person	Address	Salutation	1. Oral Reference 2. Written Reference
Foreign Ambassador	His Excellency, John Jones Ambassador of Norway *if from Great Britain* His Excellency The Right Honorable John R. Jones British Ambassador	Dear Mr. Ambassador: Dear Mr. Ambassador:	1. Mr. Ambassador or Mr. Jones 2. The Ambassador of Norway (The Ambassador or Mr. Jones) 1. Mr. Ambassador 2. The British Ambassador
American Minister	The Honorable John R. Jones American Minister to France*	Dear Mr. Minister:	1. Mr. Minister or Mr. Jones 2. The American Minister, Mr. Jones (The Minister or Mr. Jones)

*If an ambassador or minister holds a military title, omit The Honorable, thus General John R. Jones, American Ambassador (or Minister). If an ambassador is not resident in the country to which he is accredited, add the name of the country, as The American Ambassador to France.

Forms of Address 161

Foreign Minister in the United States	The Honorable John Jones Minister of France *if from Great Britain* British Minister	Dear Mr. Minister:	1. Mr. Minister or Mr. Jones 2. The Minister of France (The Minister or Mr. Jones)
High Commissioner	The Honorable John R. Jones United States High Commissioner to France	Dear Mr. Jones:	1. Commissioner Jones or Mr. Jones 2. Commissioner Jones or Mr. Jones
American Chargé d'Affaires	John R. Jones, Esq. American Chargé d'Affaires ad Interim *if in Central or South America* United States Chargé d'Affaires ad Interim	Dear Mr. Jones:	1. Mr. Jones 2. Mr. Jones

162 LETTER WRITING

Person	Address	Salutation	Oral Reference / Written Reference
Foreign Chargé d'Affaires ad Interim	Mr. John R. Jones Chargé d'Affaires ad Interim of France	Dear Mr. Jones:	1. Mr. Jones 2. Mr. Jones
Foreign Chargé d'Affaires (de missi) in the United States	Mr. John Jones Chargé d'Affaires of France	Dear Mr. Jones:	1. Mr. Jones 2. Mr. Jones

The Military

Person	Address	Salutation	Oral Reference / Written Reference
General of the Army	General of the Army John R. Jones Department of the Army	Dear General Jones:	1. General Jones 2. General Jones
General, Lieutenant General, Major General, Brigadier General	General (Lieutenant General, Major General, or Brigadier General) John R. Jones	Dear General Jones:	1. General Jones 2. General Jones
Fleet Admiral	Fleet Admiral John R. Jones, Chief of Naval Operations, Department of the Navy	Dear Admiral Jones:	1. Admiral Jones 2. Admiral Jones

Admiral, Vice Admiral, Rear Admiral	Admiral (Vice Admiral or Rear Admiral) John R. Jones	Dear Admiral Jones:	1. Admiral Jones 2. Admiral Jones
Colonel, Lieutenant Colonel	Colonel (Lieutenant Colonel) John R. Jones	Dear Colonel Jones:	1. Colonel Jones 2. Colonel Jones
Major	Major John R. Jones	Dear Major Jones:	1. Major Jones 2. Major Jones
Commodore, Commander, Lieutenant Commander	Commodore (Commander, Lieutenant Commander) John R. Jones	Dear Commodore (Commander) Jones:	1. Commodore (Commander) Jones 2. Commodore (Commander) Jones
Captain	Captain John R. Jones	Dear Captain Jones:	1. Captain Jones 2. Captain Jones
First Lieutenant, Second Lieutenant	Lieutenant John R. Jones	Dear Lieutenant Jones:	1. Lieutenant Jones 2. Lieutenant Jones

Names may be followed by a comma and the initials of the appropriate branch of the military, as U.S.A. for the Army, U.S.N. for the Navy, U.S.A.F. for the Air Force, U.S.C.G. for the Coast Guard, and U.S.M.C. for the Marine Corps.

LETTER WRITING

Person	Address	Salutation	Oral Reference / Written Reference
Junior Officers: Lieutenant, Lieutenant Junior Grade, Ensign	(Lieutenant, etc.) John R. Jones	Dear Mr. Jones:	1. Mr. Jones 2. Lieutenant, etc., Jones (Mr. Jones)
Chief Warrant Officer, Warrant Officer	Mr. John R. Jones, U.S.N. U.S.S. Texas	Dear Mr. Jones:	1. Mr. Jones 2. Mr. Jones
Chaplain	Chaplain John R. Jones, Captain, U.S.N. Department of the Navy	Dear Chaplain Jones:	1. Chaplain Jones 2. Captain Jones (Chaplain Jones)

College and University Officials

Person	Address	Salutation	Oral / Written Reference
President of a College or University	*With a doctor's degree:* Dr. John R. Jones or John R. Jones, LL.D., Ph.D. President, Tufts College	Dear Dr. Jones:	1. Dr. Jones 2. Dr. Jones

Forms of Address 165

Without a doctor's degree: Mr. John R. Jones President, Harvard University	Dear President Jones:	1. Mr. Jones 2. Mr. Jones or Mr. Jones, President of the College
Catholic priest: The Very Reverend John R. Jones, S.J., D.D., Ph.D. President, Fordham University	Dear Father Jones:	1. Father Jones 2. Father Jones
University Chancellor	Dr. John R. Jones Chancellor, University of Hartford	Dear Dr. Jones:	1. Dr. Jones 2. Dr. Jones
Dean or Assistant Dean of a College or Graduate School	Dean John R. Jones School of Law or *(If he holds a doctor's degree)* Dr. John R. Jones, Dean (Assistant Dean) School of Medicine University of Iowa	Dear Dean Jones:	1. Dean Jones 2. Dean Jones or Dr. Jones, the Dean (Assistant Dean) of the School of Law

166 LETTER WRITING

Person	Address	Salutation	1. Oral Reference 2. Written Reference
Professor	Professor John R. Jones or *(If he holds a doctor's degree)* Dr. John R. Jones or John R. Jones, Ph.D. Barnard University	Dear Professor (Dr.) Jones:	1. Professor (Dr.) Jones 2. Professor (Dr.) Jones
Associate or Assistant Professor	Mr. John R. Jones or *(If he holds a doctor's degree)* Dr. John R. Jones or John R. Jones, Ph.D. Associate (Assistant) Professor Department of Romance Languages	Dear Professor (Dr.) Jones:	1. Professor (Dr.) Jones 2. Professor (Dr.) Jones

Forms of Address

Instructor	Mr. John R. Jones or (*If he holds a doctor's degree*) Dr. John R. Jones, Ph.D. Department of Economics	Dear Mr. (Dr.) Jones:	1. Mr. (Dr.) Jones 2. Mr. (Dr.) Jones
Chaplain of a College or University	The Reverend John R. Jones, D.D. Chaplain, Trinity College or Chaplain John R. Jones Trinity College	Dear Chaplain (Dr.) Jones:	1. Chaplain Jones 2. Chaplain Jones or Dr. Jones

United Nations Officials

Secretary General	His Excellency, John R. Jones Secretary General of the United Nations	Dear Mr. Secretary General:	1. Mr. Jones or Sir 2. The Secretary General of the United Nations or Mr. Jones

168 LETTER WRITING

Person	Address	Salutation	1. Oral Reference 2. Written Reference
Under Secretary	The Honorable John R. Jones Under Secretary of the United Nations	Dear Mr. Jones:	1. Mr. Jones 2. Mr. Jones
Foreign Representative (with ambassadorial rank)	His Excellency, John R. Jones Representative of France to the United Nations	Dear Mr. Ambassador:	1. Mr. Ambassador *or* Mr. Jones 2. Mr. Ambassador *or* The Representative of France to the United Nations (The Ambassador or Mr. Jones)
United States Representative (with ambassadorial rank)	The Honorable John R. Jones, United States Representative to the United Nations	Dear Mr. Ambassador:	1. Mr. Ambassador *or* Mr. Jones 2. Mr. Ambassador *or* The United States Representative to the United Nations (The Ambassador or Mr. Jones)

Religious Personages

The Pope	His Holiness, The Pope or His Holiness Pope—— Vatican City	Your Holiness: Most Holy Father	1. Your Holiness 2. His Holiness or The Pope
Apostolic Delegate	His Excellency, The Most Reverend John R. Jones Archbishop of—— The Apostolic Delegate	Dear Archbishop Jones:	1. Your Excellency 2. The Apostolic Delegate
Cardinal in the United States	His Eminence, John Cardinal Jones Archbishop of New York	Dear Cardinal Jones:	1. Your Eminence or *less formally* Cardinal Jones 2. His Eminence or Cardinal Jones
Abbot	The Right Reverend John R. Jones Abbot of Westmoreland Abbey	Dear Father Jones:	1. Father Abbot 2. Father Jones

LETTER WRITING

Person	Address	Salutation	1. Oral Reference / 2. Written Reference
Bishop Archbishop (Catholic)	The Most Reverend John R. Jones Bishop (Archbishop) of Baltimore	Dear Bishop (Archbishop) Jones:	1. Bishop (Archbishop) Jones 2. Bishop (Archbishop) Jones
	in England The Right Reverend John R. Jones Bishop of Sussex	Dear Bishop:	1. Bishop Jones 2. Bishop Jones
Canon	The Reverend John R. Jones, D.D. Canon of St. Patrick's Cathedral	Dear Canon Jones:	1. Canon Jones 2. Canon Jones
Monsignor domestic prelate papal chamberlain	The Right Reverend Msgr. John Jones The Very Reverend Msgr. John R. Jones	Dear Monsignor Jones:	1. Monsignor Jones 2. Monsignor Jones
Brother	Brother John Jones	Dear Brother Jones:	1. Brother Jones 2. Brother Jones

Forms of Address

Superior of a Brotherhood and Priest	The Very Reverend John R. Jones, M.M. Director	Dear Father Superior:	1. Father Jones 2. Father Jones
Priest	*With scholastic degree:* The Reverend John R. Jones, Ph.D. *Without scholastic degree:* The Reverend John R. Jones	Dear Dr. Jones: Dear Father Jones:	1. Doctor (Father) Jones 2. Doctor (Father) Jones 1. Father Jones 2. Father Jones
Sister Superior	The Reverend Sister Superior *(order, if used)*	Dear Sister Superior:	1. Sister Jones or Sister St. Teresa 2. The Sister Superior or Sister Jones (Sister St. Teresa)
Sister	Sister Mary Jones	Dear Sister Jones:	1. Sister Jones 2. Sister Jones
Mother Superior of a Sisterhood (Catholic or Protestant)	The Reverend Mother Superior, O.C.A.	Dear Reverend Mother: or Dear Mother Superior:	1. Reverend Mother 2. Reverend Mother

Person	Address	Salutation	1. Oral Reference 2. Written Reference
Member of Community	Mother Mary Walker, R.S.M.	Dear Mother Jones:	1. Mother Jones 2. Mother Jones
Archbishop Anglican	The Most Reverend Archbishop of Canterbury or The Most Reverend John Jones, Archbishop of Canterbury	Dear Archbishop Jones:	1. Your Grace 2. His Grace or The Archbishop
Presiding Bishop of the Protestant Episcopal Church in America	The Most Reverend John R. Jones, D.D., LL.D. Presiding Bishop of the Protestant Episcopal Church in America	Dear Bishop Jones:	1. Bishop Jones 2. Bishop Jones
Anglican Bishop	The Right Reverend The Lord Bishop of London	My dear Bishop:	1. Bishop Jones 2. Bishop Jones

Methodist Bishop	The Very Reverend John R. Jones Methodist Bishop	My dear Bishop:	1. Bishop Jones 2. Bishop Jones
Protestant Episcopal Bishop	The Right Reverend John R. Jones, D.D., LL.D. Bishop of Denver	Dear Bishop Jones:	1. Bishop Jones 2. Bishop Jones
Archdeacon	The Venerable John R. Jones Archdeacon of Baltimore	My dear Archdeacon:	1. Archdeacon Jones 2. Archdeacon Jones
Dean	The Very Reverend John R. Jones, D.D. Dean of St. John's Cathedral	Dear Dean Jones:	1. Dean Jones or Dr. Jones 2. Dean Jones or Dr. Jones

174 LETTER WRITING

Person	Address	Salutation	1. Oral Reference 2. Written Reference
Protestant Minister	*With scholastic degree:* The Reverend John R. Jones, D.D., Litt.D. or The Reverend Dr. John R. Jones *Without scholastic degree:* The Reverend John R. Jones	Dear Dr. Jones: Dear Mr. Jones:	1. Dr. Jones 2. Dr. Jones 1. Mr. Jones 2. Mr. Jones
Episcopal Priest (High Church)	*With scholastic degree:* The Reverend John R. Jones, D.D. Litt.D. All Saint's Cathedral or The Reverend Dr. John R. Jones	Dear Dr. Jones:	1. Dr. Jones 2. Dr. Jones

	Without scholastic degree: The Reverend John R. Jones St. Paul's Church	Dear Mr. Jones: or Dear Father Jones:	1. Father Jones or Mr. Jones 2. Father Jones or Mr. Jones
Rabbi	*With scholastic degree:* Rabbi John R. Jones, Ph.D. *Without scholastic degree:* Rabbi John R. Jones	Dear Rabbi Jones: or Dear Dr. Jones: Dear Rabbi Jones:	1. Rabbi Jones or Dr. Jones 2. Rabbi Jones or Dr. Jones 1. Rabbi Jones 2. Rabbi Jones

10.

Model Letters

Letters of Acknowledgment during Employer's Absence

(1)

As Mr. Franklin is away from the office this week, I am acknowledging your letter of January 27 concerning stock transferral notices. I will bring this matter to his attention as soon as he returns, and I am sure he will be able to give you a prompt reply.

Please accept my apologies for this unavoidable delay.

(2)

This will acknowledge receipt of your estimate of the cost of the four-color printing process. As I know Mr. Stone was awaiting your reply with interest, I am sure he will get in touch with you on his return to the office at the end of next week.

(3)

Thank you for your kind invitation to Mr. Forensick to speak at the annual dinner of the Business Writers' Club. Mr. Forensick is attending a convention in Sydney, Australia and will return to the office next week. I will bring your letter to his attention at that time.

(4)

Your letter giving Mr. Kirk the details of the Hightson board meeting arrived two days after he left town on a business trip.

However, I have checked his schedule for October 24, and I see that he is to be in Washington at the Senate subcommittee hearings on that day, and, therefore, it will be impossible for him to be present at the board meeting.

I know that Mr. Kirk will want to be in touch with you on his return to make plans for the next board meeting.

(5)

Thank you for your letter of April 13 asking Mr. Stonington for details of Smith & Co.'s employee benefits plan. In his absence, I am taking the liberty of sending you several brochures that describe the plan. Mr. Stonington will be back in the office after May 30, and I know he will be in touch with you at that time to answer any questions you may have.

Reservation Letters

(1)

This will confirm our telephone conversation of this morning in which we discussed arrangements for Smith & Co.'s convention reservations at your hotel.

The following will be required:

1. Nine single rooms for December 5 through 9.
2. Fifteen double rooms for the same period.
3. Three suites of at least three rooms each.
4. The use of two conference rooms holding 300 persons for the entire period.
5. Banquet room of the same size for evening of December 9.

As we discussed, you will provide Smith & Co. with written confirmation of the above arrangements.

If you need any further information, please call me.

(2)

Thank you for your prompt confirmation of Smith & Co.'s convention reservations at your hotel.

As you requested, we are forwarding a deposit in the amount stated. A check is enclosed.

Order Letters

(1)

In confirmation of our telephone discussion this morning regarding Mr. Smith's Christmas gifts, I am sending you the order in detail.

5	Key rings (silver)	@ $22.95	$114.75
8	Swizzle sticks - 3"	@ 10	80.00
1	Watch - Model 12-X	@ 175	175.00
2	Embossed lighters	@ 37.50	75.00
	Pocket calendars		
15	No. 3	@ 4	60.00
			$504.75

I have enclosed a list of the recipients and the messages to be enclosed with each gift.

You have assured me that the gifts will be delivered by December 22.

(2)

On July 19 I placed an order for letterhead stationery, personal stationery, envelopes, and business cards for Mr. Gerald R. Smith. Because of Mr. Smith's death, the order must be cancelled.

This order was charged to Freeman & Freeman's general account. You assured me at the time of the order that in the event of cancellation, half the amount of the purchase price would be refundable. Please credit our account with that amount.

Letters regarding Errors in Accounts

(1)

Mr. Dillingham recently received a statement from your company for $275.50. The amount is not correct. As you will see from the enclosed photocopy of the receipt, the item Mr. Dillingham bought was $175.50.

Kindly send me a correct invoice.

(2)

The recent statement of Mr. Horsely's account shows a charge of $27.50 for a person-to-person call to London, England. Evidently this charge is an error as our records show that Mr. Horsely's telephone was used for no long distance calls on that date.

I have deducted $27.50 from the total amount of the statement and am enclosing a check for the remainder.

(3)

On January 5 Ms. Nancy Fortin returned for credit a silver bowl that she purchased from you on December 3 for $660. Ms. Fortin's January statement does not show this credit. Ms. Fortin would appreciate it if you would verify the credit and send her a corrected statement.

(4)

Mrs. Jefferson's checking account statement of February 11 shows a final balance of $2,407.68. According to Mrs. Jefferson's records, however, the correct figure should be $2,507.68, or $100 more than the statement shows.

In reviewing the statement, I believe a printing error occurred on Line 16 which resulted in the understatement of Mrs. Jefferson's account.

Would you kindly rectify your records.

Appointment Letters

(1)

An opening has occurred in our Overseas Production Department, and your resume in our files indicates that the position may be of interest to you.

Mr. Borowski, Personnel Director of the Overseas Division, would like to know if it would be possible to see you next week in his office on either Monday or Tuesday.

Please telephone me to arrange a convenient time.

(2)

Dear Mr. Anderson:

Would it be possible to have a brief meeting with you at your office in the near future?

I'm Safety Chairman of the 12th Street Association, and I should like to discuss some new ideas for reducing the hazards posed by some of your trucks in our neighborhood.

If it is possible to arrange such a meeting, would you be kind enough to let me know when it would be convenient?

I know your company's reputation for good citizenship is well earned, and I'm looking forward to meeting with you.

Sincerely,

(3)

Mr. Brown will be in Washington April 4 through April 8 for the committee hearings on the proposed Tariff Act. Mr. Brown would like to know if your schedule during that period would permit you to see him for an hour or so to discuss the consequences to the drug industry of the Act.

If your secretary will be kind enough to call me, we will be able to set up a mutually agreeable time.

Reminders

(1)

As we agreed when I telephoned you, I am writing to remind you that we are expecting you at the Springfield Business Society's luncheon at 2 o'clock on April 7. You have agreed to speak on the subject of government regulation of the international oil business.

We look forward to seeing you then.

(2)

This is a reminder that the quarterly board meeting will be held next month at the conference hall of the Jones Street offices rather than in the chief meeting room of the Executive Office Building.

The time, as usual, is 11 a.m.

Inquiry letter

My company is planning to hold a national sales meeting in your city around the first week of April.

We will have about twenty people at the meeting.

They will probably arrive the night before the meeting begins and stay for two additional nights.

We will need two conference rooms throughout most of the time, each capable of holding about 10 people.

We would also like to arrange special entertainment for them in the evenings.

Please let me know:

1. The rate scales for single- and double-occupancy rooms.
2. The cost for meetings rooms.
3. The details of any package plans that offer room, meals, and some form of entertainment.
4. What kind of attractions you can offer the spouses during the meeting sessions.

If you need additional information in order to answer my questions, please call or write me.

Business Agreement Letters

Dear Mr. Henderson:

This will confirm the arrangement made in our conversation this morning at your office.

You will provide men and materials to landscape the grounds of our office building at 45 Groveton Terrace, Greenfield, N.Y., during the eight week period from April 1 through May 31, at a cost not to exceed thirteen thousand dollars.

You will do the following: procure and install twelve hundred square feet of No. 1 quality turf in the designated area between the building and the parking lot; procure and plant at least ten but not more than twelve No. 4 caliper maple trees in a line bordering the parking lot; procure and plant one hundred shrub plants 1½ to 2 feet tall as foundation plantings, to consist of any mixture of azaleas, lilacs, hydrangeas, and barberries.

You will also replace free of charge any trees or plants that die within two months of planting.

Please let me know if you agree to these terms.

Complaints and Claim Letters

(1)

For the past year, I've had to discard about 10% of every shipment we've received from you because of poor quality workmanship.

I've spoken about this to Jane Dale, your sales representative, several times. She has always promised to get it corrected.

But nothing—absolutely nothing—has changed.

I like your prices and your delivery schedules. But I have to throw away too much of your merchandise.

And I can't afford this kind of waste.

Therefore, from now on, I plan to start taking a 10% discount on your bills unless you can eliminate the bad castings.

(2)

Your people have made a mistake with our order no. 12345. We asked for blue, and they sent us green. This is the third time they've made an error like this. If they can't prevent it from happening, we'll have to stop doing business with your company.

(3)

Your letter of January 15th asks me to itemize the goods that were damaged in the fire that destroyed our summer home.

I'm attaching the list to this letter, giving the approximate price of each item.

(4)

Your letter of July 19 denies benefits because you say our child, Mary, "is not a student and is over 19 years of age."

Your records are in error.

Mary is ten years old. She was born June 24, 1968, as a review of your records will certainly show.

Please, therefore, do the following things:

1. *Acknowledge receipt of this letter* by a personal acknowledgment, not a computer-written letter or card.
2. Acknowledge that you are correcting your records to show Mary's correct birthdate.
3. Acknowledge that a check for the benefits due will be forthcoming.

Several months have passed since this claim was entered. Your company's delays and errors are outrageous. If the matter is not settled within the next 30 days, I shall complain to the Better Business Bureau, the Attorney General, and the State Commissioner of Insurance.

(5)

You recently sent me a letter asking why I had failed to place my customary order with you for Christmas fruit packages.

The answer is that your prices are out of line with your competition.

Admittedly, the quality of your products and the reliability of your service are both first rate. But so are those of your competitors.

Therefore, I have chosen to do business with them this year.

If you can bring your prices more in line with other companies selling similar items, I'll be glad to consider buying from you again next year.

Replies to Complaint Letters

(1)

We're very grateful that you let us know about our billing error of $75.50.

We're correcting it at once, and are sending along a credit memo for the same amount.

Thank you for telling us about the problem so quickly. We're glad to be able to clear it up immediately.

(2)

Thank you for telling me about the salesman who waited on you last Thursday.

I've discussed the matter with him, and he has assured me that it will not happen again and that he is very sorry the incident occurred.

I believe that part of the difficulty was that we were all extremely harried that day. It was the opening of our post-Christmas sale—and in the rush, he simply got carried away.

As for myself, I'm quite sorry that the incident occurred, and I apologize for it.

We do value your friendship, and we hope that you'll come back very soon and give us the opportunity to show you that courtesy is our first order of business.

Holiday Notes

(1)

Dear Anna:

This year, I want to send Holiday wishes in my own words rather than with a card.

Over the years, you've been a good, steady friend; and although our relationship has been basically related to business, I've often felt that business was merely an excuse for something more important: a mutual respect and sincere liking for one another as human beings.

At this time of the year, when we all think of Peace on Earth, I wanted to say a few words directly to you, wishing you a very Merry Christmas and a Happy New Year.

(2)

Dear Mr. Jones:
On behalf of this company, I am happy to tell you that we are sending in your name a donation to the Children's Disease Research Institute in place of the personal gift we usually send at this season.

May the coming holidays bring to you and yours good health and happiness.

Cordially yours,

Condolence Letters

(1)

Your husband's death is a sad event for all of us who knew him.

We all held him in great respect and affection, and we shall miss him.

All of us at his office send you our condolences; if any of us can be of any assistance, please call on us.

(2)

I was grieved to hear of your son's tragic accident.

Although I did not know him, I know how proud you were of him and what joy he gave you during his life.

My wife and I send you our sincere condolences.

(3)

Jim's passing is a great loss to all of us who have known him and worked with him.

We valued his experience and the generosity with which he

shared his knowledge. Most of all, we valued his friendship; we shall all cherish the memory of his warmth and decency.

I send you my condolences, and I am joined by all of us who knew him. His memory will live with us for many, many years.

Sincerely,

(4)

I was sorry to hear about your mother's passing.

Although I had met her only once, I recall her as an intelligent and lovely human being.

I send you my warm sympathy.

(5)

I learned with regret of the death of your chairman, Elliot Knowles, who has been such a distinguished member of the business community. The directors wish me to convey their sympathy to you in the loss of an esteemed official and valued citizen.

(6)

The officers and staff of James Brother, Inc. extend their sincere sympathy to the family of Mr. Frederick Forman. We will feel his loss keenly. We greatly esteemed him for his integrity of character and depended on his clear judgment in the conduct of the affairs of the company.

(7)

We read with regret in this morning's Chronicle of the passing of Mrs. Appleby. The officers of our firm extend to you our sympathy, knowing the sorrow you must feel at her loss.

Letters of Congratulation

(1)

Dear Harriet:

How lucky the Abex Corporation is to have got you! Do they know you're the most talented marketing specialist in the field? I suppose they must: everyone else does.

I know you're going to make a tremendous impact on the firm. Good luck and happy times.

(2)

Dear Mr. Harrison:

I have a feeling that a lot of things are going to change for the better now that you're in charge of Monad Co.'s engineering.

I'm not sure who's to be congratulated more: you for taking on your new job at Monad, or Monad for getting you.

I know that you're interested in new ideas, and I have a number of thoughts I'd like to tell you about that you might find useful. I'll call you in a few days to see if we can set up a date.

In the meantime, let me offer you my warmest wishes on your new position.

(3)

Dear Mayor Jordan:

Congratulations on your victory. As a voter who believes that you'll bring youth and integrity to the office, I want you to know that you'll have my full and vocal support.

The city needs your intelligence. I hope you'll pay special attention to the needs of the business community and the aged. You'll be hearing from me periodically; for now, I'll wish you the best of luck, and remind you that the hopes of thousands of people are riding with you.

(4)

Dear Tom:

We were delighted to learn that you've won the annual Best Athlete award.

All of us are very proud of you—and we speak about your accomplishments with awe and admiration.

We send you our warm wishes for many more triumphs.

                                        Cordially,

(5)

May I congratulate you and your committee on a fine job? Your report is excellent, concise but complete, accurate, and useful. I know what a long and difficult job it represents. It was a pleasure to read.

(6)

Please accept my heartiest congratulations upon your well-deserved appointment and my best wishes for your success in your new office.

(7)

Your appointment as Commissioner of Banking is a source of great satisfaction to the members of the Greater New York Bankers' Association. At the Association's quarterly meeting last night, I was asked to send you our joint congratulations.

We extend to you our best wishes for your success and pleasure in your new work.

(8)

Please accept my sincere congratulations upon your re-election. I hope and trust that the future will bring you still higher honors and continued success.

Letters to Congressmen

Dear Senator Mason:

I strongly oppose your position on gun licensing.

I think there are three overwhelming reasons why we need a strong gun-licensing law:

First, right now, anyone can buy a gun and kill with it.

Second, the number of gun-caused deaths in this city has risen by ten percent a year for the last five years.

Third, every major law enforcement official in the state has come out in favor of strict control.

I urge you to vote in favor of the new gun control legislation. If you fail to do so, I shall definitely vote for your opponent in the next election.

Sincerely,

Reference Letters

(1)

Dear Mr. Anderson:

I am happy to recommend Richard Jones to a prospective employer.

Richard has worked for our company for five years, and we have a high regard for his abilities and his motivation.

As a bookkeeper, he has always been careful, neat, and accurate.

His character and personality are commendable; he has always worked well with his colleagues and his superiors.

We were most unhappy that the elimination of his department made it necessary to release him. But we believe that his next employer will be acquiring an efficient, productive, and cooperative employee.

Sincerely,

(2)

Dear Sir or Madame:

Ms. Fran Carney has been buying menswear from our company for about five years. As the company's general sales manager, I've had close and regular contact with her during that time.

Ms. Carney has repeatedly proved herself to be highly skilled in negotiating good prices for first-quality merchandise.

She understands the needs of the marketplace, and she buys wisely and prudently. As a salesman, I naturally am always hopeful that her orders will be larger than they are; but as a businessman, I respect her fairness and the breadth of her knowledge.

As a case in point, last year she was one of the few buyers who correctly anticipated a shift away from leisure wear and toward more formal outfits. Her company profited handsomely.

If you're looking for a skilled professional, I think you need look no further than Ms. Carney.

Sincerely,

(3)

William Orne has asked me to send you a letter of reference on his behalf. I'm happy to do it.

Bill has been an assistant programmer with us for the past two years. During that time, he's worked exclusively in the accounting department. As his supervisor, I've had a chance to see him in operation on a daily basis.

He understands the basic principles of programming and knows how to apply them to almost any kind of accounting operation. He learns quickly and has always been highly self-motivated.

He works well with other people. He tends to be quiet and self-contained, but he has never failed to contribute ideas and goodwill in conferences and in undertaking new projects.

I can recommend him to a prospective employer without reservation.

(4)

Gentlemen:

You ask for my opinions about John Smith, who has applied for admission to Bertram University.

For about five years, John has worked for me as a stock boy and delivery boy after school and during the summer. During that time, I've seen him grow into a splendid young man of excellent character. To answer your specific questions:

Learning ability: John has always shown an ability to learn quickly. He knows the names of scores of our customers, many of whom he's seen only once. He puts this knowledge to good use, addressing them by name when they come into the store. In that sense, he always helps build goodwill for us.

Initiative: Because of the nature of his work here, he has virtually no chance to undertake independent projects in connection with his work. Consequently, I am unable to comment on that aspect of his abilities.

Character: John's most outstanding personal qualities are his honesty, his cooperativeness, and his good humor.

Much of our inventory is quite valuable and could easily be

spirited away without immediate discovery. In all the years John has been with us, he has never given us any cause to doubt his complete honesty.

His cooperativeness has shown itself in his willingness to spend extra time at the store when we needed him—even when he had to give up other plans.

His good humor has always been evident, and he has made everyone who knows him feel better about life.

I believe that John will be a credit to any school, and I'm happy to be able to recommend him to you.

Sincerely,

Criticism in a Letter of Reference

When you're asked to write a reference letter for someone about whom you have doubts, there are a couple of ways to handle the problem. If your doubts are very strong, you might suggest to the person that you'd prefer not to write or that it might be more suitable if someone else wrote a letter.

Or, you might write a letter that clearly defines the limits of your recommendation. Here are some examples:

If the person is willing but is not very careful about details:

> Mr. Smith is a willing worker. When he's involved in detailed work, we think that regular supervision will be helpful to him.

If the person is good at the job but has an abrasive personality:

> Mrs. Jones has always done a highly professional job. We've found that she's at her best when she's allowed to do her work with minimal distractions from fellow workers.

If the person tends to socialize too much with other workers, letting his or her own work slip by, but is otherwise able to do a good job:

> Mr. Gold does his work well. We've found that it's useful to him to have a clear schedule so that he can meet his regular deadlines.

In other words, when you need to criticize someone in a letter of reference and you don't want to be unfairly harsh, try to phrase your comments positively. Think in terms of: what does this person need in order to turn out good work?

Letters of Introduction

(1)

This letter will introduce Howard Murphy, my colleague in the Music Department of Wayne State University.

Howard is doing a doctoral thesis on jazz musicians in Europe, and will be spending six months traveling on the Continent.

He is one of my most competent and imaginative students, and is an accomplished jazz musician in his own right.

He is especially interested in meeting both very young and very old European jazz musicians, and in discussing their contributions to the modern jazz idiom.

I have assured Howard that my European friends will respond as warmly and cordially to him as they always have to me.

And so, I shall be most appreciative of any professional or personal assistance you can offer.

Sincerely,

(2)

Dear Jack:

This letter will introduce Harry Senour, our newest salesman.

Harry used to be in Chicago, with J. B. Morton, our toughest competitor, so he knows the business very well.

I've filled him in on your operation, and he has a good idea of what your needs are and how we can help you. In fact, he has a couple of interesting ideas that you might find productive.

Thanks for taking the time to see him. I think you're going to find him a very useful visitor.

Cordially,

Formal Invitations and Replies

Formal invitation:

>Mr. and Mrs. Harrison Cobler
>request the pleasure of
>Mr. and Mrs. Carl Samovar's
>company at dinner
>on December 25th
>at eight o'clock
>10 Bristow Drive

Rules for replying to formal invitations:

1. Reply promptly.
2. Use fine, white or cream double-fold paper; write only on the first page—not on the inside. Business invitations may be answered on letterhead.
3. The reply should be handwritten, unless it is to a business invitation issued by an official or an organization.
4. Follow the same form and spacing as the invitation.

Acceptance:

>Mr. and Mrs. Carl Samovar
>accept with pleasure
>Mr. and Mrs. Cobler's
>kind invitation for dinner
>on December 25th
>at eight o'clock

If only one of you can go, the acceptance will read:

>Mrs. Carl Samovar
>accepts with pleasure
>Mr. and Mrs. Cobler's
>kind invitation for dinner
>on December 25th
>at eight o'clock
>but regrets that
>Mr. Samovar
>will be absent at that time

If neither of you can attend, the response will read:

>Mr. and Mrs. Carl Samovar
>regret that they are unable to accept
>Mr. and Mrs. Cobler's
>kind invitation for December 25th.

Notices on postcards.

>Monthly Meeting
>East Hampton Philatelic Society
>Saturday, June 25
>10:00 A.M.
>At the home of Jim Tully
>34 Anderson Avenue, Brookdale
>
>Fred Maher, Secy.
>Tel.: 123-4567

Letters of Resignation

(1)

It is with regret that I submit my resignation as chairman of the Greater Gotham Business Council. The duties required are more than I can conscientiously fulfill at present, and I therefore ask to be relieved of them.

It has been a great pleasure and honor to be associated with the Council. I regret that my health no longer permits me to share its responsibilities.

(2)

I have decided to accept a position with California Broadcasting, Inc. of Los Angeles, and I therefore tender my resignation as Chief of Programming of Crest Communications. My five years with the company have been such happy and productive ones that I sincerely regret to end my connection with it. Only the opportunity for greater responsibilities and higher salary would tempt me to do so.

Correct English Usage

11. Capitalization

Money

Checks. Write out the amount of the check with each word capitalized.

Legal documents. Spell out amounts of money and capitalize each word. Follow this with the amount in figures in parentheses, as Four Hundred Fifty Six Dollars ($456).

Enumerations

After a colon. Enumerations after a colon are capitalized if they are complete sentences. Brief items or phrases which are not sentences are not capitalized unless they are listed in tabular form.

> A document is classified Top Secret if: (1) It involves national security. (2) It is so designated by the Chiefs of Staff. (3) The President . . .

> The characteristics of a good secretary are: (1) honesty, (2) cooperativeness, (3) punctuality, (4) . . .

The characteristics of a good secretary are:
(1) Honesty
(2) Cooperativeness
(3) Punctuality

When there is no colon. Enumerations in this case are not capitalized.

We decided not to order the new product because (1) it was too expensive, (2) it did not suit our needs, (3) the director . . .

Titles and Headings

General Rule. Capitalize all important words in a title or heading. Articles, conjunction, and prepositions (except prepositions of five letters or more) are in lower case; if an article, conjunction, or preposition follows a punctuation, it may be capitalized.

How to Be a Better Secretary
Join the Army—And Like It
Talking About Children
Television: The Enemy
Secrets of a Millionaire
This Is for You

Hyphenated Compounds

General rule. Capitalize a word in hyphenation only when it is capitalized in ordinary usage.

ex-President Nixon
un-American
Afro-American woman
Jersey-cloth

Titles and headings. Capitalize all parts of hyphenated words except (1) when considered one word, and (2) compound numerals.

Quorum of Ex-Presidents
Speed-Up in Exports

but

Eighty-fifth Street
Self-preservation
Re-entry
One-fourth of a Nation
Anti-freeze
Runner-up

Quotations

General rule. Capitalize the first word of an exactly quoted passage only. Do not capitalize it if it is not a complete sentence or if it is not a direct quotation.

> The president said, "Officers over 65 must retire."
> The president said that officers over 65 "must retire."
> The president said that officers beyond the age of 65 must retire.

Resolutions

General rule. Write WHEREAS and RESOLVED in full capitals; begin That and The with a capital.

> WHEREAS, The secretary of organization . . .
> RESOLVED, That the secretary of the organization . . .

GUIDE TO CAPITALIZATION

A-bomb
abstract B, 1, etc.
Academy:
   Air Force; the Academy
   Andover; the academy
Merchant Marine; the Academy
Military; the Academy
National Academy of Sciences; the Academy of Sciences; the Academy

Naval; the Academy
but service academies
Act (Federal, State, or foreign), short or popular title or with number; the act:
Lend-Lease Act; *but* lend-lease materials, etc.
Acting, if part of capitalized title
Administration, with name; capitalized standing alone if referring to Federal unit:
Farmers Home
Food and Drug
Maritime
Veterans' (follow apostrophe)
but Roosevelt administration; administration bill, policy, etc.
Admiralty, British, etc.
Admiralty, Lord of the
Africa:
east
East Coast
north
South
South-West
West Coast
Agency, if part of name; capitalized standing alone if referring to Federal or District of Columbia unit:
Chippewa (Indian); the agency
Federal Security; the Agency
Ages:
Age of Discovery
Dark Ages
Elizabethan Age
Golden Age (of Pericles only)
Middle Ages
but atomic age; Cambrian age; copper age; ice age; missile age; rocket age; space age; stone age; etc.
Agreement, with name; the agreement:
General Agreement on Tariffs and Trade (GATT); the general agreement
International Wheat Agreement; the wheat agreement; the coffee agreement
Status of Forces; *but* status-of-forces agreements
but the Geneva agreement; the Potsdam agreement
Air Force:
Base (see Base; Station)
Civil Air Patrol; Civil Patrol; the patrol
WAF (see Women in the Air Force)
Airport: La Guardia; National; the airport
Alliance, Farmers', etc.; the alliance
Alliance for Progress; the Alliance
Alliance for Progress program
alliances and coalitions (see also powers):
Allied Powers; the powers (World Wars)
Axis, the; Axis Powers; the powers
Benelux (Belgium, Netherlands, Luxembourg)
Big Four (European); of the Pacific

Capitalization

Big Three
Central Powers; the powers (World War I)
European Economic Community (see also Common Market)
Fritalux (France, Italy, Benelux countries)
North Atlantic Treaty Organization (see Organization)
Western Powers
Western Union (powers); the union
Allied (World Wars):
  armies
  Governments
  Nations
  peoples
  Powers; the powers; *but* European powers
  Supreme Allied Commander
Allies, the (World Wars); also members of Western bloc (political entity); *but* our allies; weaker allies, etc.
Ambassador:
  British, etc.; the Ambassador; the Senior Ambassador; His Excellency
  Extraordinary and Plenipotentiary: the Ambassador; Ambassador at Large; an ambassador
amendment:
  Social Security Amendments of 1954; 1954 amendments; the social security amendments; the amendments
  Tobey amendment
  to the Constitution (U.S.); first amendment, 14th amendment, etc.
American:
  Federation of Labor and Congress of Industrial Organizations (AFL-CIO); the federation
  Gold Star Mothers, Inc.; Gold Star Mothers; a Mother
  Legion (see Legion)
  National Red Cross; the Red Cross
  Veterans of World War II (AMVETS)
  War Mothers; War Mothers; a Mother
Amtrak (National Railroad Passenger Corporation)
Ancient Free and Accepted Masons; a Mason; a Freemason
Annex, if part of name of building; the annex
Antarctic Ocean (see Arctic; Ocean)
anti-New Deal
appendix 1, A, II, etc.; the appendix; *but* Appendix II, when part of title: Appendix II: Education Directory
appropriation bill (see also bill):
  deficiency
  Department of Agriculture
  for any governmental unit
  independent offices

Arab States
Arboretum, National; the arboretum
Arabic numerals
Archipelago, Philippine, etc.; the archipelago
Archives, the, etc. (see The)
Archivist of the United States; the Archivist
Arctic:
  Circle
  Current (see Current)
  Ocean
  zone
  but subarctic
arctic (descriptive adjective):
  clothing
  conditions
  fox
  grass
  night
  seas
Arctics, the
Area, if part of name; the area:
  Cape Hatteras Recreational
  White Pass Recreation; etc.
  but area 2; free trade area; Metropolitan Washington area; bay area
Armed Forces (synonym for overall Military Establishment); British Armed Forces; the armed forces
armed services
armistice
Army, American or foreign, if part of name; capitalized standing alone only if referring to U.S. Army:
  Confederate (referring to Southern Confederacy); the Confederates
Continental; Continentals
Corps (see Corps)
Division, 1st, etc.; the division
Engineers (the Corps of Engineers); the Engineers; *but* Army engineer
Establishment
Field Establishment
Field Forces (see Forces)
Finance Department; the Department
1st, etc.
General of the Army; *but* the general
General Staff; the Staff
Headquarters, 1st Regiment
Headquarters of the; the headquarters
Hospital Corps (see Corps)
Medical Museum (see Museum)
Organized Reserves; the Reserves
Regiment, 1st, etc.; the regiment
Regular Army officer; a Regular
Revolutionary (American, British, French, etc.)
service
Surgeon General, the (see Surgeon General)
Volunteer; the Volunteers; a Volunteer army:
Lee's army; *but* Clark's 5th Army
mobile

mule, shoe, etc.
of occupation; occupation army
Red
article 15; *but* Article 15, when part of title: Article 15: Uniform Code of Military Justice
Articles of Confederation (U.S.)
Assembly of New York; the assembly (see also Legislative Assembly)
Assembly (see United Nations)
Assistant, if part of capitalized title; the assistant
assistant, Presidential (see Presidential)
Assistant Secretary (see Secretary)
Associate Justice (see Supreme Court)
Association, if part of name; capitalized standing alone if referring to Federal unit:
  American Association for the Advancement of Science; the association
  Federal National Mortgage (Fannie Mae); the Association
  Young Men's Christian; the association
Atlantic:
  Charter (see Charter)
  coast
  community
  Coast States
  Destroyer Flotilla; the destroyer flotilla; the flotilla
  Fleet (see Fleet)
  mid-Atlantic
  North
  Pact (see Pact)
  seaboard
  slope
  South
  time, standard time (see time)
  but cisatlantic; transatlantic
Attorney General (U.S.); *but* attorney general of Maine, etc.
attorney, U.S.
Authority, capitalized standing alone if referring to Federal unit:
  National Shipping; the Authority
  Port of New York; the port authority; the authority
  St. Lawrence Seaway Authority of Canada; the authority
  Tennessee Valley; the Authority
autumn
Award: Distinguished Service, Merit, Mother of the Year, etc.; the award (see also decorations, etc.)
Axis, the (see alliances)

Badlands (S. Dak. and Nebr.)
Balkan States (see States)
Baltic States (see States)
Band, if part of name; the band:
  Army, Marine, Navy, Sousa's Eastern, etc. (of Cherokee Indians)

202 CORRECT ENGLISH USAGE

Bank, if part of name; the bank; capitalized standing alone if referring to international bank:
  Export-Import Bank of Washington (Eximbank); Export-Import Bank; the Bank
  Farm Loan Bank of Dallas; Dallas Farm Loan Bank; farm loan bank; farm loan bank at Dallas
  Farmer & Mechanics, etc.
  Federal home loan bank at Cumberland
  Federal Land Bank of Louisville; Louisville Federal Land Bank; land bank at Louisville; Federal land bank
  Federal Reserve Bank of New York; Richmond Federal Reserve Bank; *but* Reserve bank at Richmond; Federal Reserve bank; Reserve bank; Reserve city
  First National, etc.
  German Central; the Bank
  International Bank for Reconstruction and Development; the Bank
  International Monetary; the Bank
  International World; the Bank *but* blood bank, central reserve, soil bank
Barracks, if part of name; the barracks:
  Carlisle
  Disciplinary (Leavenworth)
  Marine (District of Columbia)
  but A barracks; barracks A; etc.
Base, Andrews Air Force; Air Force base; the base (see also Naval Base); *but* Sandia Base
Basin (see geographic terms)
Battery, the (New York City)
Battle, if part of name; the battle:
  of Gettysburg; *but* battle at Gettysburg; etc.
  of the Bulge; of the Marne; of the Wilderness; of Waterloo; etc.
battlefield, Bull Run, etc.
battleground, Manassas, etc.
Bay, San Francisco Bay area; the bay area
Belt, if part of name; the belt:
  Corn
  Cotton
  Dairy
  Ice
  Wheat
  but Bible belt, goiter belt
Beltway, capitalized with name; the beltway
Bench (see Supreme Bench)
Benelux (see alliances)
Bible; Biblical; Scriptures; etc. (see also book)
Bill of Rights (historic document); *but* GI bill of rights
Bizonia; bizonal; bizone
black
Black Caucus (see Congressional)

Black Panther; Panther
bloc (see Western)
Bluegrass regions, etc.
B'nai B'rith
Board, if part of name; capitalized standing alone only if referring to Federal, interdepartmental, District of Columbia, or international board:
  Civil Aeronautics
  Employees' Compensation Appeals
  Federal Maritime
  Federal Reserve (see Federal)
  General (Navy)
  Loyalty Review
  Macy Board, etc. (Federal board with name of person)
  Military Production and Supply (NATO)
  of Directors (Federal unit); *but* board of directors (nongovernmental)
  of Education (District of Columbia)
  of Health of Montgomery County; Montgomery County Board of Health; the board of health; the board
  of Managers (of the Soldiers' Home)
  of Regents (Smithsonian)
  of Visitors (Military and Naval Academies)
  on Geographic Names
Bolshevik; Bolsheviki (collective plural); Bolshevist; bolshevism
bond:
  defense bond; defense savings bond; savings bond; defense savings bonds and stamps; series E bond; savings bonds and stamps
  Victory bond; the bond
  war savings bond; savings bond; war bond
  also governments, treasuries
book:
  books of the Bible
  First Book of Samuel; etc.
  Good Book (synonym for Bible)
  book 1, I, etc.; *but* Book 1, when part of title: Book 1: The Golden Legend
border, United States-Mexican
Borough, if part of name: Borough of the Bronx; the borough
Botanic Garden (National); the garden
Bowl, Dust, Ice, Rose, etc.; the bowl
Boxer Rebellion (see Rebellion)
Boy Scouts (the organization); a Boy Scout; a Scout; Scouting
Branch, if part of name; capitalized standing alone only if referring to a Federal or District of Columbia unit:
  Accounts Branch
  Public Buildings Branch

but executive, judicial, or legislative branch
Bridge, if part of name; the bridge:
 Arlington Memorial; Memorial
 Francis Scott Key; Key
 M Street
 but Pennsylvania Railroad bridge
Brother(s) (adherent of religious order)
Budget of the United States (publication); the Budget (Office implied); the budget
budget:
 department
 estimate
 Federal
 message
 performance-type
 President's
Building, if part of name; the building:
 Capitol (see Capitol Building)
 Colorado
 House (or Senate) Office
 Investment
 New House (or Senate) Office
 Old House Office
 Pentagon
 the National Archives; the Archives
 Treasury; Treasury Annex
Bureau, if part of name; capitalized standing alone if referring to Federal, District of Columbia, or international unit:

Cabinet, American or foreign, if part of name or standing alone (see also foreign cabinets):
 British Cabinet; the Cabinet
 the President's Cabinet; the Cabinet; Cabinet officer, member
Calendar, if part of name; the calendar:
 Consent; etc.
 House
 No. 99; Calendars Nos. 1 and 2 of Bills and Resolutions
 Private
 Senate
 Unanimous Consent
 Union
 Wednesday (legislative)
Cambrian age (see Ages)
Camp Gary, etc.; the camp
Canal, with name; the canal:
 Cross-Florida Barge
 Isthmian
 Panama
 Zone (Isthmian); the zone (see also Government)
Cape (see geographic terms)
Capital, Capital City, National Capital (Washington, D.C.); *but* the capital (State)
Capitol Building (with State name); the capitol
Capitol, the (Washington, D.C.):
 Building

Capitalization

Hall of Fame; the Hall
Halls (House and Senate)
Halls of Congress
Hill; the Hill
  rotunda
  Senate wing
Cemetery, if part of name: Arlington National; the cemetery
Census:
  Seventeenth Decennial (title); Seventeenth Census (title); the census
  1960 census
  1960 Census of Agriculture; the census of agriculture; the census
  the 14th and subsequent decennial censuses
Center, if part of name; the Center (Federal); the center (non-Federal):
  Agricultural Research, etc.; the Center
  Kennedy Center for the Performing Arts; the Kennedy Center; the Center
  the Lincoln Center; the center
central Asia, central Europe, etc.
Central States
central time, central standard time (see time)
century, first, 20th, etc.
Chair, the, if personified
Chairman:
  of the Board of Directors; the Chairman (Federal); *but* chairman of the board of directors (non-Federal)
chairman (congressional):
  of the Appropriations Committee
  of the Subcommittee on Banking
Chamber of Commerce: the chamber:
  of Ada; Ada Chamber of Commerce; the chamber of commerce
  of the United States; U.S. Chamber of Commerce; the chamber of commerce; national chamber
Chamber, the (Senate or House)
channel 3 (TV); the channel (see also geographic terms)
Chaplain (House or Senate); *but* Navy chaplain
chapter 5, II, etc.; *but* Chapter 5, when part of title: Chapter 5: Research and Development; Washington chapter, Red Cross
Chargé d'Affaires, British, etc.; the Chargé d'Affaires; the Chargé
chart 2, A, II, etc.; *but* Chart 2, when part of legend: Chart 2.—Army strength
Charter, capitalized with name; the charter:
  Atlantic
  United Nations
cheese: Camembert, Cheddar, Roquefort, etc.
Chicano

Chief, if referring to head of Federal or District of Columbia unit; the Chief:
  Justice (U.S. Supreme Court); *but* chief justice (of a State)
  Magistrate (the President)
  of Staff
Chief Clerk, if referring to head of Federal or District of Columbia unit
Christian; Christian name, etc.; Christendom; Christianity; Christianize; *but* christen
church and state
church calendar:
  Christmas
  Easter
  Lent
  Whitsuntide (Pentecost)
Church, if part of name of organization or building
Circle, if part of name; the circle:
  Arctic
  Logan
  but great circle
Circular 420
cities, sections of, official or popular names:
  East Side
  Latin Quarter
  North End
  Northwest Washington, etc. (District of Columbia); the Northwest; *but* northwest (directional)
  the Loop
City, if part of corporate or popular name; the city:
  Kansas City; the two Kansas Citys
  Mexico City
  New York City
  Twin Cities
  Washington City; *but* city of Washington
  Windy City
  but Reserve city (see Bank)
civil action No. 46
civil defense
Civil Air Patrol (see Air Force)
Civil Service, capitalize only when word "Commission" follows or is implied:
  the Civil Service has ruled
  but civil service employee, examination, etc.
Civil War (see War)
Clan, if part of tribal name; the clan
class 2, A, II, etc.; *but* Class 2 when part of title: Class 2: Leather Products
Clerk, the, of the House of Representatives; of the Supreme Court of the United States
coal sizes: pea, barley, buckwheat, stove, etc.
coast: Atlantic, east, gulf, west, etc.
Coast Guard, U.S.; the Coast Guard; Coastguardsman Smith; *but* a coastguardsman; a guardsman
Coastal Plain (Atlantic and Gulf)
Code (in shortened title of a

Capitalization 207

publication); the code:
District
Federal Criminal
Internal Revenue
International (signal)
of Federal Regulations
Penal; Criminal; etc.
Pennsylvania State
Radio
Television
Uniform Code of Military Justice
United States
but civil code; flag code; Morse code; ZIP code
collection, Brady, etc.; the collection
collector of customs
College, if part of name; the college:
of Bishops
but electoral college
college degrees: bachelor of arts, master's, etc.
Colonials (American Colonial Army); *but* colonial times, etc.
Colonies, the:
Thirteen
Thirteen American
Thirteen Original
but 13 separate Colonies
colonist, the
Colony: Cyprus, Crown Colony of Hong Kong; the colony, crown colony
Cominform (see U.S.S.R.)
Command, capitalize with name; the command:
Air Materiel
GHQ Far East
Joint Far Eastern
Potomac River Naval
Zone of Interior
Commandant, the (Coast Guard or Marine Corps only)
Commandos, the; Commando raid; a commando; a commandoman
Commission, if part of name; capitalized standing alone if referring to Federal, District of Columbia, or international commission:
Atomic Energy
Civil Service
District (District of Columbia)
Electoral
International Boundary, United States, Alaska and Canada
Commissioner, if referring to Federal, District of Columbia, or international commission; the Commissioner:
Land Bank; *but* land bank commissioner loans
U.S. (International Boundary Commission, etc.)
but a U.S. commissioner
Committee, if part of name; the Committee, if referring to international or noncongressional Federal committee or to the Committee of the Whole, the Committee of the Whole House, or

208 CORRECT ENGLISH USAGE

    the Committee of the Whole House on the State of the Union:
American Medical Association Committee on Education; the committee
Appropriations, etc.; the committee, Subcommittee on Appropriations; the subcommittee; subcommittee of the Appropriations Committee
Democratic National; the national committee; the committee; national committeeman
Democratic policy committee; the committee
Joint Committee on Atomic Energy; the Joint Committee; the committee; *but* a joint committee.
of Defense Ministers (NATO); the Committee (see also Organization, North Atlantic Treaty)
of One Hundred, etc.; the committee
Republican National; the national committee; the committee; national committeeman
Republican policy committee; the committee
Senate policy committee
Subcommittee No. 5, etc.; the subcommittee
Subcommittee on Immigration
but Kefauver committee
ad hoc committee

Committee Print No. 32; Committee Prints Nos. 8 and 9; committee print
Common Market; the market (European Economic Community); *also* Common Market Treaty; Inner Six; Outer Seven
Commonwealth of Australia, Massachusetts, etc.; British Commonwealth; the Commonwealth
Commune (of Paris)
Communist; communism; communistic
Communist government, etc. (see U.S.S.R.)
Community, European Coal and Steel; European Economic; the Community; *but* the Atlantic community
compact, U.S. marine fisheries, etc.; the compact
Company, if part of name; capitalized standing alone if referring to unit of Federal Government:
    Panama Railroad Company; the Company
    Procter & Gamble Co.; the company
Comptroller:
    of the Currency; the Comptroller of the Post Office Department; the Comptroller
Comptroller General (U.S.); the Comptroller
Comsat
conelrad

Capitalization

Confederacy (of the South)
Confederate:
  Army
  government
  soldier
  States
Confederation, Swiss; the Confederation
Conference, if referring to governmental (U.S.) or international conference:
  Bretton Woods; the Conference
  Sixth Annual Conference of Southern Methodist Churches; the conference
Confession, Augsburg
Congress (convention), if part of name; capitalized standing alone if referring to international congress:
  of Parents and Teachers, National; the congress
Congress (legislature), if referring to national congress:
  of Bolivia, etc.; the Congress
  of the United States; First, Second, 11th, 82d, etc.; the Congress
Congressional:
  Directory; the directory
  District, First, 11th, etc.; the First District; the congressional district; the district
  Library; the Library
  Medal of Honor (see decorations)
  but congressional action, committee, etc.
Congressman; Congressman at Large; Member of Congress; Member; membership
Constitution, with name of country; capitalized standing alone when referring to a specific national constitution; *but* New York State constitution; the constitution
constitutional
consul, British, etc.
consul general, British, etc.
consulate, British, etc.
Consumer Price Index (official title); the price index; the index; *but* a consumers' price index (descriptive)
Continent, only if following name; American Continent; the continent; *but* the Continent (continental Europe)
Continental:
  Army; the Army
  Congress; the Congress
  Divide (see Divide)
  Outer Continental Shelf
  Shelf; the shelf; a continental shelf
continental:
  care not a continental, etc.
  Europe, United States, etc.
Continentals (Revolutionary soldiers)
Convention, governmental (U.S.), international, or national political; the convention:
  Constitutional (United States, 1787); the Convention

Democratic National; Democratic
Genocide
19th Annual Convention of the American Legion
on International Civil Aviation
Universal Postal Union; Postal Union *also* International Postal; Warsaw convention of 1907 (not formal name)
Coordinator of Information; the Coordinator
copper age (see Ages)
Corn Belt (see Belt)
Corporation, if part of name; the Corporation, if referring to unit of Federal Government:
  Commodity Credit
  Federal Deposit Insurance
  National Railroad Passenger (Amtrak)
  Petroleum Reserves
  Rand Corp.; the corporation
  St. Lawrence Seaway Development Corporation
  Union Carbide Corp.; the corporation
  Virgin Islands
corridor, Northeast
Corps, if part of name; the corps (military); the Corps (nonmilitary) (see also Reserve):
  Foreign Service Officer (see Foreign Service)
  Job
  Marine (See Marine Corps)
  of Engineers; Army Engineers; the Engineers; *but* Army engineer; the corps
  Peace; Peace Corpsman; the corpsman
  Reserve Officers' Training (ROTC)
  VII Corps, etc.
  Signal
  Teachers; *but* Teacher Corps Act
  Women's Army (WAC); a Wac; the Wacs
  Youth
  but diplomatic corps
  corpsman; hospital corpsman
Cotton Belt (see Belt)
Council, if part of name; capitalized standing alone if referring to Federal or international unit (see also United Nations):
  Boston City; the council
  Choctaw, etc.; the council
  Federal Personnel; the Council
  His Majesty's Privy Council; the Privy Council; the Council
  National Security; the Council
  of Foreign Ministers (NATO); the Council
  of the Organization of American States; the Council
  Philadelphia Common; the council
councilor, privy
Counsel (see General Counsel)
County, Fairfax; county of Fairfax; County Kilkenny,

Capitalization

etc.; Loudoun and Fauquier Counties; the county Court (of law) capitalized if part of name of national or international court, U.S. court, district court, or State court; lowercased if city or county court; capitalized standing alone if referring to the Supreme Court of the United States, to Court of Impeachment (U.S. Senate), or to international court:

Circuit Court of the United States for the Second Circuit; Circuit Court for the Second Circuit; the circuit court; the court; the second circuit

  Court of Appeals of the State of Wisconsin, etc.; the court of appeals; the court
  Court of Claims; the court
  Court of Customs and Patent Appeals; the court
  Court of Impeachment, the Senate; the Court
  District Court of the United States for the Eastern District of Missouri; the district court; the court
  Emergency Court of Appeals, United States; the court
  International Court of Justice; the Court
  Permanent Court of Arbitration; the Court
  Superior Court of the District of Columbia; the superior court; the court
  Supreme Court of the United States (see Supreme Court)
  Supreme Court of Virginia, etc.; the supreme court; the court
  Tax Court; the court
  U.S. Court of Appeals for the District of Columbia; the court

Covenant, League of Nations; the covenant
Creed, Apostles'; the Creed
Croix de Guerre (see decorations)
Crown, if referring to a ruler; *but* crown colony, lands, etc.
Current, if part of name; the current:
  Arctic
  Humboldt
  Japan
  North Equatorial
customhouse; customs official
czar; czarist

Dairy Belt (see Belt)
Dalles, The; *but* the Dalles region
Dam (see geographic terms)
Dark Ages (see Ages)
Dark Continent (Africa)
Daughters of the American Revolution; a Real Daughter; King's Daughters; a Daughter
days (see holidays)
D-day, etc. (see holidays)
dean of the diplomatic corps
Declaration, capitalized with

name: of Independence; the Declaration of Panama; the declaration

decorations, medals, etc., awarded by United States or any foreign national government; the medal, the cross, the ribbon (see also awards):
  Air Medal
  Bronze Star Medal
  Commendation Ribbon
  Congressional Medal of Honor
  Croix de Guerre
  Distinguished Flying Cross
  Distinguished Service Cross
  Distinguished Service Medal
  Good Conduct Medal
  Iron Cross
  Legion of Merit
  Medal for Merit
  Medal of Freedom
  Medal of Honor
  Purple Heart
  Silver Star
  Soldier's Medal
  Victoria Cross
  Victory Medal
  also Carnegie Medal, etc.

Decree (see Executive; Royal Decree)
Deep South
defense bond (see bond)
Defense Establishment (see Establishment)
De Gaulle Free French; Free French; Fighting French; *but* General de Gaulle; de Gaullist

Diety, words denoting, capitalized
delegate (to a conference); the delegate; the delegation
Delegate (U.S. Congress)
Delta, Mississippi River; the delta
Department, if part of name; capitalized standing alone if referring to Federal, District of Columbia, or international unit:
  Highway (District of Columbia)
  Post Office
  Treasury
  Yale University Department of Economics; the department of economics; the department
Department of New York, American Legion
department:
  clerk
  legislative, executive, judicial departments
Depot, if part of name; the depot (see also Station)
Deputy, if part of capitalized title; *but* the deputy
deutsche mark
Diet, Japanese (legislative body)
diplomatic corps (see also Corps; service)
Director, if referring to head of Federal, District of Columbia, or international unit; the Director:
  District Director of Internal

Revenue
of Coast and Geodetic Survey
of Fish and Wildlife Service
of the Budget
of the Mint
of Vehicles and Traffic
but director, board of directors (nongovernmental)
Director General of Foreign Service; the Director General; the Director
Distinguished Service Medal, etc. (see decorations)
District, if part of name; the district:
 Alexandria School District No. 4; the school district
 Chicago Sanitary; the sanitary district
 Congressional (see Congressional)
 Federal (see Federal)
 1st Naval; naval district
 Grant County Public Utility; the utility district
 Imperial Valley Irrigation; the irrigation district
 Los Angeles Water; the water district
 but customs district No. 2; first assembly district; school district No. 4
District of Columbia; the District
Divide, Continental (Rocky Mountains); the divide
Divine Father; *but* divine guidance, divine providence, divine service
Division, Army, if part of name: 1st Division; the division
Division, if referring to Federal or District of Columbia governmental unit; the Division:
 Electro-Motive Division; the division; *but* division of General Motors
 of Air Services
 of Parcel Post
 of Railway Mail Service
 of the Federal Register Passport
 Trinity River division (reclamation); the division
Dixie; Dixiecrat
docket No. 66; dockets Nos. 76 and 77
Doctrine, Monroe; the doctrine; *but* Truman, Eisenhower doctrine
Document, if part of name; the document:
 Document No. 2
 Document Numbered One Hundred and Thirty
Dominion of Canada, of New Zealand, etc; the Dominion; *but* British dominions; a dominion; dominion status
drawing II, A, 3, etc.; *but* Drawing 2 when part of title: Drawing 2.— Hydroelectric Power Development
Driftless Area (Mississippi Valley)
Dust Bowl (see Bowl)

eagle boat (class)
Earth (planet)
East:
  Coast (Africa)
  Europe (political entity)
  Germany (political entity)
  Middle, Mideast (Asia)
  Near (Balkans)
  South Central States
  the East (section of United States); *also* Communist political entity
east:
  Africa
  coast (U.S.)
  Pennsylvania
Eastern:
  Europe (political entity)
  Far (Orient) (see Far East)
  Germany (political entity)
  Gulf States
  Hemisphere (see Hemisphere)
  Middle, Mideastern (Asia)
  North Central States
  Shore (Chesapeake Bay)
  States
  United States
eastern:
  France
  seaboard
  time, eastern standard time (see time)
  Wisconsin
easterner
E-bond
electoral college, the electors
Elizabethan Age (see Ages)
Emancipation Proclamation (see Proclamation)
Embassy, British, etc.; the Embassy
Emperor, Ethiopian, etc.; the Emperor
Empire, Ethiopian, etc.; the Empire; *but* an empire
Engine Company, Bethesda; engine company No. 6; No. 6 engine company; the company
Engineer Commissioner (see District of Columbia)
Engineer Department (see District of Columbia)
Engineer officer, etc. (of Engineer Corps); the Engineers
Engineers, Chief of (see Chief)
Engineers, Corps of (see Corps)
Envoy Extraordinary and Minister Plenipotentiary; the Envoy; the Minister
Equator, the; equatorial
Establishment, if part of name; the establishment:
  Defense
  Federal
  Military
  Naval; *but* naval establishments
  Postal
  Regular
  Reserve
  Shore
  but civil establishment; legislative establishment
Estate, Girard (a foundation); the estate
estate, third (the commons); fourth (the press); etc.
Eurodollar

European theater of operations; the European theater; the theater
Excellency, His; Their Excellencies
Exchange, New York Stock; the stock exchange; the exchange
Executive (President of United States):
  Chief
  Decree No. 100; Decree 100; *but* Executive decree; direction
  Document No. 95
  Mansion; the mansion; the White House
  Office; the Office
  Order No. 34; Order 34; *but* Executive order
  power
executive:
  agreement document
  branch paper
  communication privilege
  department
exhibit 2, A, II, etc.; *but* Exhibit 2, when part of title: Exhibit 2: Capital Expenditures, 1935–49
Expedition, Byrd; Lewis and Clark; the expedition
Experiment Station (see Station)
Explorer I, etc.
Exposition, California-Pacific International, etc.; the exposition
Express, if part of name: Federal Express, the
Fair Deal
Fair, World's, etc.; the fair; Texas State Fair
Falangist
fall (season)
Falls, Niagara; the falls
fanciful appellations capitalized:
  Bay State (Massachusetts)
  Big Four (powers, railroad, etc.)
  City of Churches (Brooklyn)
  Fair Deal
  Great Father (the President)
  Great Society
  Keystone State (Pennsylvania)
  New Deal
  New Frontier
  the Hub (Boston)
Far East, Far Eastern (the Orient); Far West (U.S.); *but* far western
Farm, if part of name; the farm: Johnson Farm; *but* Johnson's farm
  San Diego Farm
  Wild Tiger Farm
Fascist; Fascisti; fascistic; fascism
Father of his Country (Washington)
Fed, the (no period)
Federal (synonym for United States or other sovereign power):
  District (Mexico)
  Establishment

Government (of any national government)
grand jury; the grand jury
land bank (see Bank)
Personnel Council (see Council)
Register (publication); the Register
Reserve bank (see Bank)
Reserve Board, the Board; *also* Federal Reserve System, the System; Federal Reserve Board Regulation W, *but* regulation W
but a federal form of government
federally
fellow, fellowship (academic); lowercase with name
Field, Byrd, Stewart, etc.; the field
fifth column; fifth columnist
figure 2, A, II, etc. (illustration); *but* Figure 2, when part of legend: Figure 2.—Market scenes
First Lady (wife of President)
First World War (see War)
flag code
flag, U.S.:
 Old Flag, Old Glory
 Stars and Stripes
 Star-Spangled Banner
flags, foreign:
 Tricolor (French)
 Union Jack (British)
 United Nations
Flats, Anacostia (see District of Columbia)
Fleet, if part of name; the fleet:
 Atlantic
 Channel
 Grand
 High Seas
 Marine Force
 Naval Reserve
 Pacific, etc. (naval)
 6th Fleet, etc.
 U.S.
floor (House or Senate)
flyway; Canadian flyway, etc.
Force(s), if part of name; the force(s):
 Active Forces
 Air (see also Air Force)
 Armed Forces (synonym for overall Military Establishment)
 7th Task; the task force; *but* task force report (Hoover Commission)
 United Nations Emergency; the Emergency Force; the Force; *but* United Nations police force
foreign cabinets:
 Foreign Office; the Office
 Minister of Foreign Affairs; the Minister
 Ministry of Foreign Affairs; the Ministry
 Premier
 Prime Minister
Foreign Legion (French); the legion
Foreign Service; the Service: officer
 Officer Corps; the corps
 Reserve officer; the Reserve officer
 Reserve Officer Corps; the Reserve Corps; the corps

Capitalization   217

Staff officer; the Staff officer
Staff Officer Corps; the Staff Corps; the corps
Forest, if part of name; the national forest; the forest:
   Angeles National
   Black
   Coconino and Prescott National Forests
   but State and National forests
Forester (Chief of Forest Service); the Chief; *also* Chief Forester
form 2, A, II, etc; *but* Form 2, when part of title: Forum 1040: Individual Income Tax Return; *but* withholding tax form
Fort McHenry, etc.; the fort
Foundation, if part of name; capitalized standing alone if referring to Federal unit:
   Chemical; the foundation
   Infantile Paralysis; the foundation
   National Science; the Foundation
   Russell Sage; the foundation
Founding Fathers (colonial)
four freedoms
Four Power Pact (see Pact)
free list; *but* Title I: Free List
free trade area
free world
Frisco (for San Francisco; no apostrophe)
Fritalux (see alliances)
Fund, if part of name; capitalized standing alone if referring to international or United Nations fund:
Common Market Development Loan Fund; the Fund (U.S. Government corporation)
International Monetary
Rockefeller Endowment; the fund
Special Projects (U.N.)
but civil service retirement fund; mutual security fund; national service life insurance fund; revolving fund

Gadsden Purchase
Gallery of Art, National (see National)
Garand rifle
Geiger counter
general agreement (see Agreement)
General Board (of Navy) (see Board)
General Counsel; the Counsel (Federal)
General Order No. 14; General Orders, No. 14; a general order
gentile
Geographer, the (State Department)
geographic terms, such as those listed below,[1] capitalized if part of name; lowercased in general sense (rivers of Virginia and Maryland)

Archipelago	Arroyo
	Atoll
Area	Bank

Bar
Basin, Upper (Lower) Colorado River, etc. (legal entity); *but* Hansen flood-control basin; Missouri River basin (drainage); upper Colorado River storage project
Bay
Bayou
Beach
Bench
Bend
Bight
Bluff
Bog
Borough (boro)
Bottom
Branch (stream)
Brook
Butte
Canal; the canal (Panama)
Canyon

Cape
Cascade
Cave
Cavern
Channel; *but* Mississippi River channel(s)
Cirque
Coulee
Cove
Crag
Crater
Creek
Crossroads
Current (ocean feature)
Cut
Cutoff
Dam
Delta
Desert
Divide
Dome (not in geologic sense)
Draw (stream)
Dune
Escarpment
Estuary
Falls
Fault
Flat(s)
Floodway
Ford
Forest

Fork (stream)
Gap
Geyser
Glacier
Glen
Gorge
Gulch
Gulf
Gut
Harbor
Head
Hill
Hogback
Hollow
Hook
Hot Spring
Icefield
Ice Shelf
Inlet
Island
Isle
Islet
Keys (Florida only)
Knob
Lagoon
Lake
Landing
Ledge
Lowland
Marsh
Massif
Mesa
Monument
Moraine
Mound
Mount
Mountain
Narrows
Neck

Needle
Notch
Oasis
Ocean
Oxbow
Palisades
Park
Pass
Passage
Peak
Peninsula
Plain
Plateau
Point
Pond
Pool
Port (water body)
Prairie
Range (mountain)
Rapids
Ravine
Reef
Reservoir
Ridge
River
Roads (anchorage)
Rock
Run (stream)
Sea
Seaway
Shoal
Sink
Slough
Sound
Spit
Spring

Spur
Strait
Stream
Summit
Swamp
Terrace
Thorough-
 fare
Trench
Trough
Valley
Volcano
Wash
Waterway
Woods

[1] List compiled with the cooperation of the U.S. Board on Geographic Names.

Geological Survey (see Survey)
German measles
GI bill of rights
Girl Scouts (organization); a Girl Scout; a Scout; Scouting
G-man
Gold Star Mothers (see American)
Golden Age (see Ages)
Golden Rule
Gospel, if referring to the first four books of the New Testament; *but* gospel truth
Government:
  British, Soviet, etc.; the Government
  Canal Zone; the government department, officials, -owned, publications, etc. (U.S. Government)
  National and State Governments
  Printing Office (see Office)
  U.S.; National; Federal; Central; General
government:
  Churchill
  Communist
  District (of Columbia)
  European governments
  Federal, State, and municipal governments
  insular; island
  military
  seat of
  State
  State and Provincial governments
  Territorial
governmental
Governor:
  of Puerto Rico; the Governor of the Federal Reserve Board; the Governor of the Panama Canal; the Governor of Wisconsin, etc.; the Governor
  but State Governor(s); Governors' conference; a Governor
Governor General of Canada; the Governor General
grade, market (see market grades)
grand jury (see Federal)
Grange, the (National)
graph 2, A, II, etc.; *but* Graph 2, when part of title: Graph 2.—Production Levels
Great:
  Basin
  Beyond
  Divide
  Father (see fanciful appellations)
  Lakes; the lakes; lake(s) traffic
  Plains; *but* southern Great Plains

Rebellion (see Rebellion)
War (see War)
White Way (New York City)
great circle (navigation)
Greater Los Angeles, Greater New York
gross national product (GNP)
Group:
   Military Advisory Group; the group
   Standing (see Organization)
group 2, II, A, etc.; *but* Group 2, when part of title: Group II: List of Counties by States
guaranteed annual wage (GAW)
Guard, National (see National)
guardsman (see Coast Guard; National Guard)
Gulf:
   Coast States; *but* gulf coast of Mexico; the gulf States
   Stream; the stream

Hall (U.S. Senate or House)
Halls of Congress
H-bomb; H-hour
Headquarters:
   Alaska Command; the command headquarters
Heaven (Deity); heaven (place)
Hells (no apostrophe) Canyon
Hemisphere, Eastern; Western; etc.; the hemisphere
High Church
High Commissioner
High Court (see Supreme Court)
High School, if part of name: Western; the high school
Highway No. 40; Route 40; State Route 9; the highway
Hill (the Capitol)
His Excellency the Duke of Athol, etc.; His Excellency; Their Excellencies
His Majesty; Her Majesty; Their Majesties
historic events and epochs:
   Reformation, the
   Renaissance, the
   Restoration, the (English)
   Revolution of July (French)
   Revolution, the (American, 1775; French, 1789; English, 1688)
holidays and special days:
   Admission Day
   All Fools'
   Arbor Day
   Armed Forces Day
   Christmas Day, Eve
   Columbus Day
   D-day; D-plus-4-day
   Father's Day
   Flag Day
   Founders' Day
   Fourth of July
   Halloween
   Inauguration Day
   Independence Day
   Labor Day
   Lincoln's Birthday
   Lord's day
   M-day
   Memorial Day (also Decoration Day)
   Mother's Day
   New Year's Day, Eve

S-D Day (Safe-Driving Day)
Thanksgiving Day
V-E Day; V-J Day
Veterans (no apostrophe) Day
Washington's Birthday
but election day; primary day
Holy Scriptures; Holy Writ (Bible)
Home (see Naval; Soldiers')
Hospital, if part of name; the hospital:
    District of Columbia General
    5th Regiment
    Freedmen's
    St. Elizabeths (no apostrophe)
    but naval (marine or Army) hospital
hospital corpsman (see corpsman)
House, if part of name:
    Johnson house (private residence)
    Lee (hotel); the house
    of Representatives; the House (U.S.)
    of the Woods (palace); the house
    Office Building (see Building)
    Ohio (State); the house
    but both Houses; lower (or upper) House (Congress)
House of Representatives (U.S.), titles of officers standing alone capitalized:
    Chairman (Committee of the Whole)
    Clerk; *but* legislative clerk, etc.
    Official Reporter(s) of Debates
    Speaker pro tempore
    Speaker; speakership
HUD (Department of Housing and Urban Development)
Hudson's Bay Co.
Hurricane Carol, etc.

ice age (see Ages)
independence; in the year of our independence the one hundred and ninety-seventh
Indians:
    Absentee Shawnee
    Alaska (see Native)
    Eastern (or Lower) Band of Cherokee; the band
    Five Civilized Tribes; the tribes
    Shawnee Tribe; the tribe
    Six Nations (Iroquois Confederacy)
Inquisition, Spanish; the Inquisition
Institute, if part of name; capitalized standing alone if referring to Federal or international organization:
    National Cancer; the Cancer Institute; the Institute
    National Institutes of Health; the Institutes
    of International Law; the Institute
    Woman's Institute; the institute
Institution, if part of name;

capitalized standing alone if referring to Federal unit:
Carnegie Institution; the institution
Smithsonian Institution; the Institution
insular government; island government
intercoastal waterway (see waterway)
interdepartmental
International Court of Justice (see Court)
International Geophysical Year (see Year)
International Hydrological Decade; the Decade (UNESCO)
International Postal Convention (see Convention)
international:
  banks (see Bank)
  dateline
  boundary
  law
  Morse code (see Code)
interprovincial
interstate
Intracoastal Waterway; the waterway (see also waterway)
intrastate
Irish potato
Iron Cross (see decorations)
Iron Curtain; the curtain
irrigation district (see District)
Isthmian Canal (see Canal)
Isthmus of Panama; the isthmus
Ivory Coast

Japan Current (see Current)
Jersey cattle
Jim Crow law, car, etc.
Job Corps
Joint Chiefs of Staff; Chiefs of Staff
Joint Committee on Atomic Energy (see Committee)
Journal clerk; the clerk
Journal (House or Senate)
Judge Advocate General, the
judiciary, the

Kennedy round
King of England, etc.; the King
Koran, the; Koranic
K-ration
Ku Klux Klan; the Klan

Laboratory, if part of name: Forest Products; the Laboratory; *but* the laboratory (non-Federal)
Lake: Erie, of the Woods, Salt; the lake
Lakes, Great (see Great Lakes)
Lane, if part of name: Maiden; the lane
Latin American States (see States)
Latter-day Saints
law of nations
law, Walsh-Healey, etc.; law 176; law No. 176; copyright law; Ohm's, etc.
League, Urban; the league
Legal Adviser of the Department of State; the Legal Adviser
Legation, Finnish, etc.; the Legation

Capitalization

Legion:
    American; the Legion; a Legionnaire; French Foreign; the legion
Legislative Assembly, if part of name:
    of New York; the legislative assembly; the assembly
    of Puerto Rico; the legislative assembly; the assembly
legislative branch, clerk, session, etc.
Legislature:
    National Legislature (U.S. Congress); the Legislature
    Ohio Legislature; Legislature of Ohio; the legislature
lend-lease materials, etc. (see also Act)
Letters Patent No. 378,964; *but* patent No. 378,964; letters patent
Levant, the (Mediterranean region)
Liberty Bell; Liberty ship
Librarian of Congress; the Librarian
Library:
    Army; the library
    Franklin D. Roosevelt; the library of Congress; the Library
    Public (District of Columbia); the library
Lieutenant Governor of Idaho, etc.; the Lieutenant Governor
Light, if part of name; the light:
    Boston
    Buffalo South Pier Light 2; *but* light No. 2; light 2
    but Massachusetts Bay lights
Lighthouse (see Light Station)
Lightship, if part of name; the lightship:
    Grays Reef Lightship
    North Manitou Shoal Lightship
Light Station, if part of name; the light station; the station:
Line(s), if part of name; the line(s):
    Burlington Lines (railroad)
    Greyhound Line (bus)
    Holland-America Line (steamship) line:
    DEW
    maginot
    Mason-Dixon line *or* Mason and Dixon's line
    Pinetree
    State
Little Inch; Big Inch (pipelines)
Little Steel formula, etc.
Local: Teamsters Local Union No. 15; *but* local No. 15
local time, local standard time (see time)
Loop, the (see cities)
Louisiana Purchase
Low Church
Lower, if part of name:
    California (Mexico)
    Colorado River Basin
    Egypt
    Peninsula (of Michigan)
    but lower (or upper) House of

Congress; lower Mississippi
Mafia
Magna Carta
Majesty, His, Her (see His Majesty)
Majority Leader Mansfield; *but* the majority leader (U.S. Congress)
Mall (see District of Columbia)
Manager, General Manager (AEC), if referring to head of Federal or District of Columbia unit
Mansion, Executive (see Executive)
map 3, A, II, etc.; *but* Map 2, when part of title: Map 2.—Railroads of Middle Atlantic States
Marine Corps; the corps:
  man
  Marines (the corps); *but* marines (individuals)
  Organized Reserve; the Reserve
  also a marine, a woman marine, the women marines (individuals)
Maritime Provinces (Canada) (see Province)
market grades and classes:
  U.S. grade A
  Prime, Choice, Good (cattle)
Marshal (see Supreme Court)
Marshall plan (see plan)
Mason-Dixon line (see line)
M-day
medals (see decorations)
Medicare Act; medicare plan
Member, if referring to Senator, Representative, Delegate, or Resident Commissioner of U.S. Congress; *also* Member at Large; Member of Parliament, etc.; *but* membership; member of U.S. congressional committee
Merchant Marine Reserve; the Reserve; *but* U.S. merchant marine; the merchant marine
Metropolitan Washington, etc.; *but* Washington metropolitan area
midcontinent region
Middle Ages (see Ages)
Middle Atlantic States
Middle East; Mideast; Mideastern; Middle Eastern (Asia)
middle Europe
Middle West, Midwest (section of United States)
Middle Western States; Midwestern States; *but* midwestern farmers, etc.
Midsouth (section of United States)
Military Academy (see Academy)
Military Establishment (see Establishment)
Militia, if part of name; the militia:
  1st Regiment Ohio
  Indiana
  Naval
  of Ohio
  Organized
milkshed, Ohio, etc. (region)

Minister Plenipotentiary; the Minister; Minister Without Portfolio (see also foreign cabinets)
Ministry (see foreign cabinets)
Minority Leader Martin; *but* the minority leader (U.S. Congress)
Mint, Philadelphia, etc.; the mint
minutemen (colonial)
Mission, if part of name; the mission:
  Gospel Mission
  Mission 66
  but diplomatic mission; military mission; Jones mission
Monroe Doctrine (see Doctrine)
Monument:
  Bunker Hill; the monument
  Grounds; the grounds (District of Columbia)
  National (see National)
  Washington; the monument (District of Columbia)
Moon
Mountain States
mountain time, mountain standard time (see time)
Mr. Chairman; Mr. Secretary; etc.
Museum, capitalize with name; the museum:
  Army Medical; the Medical Museum
  Field
  National
  National Air; the Air Museum

mutual defense assistance program

Nation (synonym for United States); *but* a nation; nationwide; *also* French nation, Balkan nations
Nation, Creek; Osage; etc.; the nation
nation, in general, standing alone
National, in conjunction with capitalized name:
  Academy of Sciences (see Academy) and State institutions, etc.
  Archives, the (see The)
  Capital (Washington); the Capital
  Forest (see Forest)
  Gallery of Art; the National Gallery; the gallery
  Grange; the Grange
  Guard, Ohio, etc.; Air National; the National Guard; the Guard; a guardsman; *but* a National Guard man; National Guardsman
  Institute (see Institute)
  Legislature (see Legislature)
  Monument, Muir, etc.; the national monument; the monument
  Museum (see Museum)
  Naval Medical Center (Bethesda, Md.)
  Park, Yellowstone, etc.; Yellowstone Park; the national park; the park
  Treasury; the Treasury

War College
Woman's Party; the party
Zoological Park (see Zoological)
national:
  agency check (NAC)
  anthem, customs, spirit, etc.
  British, Mexican, etc.
  defense agencies
  stockpile
  water policy (see policy)
Native, Alaska; *but* Ohio native, etc.
Naval, if part of name:
  Academy (see Academy)
  Base, Guam Naval; the naval base
  District, 1st Naval (see District)
  Establishment (see Establishment)
  Home (Philadelphia); the home
  Militia; the militia
  Observatory (see Observatory)
  Potomac River Naval Command (see Command)
  Reserve; the Reserve; a reservist
  Reserve Force; the force
  Reserve officer; a Reserve officer
  Shipyard (if preceding or following name): Brooklyn Naval Shipyard; Naval Shipyard, Brooklyn; *but* the naval shipyard
  Station (if preceding or following name): Key West Naval Station; Naval Station, Key West; the station
  Volunteer Naval Reserve
  War College; the War College; the college
  Weapons Plant; the weapons plant; the plant
naval, in general sense:
  command (see Command)
  district (see District)
  expenditures, maneuvers, officer, service, stores, etc.
  petroleum reserves; *but* Naval Petroleum Reserve No. 2 (Buena Vista Hills Naval Reserve); reserve No. 2
  navel orange
Navy, American or foreign, if part of name; capitalized standing alone only if referring to U.S. Navy:
  Admiral of the; the admiral
  Establishment; the establishment
  Hospital Corps; hospital corpsman; the corps
  navy yard
  Regular
  regulation 56
  7th Task Force (see Force)
Nazi; nazism
Near East (Balkans, etc.)
Negro; Negress
Network, Red, Blue; the network
New Deal; anti-New Deal
New, if part of name: New Willard
New England States
New World
Niagara Frontier; the frontier
Nike-Ajax, etc.

Capitalization

Nine Power Treaty; the treaty
North:
  Atlantic
  Atlantic Pact (see Pact)
  Atlantic States
  Atlantic Treaty (see Treaty)
  Atlantic Treaty Organization (see Organization)
  Equatorial Current (see Current)
  Korea
  Pole
  Slope (Alaska)
  Star (Polaris)
  the North (section of United States)
  Vietnam
north:
  Africa
  Ohio
north-central region, etc.
northern Ohio
Northern States
northerner
Northwest Pacific
Northwest Territory (1799)
Northwest, the (section of United States)
Northwestern:
  States
  United States
numbers capitalized if spelled out as part of a name:
  Charles the First
  Committee of One Hundred
  Fourteenth Censes (see Census)

Observatory, capitalized with name:
  Astrophysical; the Observatory
  Lick; the observatory
  Naval; the Observatory
Occident, the; occidental
Ocean, if part of name; the ocean:
  Antarctic
  Arctic
  Atlantic
  North Atlantic, etc.
  Pacific
  South Pacific, etc.
  Southwest Pacific, etc.
Oceanographer (the Hydrographer), Navy
Office, if referring to unit of Federal or District of Columbia Government; the Office:
  Chicago Operations Office, etc. (AEC); the Operations Office
  Executive
  Foreign (see foreign cabinets)
  Government Printing; the Printing Office
  New York regional office (including branch, division, or section therein); the regional office; the office
  Patent
officer:
  Army
  Marine; *but* naval and marine officers
  Navy; Navy and Marine officers
  Regular Army; Regular; a Regular

Reserve
WAC, WAVE
Old Dominion (Virginia)
Old South
Old World
Olympic games; Olympiad; XI Olympic games
Operation Deep Freeze, Snowdrop, etc.; *but* Deep Freeze operation
Order of Business No. 56 (congressional calendar)
Ordnance:
 Corps (see Corps)
 Department; the Department
 Depot (see Depot)
Organization, if part of name; capitalized standing alone if referring to international unit:
 Educational, Scientific, and Cultural (UNESCO)
 International Labor
 North Atlantic Treaty (NATO)
 of American States (formerly Pan American Union)
Organized:
 Marine Corps Reserve; Marine Reserve; the Reserve
 Militia; the militia
 Naval Militia; the Naval Militia; the militia
 Reserve Corps; the Reserve
Orient, the oriental
Outer Continental Shelf (see Continental)

Pacific (see also Atlantic):
 coast
 Coast (*or* Slope) States
 Northwest
 Northwest Pacific
 seaboard
 slope
 South Pacific
 States
 time, Pacific standard time (see time) *but* cispacific; transpacific
Pact, capitalized with name; lowercased standing alone:
 Atlantic; Atlantic Defense
 North Atlantic; North Atlantic Defense
pan-American games; *but* Pan American Day
Pan American Union (see Organization of American States)
Panel, Atomic Energy Labor-Management Relations (Federal), etc; the Panel
Panhandle of Texas; Texas Panhandle; the panhandle; etc.
papers, Woodrow Wilson, etc.; the papers; *but* white paper.
Parish, Caddo, etc.; *but* parish of Caddo (Louisiana civil division); the parish
Park, Fairmount, etc.; the park (see also National)
Park Police, U.S. (District of Columbia); park policeman
Park, Zoological (see Zoological)
Parkway, George Washington

Capitalization

Memorial; the memorial parkway; the parkway
Parliament, Houses of; the Parliament
Parliamentarian (U.S. Senate or House)
part 2, A, II, etc.; *but* Part 2, when part of title: Part 2: Iron and Steel Industry
party, political (see political parties)
Pass, Brenner, capitalized if part of name; the pass
patent (see Letters Patent)
Peninsula, Upper (Lower) (Michigan); the peninsula
Penitentiary, Albany, etc.; the penitentiary
Permanent Court of Arbitration (see Court)
phase 2
Philippine Republic (see Republic)
Pilgrim Fathers (1620); the Pilgrims; a Pilgrim
Place, if part of name: Jefferson Place; the place
Plains (Great Plains), the
plan:
  Colombo
  controlled materials
  5-year
  Marshall (European recovery program)
  Reorganization Plan No. 6 (Hoover Commission); plan No. 1
Planetarium, Fels, Hayden; the planetarium
Plant, Rockford Arsenal; the plant; *but* Savannah River (AEC) plant; United States Steel plant
plate 2, A, II, etc.; *but* Plate 2, when part of title: Plate 2.—Rural Structures
Pledge of Allegiance
point 4; point 4 program
Pole: North, South; the pole; subpolar
Pole Star (Polaris); polar star
Police, if part of name; the police
policy, national water
political parties and adherents (Party, if part of name; the party):
  Communist; a Communist; A Commie
  Conservative; a Conservative
  Democratic; a Democrat
  Independent; an Independent
  National Woman's; Woman's Party
  Progressive; a Progressive
  Republican; Grand Old Party; *but* grand old Republican Party; a Republican
  Socialist; a Socialist
  States' Rights; States' Righter; a Dixiecrat; *but* States rights (in general sense)
Pool, Northwest Power, etc.; the pool
Pope; *but* papal, patriarch, pontiff, primate
Port, if part of name; Port of Norfolk; Norfolk Port; the port (see Authority)

Post Office, Chicago, etc.
P.O. Box (with number); *but* post office box (in general sense)
Postal Union (see Union)
Postmaster General
Powers, if part of name; the powers (see also alliances)
  Allied (World Wars I and II)
  Axis (World War)
  Big Four
  Western Powers
  but European powers
precinct; first, 11th precinct
Premier (see foreign cabinets)
Preserve, Wichita National Forest Game, etc.; Wichita Game Preserve; Wichita preserve
Presidency (office of head of government)
President:
  of the United States; the Executive; the Chief Magistrate; the Commander in Chief; the President-elect; ex-President; former President; also preceding name
  of any other country; the President
  of Federal or international unit
  but president of the Erie Railroad; president of the Federal Reserve Bank of New York
Presidential assistant, authority, order, proclamation, candidate, election, timber, year, etc.

Prime Minister (see foreign cabinets)
Prison, Auburn, etc.; the prison
Privy Council, His Majesty's (see Council)
Prize, Nobel, Pulitzer, etc.; the prize
Proclamation, Emancipation; Presidential Proclamation No. 24; Proclamation No. 24; the proclamation; *but* Presidential proclamation
Project Farside, Sidewinder, Vanguard, etc.; *but* Vanguard project
Project Head Start
Province, Provincial, if referring to an administrative subdivision: Ontario Province; Province of Ontario; Maritime Provinces (Canada); the Province
Proving Ground, Aberdeen, etc.; the proving ground
Public Act 26; Public Law 9; Public 37; Public Resolution 3; *also* public enemy No. 1
Public Printer; the Government Printer; the Printer
public utility district (see District)
Pueblo, Santa Clara; the pueblo
Puerto Rico:
  government
  Governor of; the Governor
  Legislative Assembly of; the legislative assembly
  Provisional Regiment; *but* Puerto Rico regiment

Capitalization 231

Resident Commissioner
Purchase, Gadsden, Louisiana, etc.
Puritan; puritanical

Quad Cities (Davenport, Rock Island, Moline, and East Moline)

Radio Free Europe
Railroad, Alaska; the Railroad
Ranch, King, etc.; the ranch
Range, Cascade, etc. (mountains); the range
Rebellion, if part of name; the rebellion:
  Boxer
  Great (Civil War)
  War of the
  Whisky
Reconstruction period (post-Civil War)
Red army
Red Cross, American (see American)
Reds, the; a Red (political)
Reformation, the
Reformatory, Elmira, etc.; the reformatory
Refuge, Blackwater Migratory Bird, etc.; Blackwater Bird Refuge; Blackwater refuge
region, north-central, etc.; first region, 10th region; mid-continent
Register of the Treasury; the Register
Regular Army, Navy; a Regular (see also, officer)
regulation:
  ceiling price regulation 8
  56 (Navy)
  supplementary regulation 22
  Veterans Regulation 8; *but* veterans regulations
  W (see also Federal Reserve Board)
Reign of Terror (France, 1792)
religious terms:
  Bahai
  Baptist
  Brahman
  Buddhist
  Catholic; Catholicism; *but* catholic (universal)
  Christian
  Christian Science
  Evangelical United Brethren
  Hebrew
  Latter-day Saints
  Mohammedan
  New Thought
  Protestant; Protestantism
  Seventh-day Adventists
  Seventh-Day Baptists
  Zoroastrian
Renaissance, the (era)
reorganization plan (see plan)
Report, if part of name (with date or number); the annual report; the report:
  Hoover Commission Report on Paperwork; *but* Hoover Commission report; Hoover report; task force report
  U.S. Reports (publication)
Reporter, the (U.S. Supreme Court)
Representative; Representative at Large (U.S. Congress); U.N.

Republic, capitalized if part of name; capitalized standing alone if referring to a specific government:
French
Irish
of Panama
of the Philippines; Philippine Republic
United Arab
United States
also the American Republics; the Latin American Republics; South American Republics; the Republics
Reservation (forest, military, or Indian), if part of name; the reservation:
Great Sioux
Hill Military
Reserve, if part of name; the Reserve (see also Air Force; Army Corps; Foreign Service; Marine Corps; Merchant Marine; Naval):
Active
Air Force
Army
bank (see Bank)
Board, Federal (see Federal)
city (see Bank)
Civil Air Patrol
components
Enlisted
Establishment
Inactive
Naval
officer
Officers' Training Corps
Ready
Retired
Standby
Volunteer Naval
Women's (see Women's Reserve)
Reserves, the; reservist
Resident Commissioner (see Member; Puerto Rico)
Resolution, with number; the resolution:
House Joint Resolution 3
Public Resolution 6
Resolution 42
Senate Concurrent Resolution 18
but Kefauver resolution
Revised Statutes (U.S.); Supplement to the Revised Statutes; the statutes
Revolution, Revolutionary (if referring to the American, French, or English Revolution) (see also War)
Road, if part of name: Benning; the road
Roman numerals, common nouns used with, not capitalized:
book II; chapter II; part II; etc.
but Book II: Modern Types (complete heading); Part XI: Early Thought (complete heading)
route No. 12466; mail route 1742; railway mail route 1144; *but* Route 40, State Route 9 (highways)
Royal Decree No. 24; Decree 24; the royal decree

rule 21; rule XXI; *but* Rule 21, when part of title: Rule 21: Renewal of Motion
Ruler of the Universe (Deity)
Rules:
   of the House of Representatives; *but* rules of the House
   Standing Rules of the Senate (publication); *but* rules of the Senate
   also Commission rules

Sabbath; Sabbath Day
sanitary district (see District)
savings bond (see bond)
schedule 2, A, II, etc.; *but* Schedule 2, when part of title: Schedule 2: Open and Prepay Stations
School, if part of name; the school:
   any school of the U.S. Army or Navy
   Hayes
   Pawnee Indian
school district (see District)
Scriptures; Holy Scriptures (the Bible)
Seabees (see Navy)
seaboard, Atlantic, eastern, etc.
seaway (see geographic terms; Authority; Corporation)
Second World War (see War)
Secretariat (see United Nations)
Secretaries of the Army and the Navy; *but* Secretaries of the military departments; secretaryship
Secretary, head of national governmental unit:
   of Defense; of State; etc.; the Secretary
   of State for Foreign Affairs (British); for the Colonies; etc.; the Secretary
   also the Assistant Secretary; the Executive Secretary
   but secretary of the Interstate Commerce Commission; secretary of state of Iowa
Secretary General: the Secretary General:
   Organization of American States (formerly Pan American Union)
   South Pacific Commission
   United Nations
section 2, A, II, etc.; *but* Section 2, when part of title: Section 2: Test Construction Theory
Selective Service (see Service; System)
Senate (U.S.), titles of officers standing alone capitalized:
   President of the
   President pro tempore
   Presiding Officer
   Secretary
Senate, Ohio (State); the senate
Senator (U.S. Congress); *but* lowercased if referring to a State senator, unless preceding a name
senatorial
Sergeant at Arms (U.S. Senate or House)

Sermon on the Mount
Service, if referring to Federal or District of Columbia unit; the Service:
  Customs Agency
  Employment
  Extension
  Fish and Wildlife
  Foreign (see Foreign Service)
  Forest
  Immigration and Naturalization
  Internal Revenue
  Mediation and Conciliation
  National Park
  Officer Procurement
  Postal
  Postal Transportation
  Secret (Treasury)
  Selective (see also System); *but* selective service, in general sense; selective service classification I-A, 4-F, etc.
  Soil Conservation
service:
  airmail
  Army
  city delivery
  consular
  customs (see Bureau)
  diplomatic
  employment (State)
  extension (State)
  general delivery
  naval
  Navy
  parcel post
  postal field
  railway mail (see Division)
  rural free delivery; rural delivery; free delivery
  special delivery
  star route
Shelf, Continental (see Continental) ship of state (unless personified)
Sister(s) (adherent of religious order)
Six Nations (see Indians)
Smithsonian Institution (see Institution)
Social Security district officer
Social Security representative
Social Security (Administration implied in these examples)
But in general sense:
  social security application
  social security medical report
Socialist; socialism; socialistic (see also political parties)
Society, if part of name; the society:
  American Cancer Society, Inc.
  Boston Medical
  of the Cincinnati
soil bank
Soldiers' Home, if part of name:
  Ohio Soldiers' Home; the soldiers' home; etc.
Soldiers' Home, the (District of Columbia only); the home
Solicitor for the Department of Commerce, etc.; the Solicitor
Solicitor General (Department of Justice)
Son of Man (Christ)

Sons of the American Revolution (organization); a Son; a Real Son
South:
  American Republics (see Republic)
  American States
  Atlantic
  Atlantic States
  Deep South (U.S.)
  Korea
  Midsouth (U.S.)
  Pacific
  Pole
  the South (section of United States); Southland
  Vietnam
Southeast Asia
southern California, southeastern California, etc.
Southern States
Southern United States
southerner
Southwest, the (section of United States)
Soviet (see U.S.S.R.)
Spanish-American War (see War)
Special Order No. 12; Special Orders, No. 12; a special order
Speedway, the (see District of Columbia)
Spirit of '76 (painting); *but* spirit of '76 (in general sense)
spring (season)
sputnik; *but* Sputnik I, etc.
Square, Lafayette, etc.; the square
Staff, Foreign Service (see Foreign Service); Air
Staked Plain
standard time (see time)
Star of Bethlehem
Star-Spangled Banner (see flag)
state:
  and church
  of the Union message
  statehood, statehouse, stateside, statewide
  downstate, tristate, upstate
  welfare
State:
  government
  legislature (see Legislature)
  line, Iowa, Ohio-Indiana, etc.
  New York
  of Israel
  of Pennsylvania
  of Veracruz
  out-of-State (adjective); *but* out-of-stater
  prison
  rights; States rights
  Vatican City
State's attorney
state's evidence
States:
  Arab
  Balkan
  Baltic
  Communistic
  Eastern; *but* eastern industrial States
  East North Central
  East South Central
  Eastern Gulf
  Eastern North Central, etc.
  Far Western
  Gulf; Gulf Coast

236 CORRECT ENGLISH USAGE

Lake
Latin American
Middle
Middle Atlantic
Middle Western
Midwestern
Mountain
New England
North Atlantic
Northern
Northwestern, etc.
Organization of American
Pacific
Pacific Coast
rights
South American
South Atlantic
Southern
the six States of Australia; a foreign state
Thirteen Original; original 13 States
West North Central
West South Central
Western; *but* western Gulf; western farming States
Station, if part of name; the station; not capitalized if referring to surveying or similar work:
Grand Central
Key West Naval (see Naval)
Nebraska Experiment Station; Experiment Station, Nebraska; Nebraska station
Syracuse Air Force
television station WSYR-TV
Union; Union Depot; the depot
WRC station; station WRC; radio station WRC; broadcasting station WRC
substation A
Statue of Liberty; the statue
Statutes at Large (U.S.) (see also Revised Statutes)
stockpile, national
stone age (see Ages)
Stream, Gulf (see Gulf; Geographic terms)
Street, if part of name; the street:
I Street (not Eye)
Fifteen-and-a-Half
110th Street
subcommittee (see Committee)
Subtreasury, New York, etc.; subtreasury at New York; the subtreasury
subtropical, subtropic(s) (see tropical) summer
Summer
summit meeting
Superintendent, if referring to head of Federal; the Superintendent:
of Documents (Government Printing Office)
of the Naval (or Military) Academy
Supreme Bench; the Bench; *also* High Bench; High Tribunal
Supreme Court (U.S.); the Court; *also* High Court; titles of officers standing alone capitalized:
Associate Justice; Justice
Chief Justice
Clerk
Marshal

Capitalization

Reporter
Surgeon General, the (Army, Navy, and Public Health Service)
Survey, if part of name of Federal or District of Columbia unit; the Survey: Coast and Geodetic; Geological; National Wilderness Preservation
System, if referring to Federal or District of Columbia unit; the System:
  Federal Credit
  Federal Home Loan Bank
  Federal Reserve
  National System of Interstate and Defense Highways; National System of Interstate Highways; Interstate System of Highways; Interstate Highway System; the Interstate System; the National, System; the system; *but* highway system; Federal road system
  New York Central System
  Selective Service (see also Service)
  but Pennsylvania Railway system; Pennsylvania system; Bell System, the system
  also Federal land bank system

table 2, II, A, etc.; *but* Table 2, when part of title: Table 2: Degrees of Land Deterioration

task force (see Force; Report)
Teacher Corps
Team, USAREUR Field Assistance, etc.; the team
television station (see Station)
Territorial, if referring to a political subdivision
Territory:
  Northwest (1799); the territory
  Trust Territory of the Pacific Islands, Pacific Islands Trust Territory; the trust territory, the territory
  Yukon, Northwest Territories; the Territory(ies), Territorial (Canada)
  but territory of: American Samoa, Guam, Virgin Islands
The, part of name, capitalized:
  The Adjutant General (only when so in copy)
  The Dalles; The Gambia; The Hague; The Weirs; *but* the Dalles Dam; the Dalles region; the Hague Conference; the Weirs streets
  but the National Archives; the Archives; the Times; the *Mermaid;* the Federal Express
Thirteen American Colonies, etc. (see Colonies)
Thirteen Original States
Thruway, New York; the thruway
time:
  Atlantic, Atlantic standard
  central, central standard
  eastern, eastern daylight,

eastern standard
Greenwich civil, etc.
local, local standard
mountain, mountain standard
Pacific, Pacific standard
universal
title 2, II, A, etc.; *but* Title 2, when part of title: Title 2: General Provisions
Tomb:
  Grant's; the tomb
  of the Unknown Soldier; Unknown Soldier's Tomb; Tomb of the Unknowns; the tomb (see also Unknown Soldier)
Tower, Eiffel, etc.; the tower
Township, Union; township of Union
transatlantic; transpacific; trans-Siberian, etc.; *but* Transjordan
Treasurer, Assistant, of the United States; the Assistant Treasurer; *but* assistant treasurer at New York, etc.
Treasurer of the United States; the Treasurer
Treasury notes; Treasurys
Treasury, of the United States; General; National; Public; Register of the
Treaty, if part of name; the treaty:
  Jay Treaty
  North Atlantic; North Atlantic Defense
  of Versailles
  but treaty of 1919

Tribunal, standing alone capitalized only in minutes and official reports of a specific arbitration; *also* High Tribunal; the Tribunal (Supreme Court)
Tricolor (see flags)
Triple A (any three A group)
Trizonia; trizonal; trizone
Tropic of Cancer, of Capricorn; the Tropics
tropical; neotropic, neotropical; subtropic(s), subtropical
Trust, Power, etc.
trust territory (see Territory)
Tunnel, Lincoln, etc.; the tunnel; *but* irrigation, railroad, etc., tunnel
Turnpike, Pennsylvania, etc.; the turnpike
Twin Cities (Minneapolis and St. Paul)

U-boat
Under Secretary, if referring to officer of Federal Government; the Under Secretary:
  of Agriculture
  of State
  of the Treasury
Union, if part of proper name; capitalized standing alone if synonym for United States or if referring to international unit:
  International Typographical; the Typographical Union; the union
  Pan American (see Organi-

Capitalization

zation of American States)
Teamsters Union; the Teamsters; the union; *also* the Auto Workers, etc.
Universal Postal; the Postal Union; the Union
Western (see alliances)
Woman's Christian Temperance
but a painters union; printers union
Union Jack (see flags)
Union of Soviet Socialist Republics (see U.S.S.R.)
Unit, if referring to Federal or District of Columbia branch; the Unit:
  Alcohol Tax
  Income Tax
  but Pasco unit
United Nations:
  Charter; the charter
  Children's Fund (UNICEF); the Fund
  Conference on International Organization; the Conference
  Economic and Social Council; the Council
  Educational, Scientific, and Cultural Organization (UNESCO) (see Organization)
  Food and Agriculture Organization (FAO); the Organization
  General Assembly; the Assembly
  International Court of Justice; the Court
  International Labor Organization (see Organization)
  Little Assembly; the Assembly
  Permanent Court of Arbitration (see Court)
  Secretariat, the
  Secretary General
  Security Council; the Council
  Special United Nations Fund for Economic Development (SUNFED)
  Trusteeship Council; the Council
  World Health Organization (WHO); the Organization
universal:
  military training (see program)
  time (see time)
Universal Postal Union (see Union)
University, if part of name: Stanford; the university
Unknown Soldier; Unknown of World War II; World War II Unknown; Unknown of Korea; Korea Unknown; the Unknowns (see also Tomb)
Upper, if part of name:
  Colorado River Basin
  Egypt
  Peninsula (of Michigan)
  but upper House of Congress
U.S.S.R. (Union of Soviet Socialist Republics):
  Cominform (Communist Information Bureau)
  Communist International
  Communist States

Politburo
Red army
Reds, the; a Red
Soviet, if part of name; capitalized standing alone if referring to central governmental unit:
  Government; *but* Communist government
  Moscow
  National
  of Labor and Defense
  S.S.S.R. (Siberian Soviet Socialist Republics)
  but a soviet; sovietic; sovietism; sovietize

Valley, Shenandoah, etc.; the valley; *but* the valleys of Maryland and Virginia
Vari-Typer (trade name); *but* varityped, varityping
V-E Day; V-J Day (see holidays)
veteran, World War
Veterans' Administration (see Administration)
Veterans Day (see holidays)
vice consul, British, etc.
Vice President (same as President)
Victoria Cross (see decorations)
Victory:
  bond (see bond)
  ship (pl., Victorys)
  but victory garden, speaker, etc.
Vietcong
Voice of America; the Voice
volume 2, A, II, etc.; *but* Volume 2, when part of title:
  Volume 2: Five Rivers in America's Future

WAC (see Corps)
War, if part of name:
  Between the States
  Civil
  First World War; World War I; World War; Great War; Second World War; World War II
  French and Indian (1754–63)
  Mexican
  of the Nations
  of the Rebellion; the rebellion
  of the Revolution; the Revolution
  of 1812; *but* war of 1914
  Philippine Insurrection
  Revolutionary
  Seven Years'
  Spanish
  Spanish-American
  the two World Wars
  also post-World War II
war:
  cold, hot
  European
  French and Indian wars
  Indian
  Korean
  third world; world war III
  with Mexico
  with Spain
war bond
War Mothers (see American)
ward 1, 2, etc.; first, 11th, etc.
Washington's Farewell Address
water district (see District)

Capitalization

waterway, inland, intercoastal, etc.; *but* Intracoastal Waterway
Week, Fire Prevention; etc.
welfare state
West:
  Coast (Africa); *but* west coast (U.S.)
  End, etc. (section of city)
  Europe (political entity)
  Far West; Far Western States
  Florida (1763–1819)
  Germany (political entity)
  Middle (United States); Midwest
  South Central States, etc.
  the West (section of United States; *also* world political entity)
west, western Pennsylvania
Western:
  bloc
  civilization
  countries
  Europe(an) (political entity)
  Germany (political entity)
  Hemisphere; the hemisphere
  ideas
  North Central States
  Powers
  States
  Union (see alliances)
  United States
  World
  but far western; western farming States (U.S.)
Wheat Belt (see Belt)
whip, the (of political party in Congress)
Whisky Rebellion (see Rebellion)
white paper, British, etc.
Wilderness, capitalized with name; San Joaquin Wilderness, Calif.; the wilderness; *but* the Wilderness (Virginia battlefield)
winter
woman marine, etc. (see Marine Corps)
Women's Army Corps (see Corps)
Women in the Air Force (WAF); a Waf, Wafs (individuals)
women's lib
Women's Reserve of the Coast Guard
  Reserve; Women's Reserve; the Reserve; SPAR, popular name, made up of initial letters of motto *semper paratus—always ready;* a Spar
Women's Reserve of the Naval Reserve; Women's Reserve; the Reserve; WAVES (*w*omen *a*ccepted for *v*olunteer *e*mergency *s*ervice); a Wave
Wood, if part of name:
  Belleau Wood
  House of the Woods (palace)
World, New, Old
World War (see War)
World War II veteran
world's series

X-ray

Year, International, Geophysical; the Geophysical Year; the Year

Young Men's Christian Association
Your Excellency; Your Honor; Your Majesty; etc.
Youth Corps; the Corps

ZIP Code number
Zone, if part of name; the zone:
  Bizonia; bizonal
  British (in Germany)
  Canal (Panama)
  Canal Zone Government
  Eastern, Western (Germany)
  Frigid
  New York Foreign Trade; Foreign Trade Zone No.1; *but* the foreign trade zone
  of Interior (see Command)
  Temperate, Torrid; the zone
  Trizonia; trizonal
  but Arctic, eastern standard time, polar, tropical zone, etc.
Zoological Park (National); the zoo; the park

12. Punctuation

Comma

The comma is used—

1. To separate the parts of a compound sentence joined by *and, but, or, for, either, neither,* or *nor.*

    > Fish swam in the lakes, and turtles frequented the shores.
    > The boy went home, but his sister remained with the crowd.

    However, compound predicates are not separated by commas.

    > Fish swam in the lakes and frequented the shores.

2. To set off descriptive (nonessential) words, phrases, or clauses. But when the words, phrases, or clauses are essential (that is, they identify the subject), they are not set off by commas.

    > Mr. Jefferson, who was then Secretary of State, favored the location of the National Capital at Washington.

It must be remembered, however, that the Government had no guarantee.

It is obvious, therefore, that this office cannot function.

The atom bomb, which was developed at the Manhattan project, was first used in World War II.

Their high morale might, he suggested, have caused them to put success of the team above the reputation of the college.

The restriction is laid down in title IX, chapter 8, section 15, of the code.

but

The man who fell [restrictive clause] broke his back.

The dam which gave way [restrictive clause] was poorly constructed.

He therefore gave up the search.

3. To set off words or phrases in apposition or in contrast.

Mr. Green, the lawyer, spoke for the defense.
Mr. Jones, attorney for the plaintiff, signed the petition.
Mr. Smith, not Mr. Black, was elected.
James Roosevelt, Democrat, of California.

But do not separate two nouns, one of which is necessary to identify the other.

The witness Smith took the stand.
The booklet *How to Type Reports* is enclosed.

4. To separate two words or figures that might otherwise be misunderstood.

Instead of hundreds, thousands came.
Instead of 20, 50 came.
February 10, 1929.
In 1930, 400 men were dismissed.
To John, Smith was very kind.

What the difficulty is, is not known; *but* he suggested that that committee be appointed.

5. Before a direct quotation of only a few words following an introductory phrase.

   —He said, "Now or never."
6. To indicate the omission of a word or words.

   Then we had much; now, nothing.

7. After each of a series of coordinate qualifying words.

   short, swift streams; *but* short tributary streams

8. Between an introductory modifying phrase and its subject.

   Beset by the enemy, they retreated.

9. Before and after *Jr., Sr., Esq., Ph.D., F.R.S.*, etc., within a sentence except where possession is indicated.

Henry Smith, Jr., chairman	Brown, A. H., Jr. (*not* Brown, Jr., A. H.)
Peter Johns, F.R.S., London	*but* John Smith 2d (*or* II); Smith, John, II
Washington, D.C., schools	Mr. Smith, Junior, also spoke (where only last name is used)
Motorola, Inc., factory	

10. After each member within a series of three or more words, phrases, letters, or figures used with *and, or,* or *nor*.

    red, white, and blue
    horses, mules, and cattle; *but* horses and mules and cattle
    by the bolt, by the yard, or in remnants
    a, b, and c
    neither snow, rain, nor heat
    2 days, 3 hours, and 4 minutes (series); *but* 2 days 3 hours 4 minutes (age)

11. After a noun or phrase in direct address.

> Senator, will the measure be defeated?
> Mr. Chairman, I will reply to the gentleman later.
> Yes, sir, he did see it.
> No, sir, I do not recall.

12. After an interrogative clause, followed by a direct question.

> You are sure, are you not? You will go, will nou not?

13. Between title of person and name of organization in the absence of the words *of* or *of the*.

> Chief, Division of Finance
> chairman, Committee on Appropriations
> colonel, 7th Cavalry
> president, Yale University

14. Inside closing quotation mark.

> He said "four," not "five."
> "Freedom is an inherent right," he insisted.
> Items marked "A," "B," and "C," inclusive, were listed.

15. To separate thousands, millions, etc., in numbers of four or more digits.

> 4,230   50,491   1,250,000

16. After year in complete dates within sentence when used parenthetically.

> The reported dates of September 11, 1943, to June 12, 1944, were proved erroneous; *but* production for June 1950 was normal.

The comma is omitted—

1. Before ZIP postal-delivery number.

   > Government Printing Office, Washington, D.C. 20401
   > Washington, D.C. 20401, is the * * *

2. Between month and year in dates.

   > June 1938; 22d of May 1938; February and March 1938; January, February, and March 1938; January 24 A.D. 1938; 15th of June A.D. 1938; 150 B.C.; Labor Day 1966; Easter Sunday 1966; 5 January 1944 (military usage)

3. Between the name and number of an organization.

   > Columbia Typographical Union No. 101
   > General U.S. Grant Post No. 25

4. In built-up fractions, in decimals, and in serial numbers, except patent numbers.

   > $^1/_{2500}$
   > 1.0947
   > page 2632
   > Metropolitan 5–9020 (telephone number)
   > 1721–1727 St. Clair Avenue
   > Executive Order 11242
   > motor No. 189463
   > 1450 kilocycles; 1100 meters (no comma unless more than four figures radio only)

5. Between superior figures or letters in footnote references.

   > Numerous instances may be cited.[1] [2]
   > Data are based on October production.[a] [b]

6. Before ampersand (&).

>Brown, Wilson & Co.
>Mine, Mill & Smelter Workers

7. Before a dash.

8. In bibliographies, between name of publication and volume or similar number.

>American Library Association Bulletin 34:238, April 1940.

9. Wherever possible without danger of ambiguity.

>$2 gold
>$2.50 U.S. currency
>$3.50 Mexican
>Executive Order No. 21
>General Order No. 12; *but* General Orders, No. 12
>Public Law 85–1
>My age is 30 years 6 months 12 days
>John Lewis 2d (*or* II)
>Murphy of Illinois; Murphy of New York; *but* Robert C. Byrd, of West Virginia; Byrd of Virginia (duplicate names of Senators or Representatives in U.S. Congress)
>Carroll of Carrollton; Henry of Navarre (places closely identified with the persons); *but* John Anstruther, of New York; President Hadley, of Yale University
>James Bros. et al.; *but* James Bros., Nelson Co., et al. (last element of series)

Period

The period is used—

1. After a declarative sentence that is not exclamatory or after an imperative sentence.

Punctuation

Stars are suns.
He was employed by Sampson & Co.
Do not be late.
On with the dance.

2. After an indirect question or after a question intended as a suggestion and not requiring an answer.

    Tell me how he did it.
    May we hear from you.
    May we ask prompt payment.

3. In place of parentheses after a letter or number denoting a series.

    a. Bread well baked.
    b. Meat cooked rare.
    c. Cubed apples stewed.

    1. Punctuate freely.
    2. Compound sparingly.
    3. Index thoroughly.

    Sometimes to indicate ellipsis. See "Ellipsis."

4. To separate integers from decimals in a single expression.

    3.75 percent $3.50   1.25 meters

5. In continental European languages, to indicate thousands.

    1.317   72.190.175

6. After abbreviations, unless otherwise specified.

    Apr.   NE.   *but* in (inch, see
    fig.   N.Y.   rule 9.3)
    Ph.D.   RR.   m (meter)
                           kc (kilocycle)

7. After legends and explanatory matter beneath illustrations. However, legends without descriptive language do not require periods.

    FIGURE 1.—Schematic drawing.
    FIGURE 1.—Continued.
    but FIGURE 1 (no period)

The period is omitted—

1. After—

    Lines in title pages.
    Center, side, and running heads.
    Continued lines.
    Boxheads of tables.
    Scientific, chemical, or other symbols.

    This rule does not apply to abbreviation periods.

2. After a quotation mark that is preceded by a period.

    He said, "Now or never."

3. After letters used as names without specific designation.

    A said to B that all is well.
    Mr. A told Mr. B that the case was closed.
    but Mr. A. [for Mr. Andrews]. I do not want to go.
    Mr. K. [for Mr. King]. The meeting is adjourned.

4. After Roman numerals used as ordinals.

    King George V   Apollo XII insigne

Colon

The colon is used—

1. Before a final clause that extends or amplifies preceding matter.

    Give up conveniences; do not demand special privileges; do not stop work: these are necessary while we are at war.
    Railroading is not a variety of outdoor sport: it is service.

2. To introduce formally any matter which forms a complete sentence, question, or quotation.

> The following question came up for discussion: What policy should be adopted?
> He said: [if direct quotation of more than a few words follows].
> There are three factors, as follows: First, military preparation; second, industrial mobilization; and third, manpower.

3. After a salutation.

> MY DEAR SIR:
> *Ladies and Gentlemen:*
> *To Whom It May Concern:*

4. In expressing clock time.

> 2:40 p.m.

5. After introductory lines in lists, tables, and leaderwork, if subentries follow.

> Seward Peninsula:
>   Council district:
>   Northern Light Mining Co.
>   Wild Goose Trading Co.
>   Fairhaven district: Alaska Dredging Association (single subitem runs in).
> Seward Peninsula: Council district (single subitem runs in)
>   Northern Light Mining Co.
>   Wild Goose Trading Co.

6. In Biblical and other citations (full space after colon).

> Luke 4: 3.
> I Corinthians xiii: 13.
> Journal of Education 3: 342–358.

7. In bibliographic references, between place of publication and name of publisher.

> Congressional Directory, Washington: U.S. Government Printing Office.

8. To separate book titles and subtitles.

> Financial Aid for College Students: Graduate
> Germany Revisited: Education in the Federal Republic

9. In imprints before the year (space each side of colon).

> U.S. Government Printing Office
> Washington : 1966

10. In proportions.

> Concrete mixed 5:3:1 (equal space each side of colon)

Semicolon

The semicolon is used—

1. To separate the parts of a compound sentence when a conjunction is not used.

> The vote has been taken; the issue is decided.
> The jury has made its decision; the case is closed.

2. To separate clauses containing commas.

> Donald A. Peters, president of the First National Bank, was also a director of New York Central; Harvey D. Jones was a director of Oregon Steel Co. and New York Central; Thomas W. Harrison, chairman of the board of McBride & Co., was also on the board of Oregon Steel Co.
> Reptiles, amphibians, and predatory mam-

Punctuation

> mals swallow their prey whole or in large pieces, bones included; waterfowl habitually take shellfish entire; and gallinaccous birds are provided with gizzards that grind up the hardest seeds.

but Yes, sir, he did see it.
No, sir, I do not recall.

3. To separate statements that are too closely related in meaning to be written as separate sentences, and also statements of contrast.

> Yes; that is right.
> No; we received one-third.
> It is true in peace; it is true in war.
> War is destructive; peace, constructive.

4. To set off explanatory abbreviations or words which summarize or explain preceding matter.

> The industry is related to groups that produce finished goods; i.e., electrical machinery and transportation equipment.
> There were involved three metal producers; namely, Jones & Laughlin, Armco, and Kennecott.

5. The semicolon is to be avoided where a comma will suffice.

> Regional offices are located in New York, N.Y., Chicago, Ill., and Dallas, Tex.

Apostrophes

1. The possessive case of a singular or plural noun not ending in *s* is formed by adding an apostrophe and *s;* the possessive case of a singular or plural noun ending in *s* or with an *s* sound is formed by adding an apostrophe only.

> | man's, men's | Corps' | Jesus' |
> |---|---|---|
> | prince's, | hostess' | Mars' |

CORRECT ENGLISH USAGE

princes'	hostesses'	Dumas'
Essex's, Essexes'	princess', princesses'	Schmitz'
Co.'s, Cos.'	Jones', Joneses'	

2. In compound nouns, the *'s* is added to the element nearest the object possessed.

   comptroller general's decision
   attorneys general's appointments
   Mr. Brown of New York's motion
   attorney at law's fee
   John White, Jr.'s (no comma) account

3. Joint possession is indicated by placing an apostrophe on the last element of a series, while individual or alternative possession requires the use of an apostrophe on each element of a series.

soldiers and sailors' home	editor's or proofreader's opinion
Brown & Nelson's store	Roosevelt's or Truman's administration
men's, women's, and children's clothing	Mrs. Smith's and Mrs. Allen's children
St. Michael's Men's Club	the Army's and the Navy's work
	master's and doctor's degrees

4. In the use of an apostrophe in geographic names, firm names, the names of organizations and institutions, and the titles of books, the authentic form is to be followed. (Note abbreviation of "St." throughout.)

Harpers Ferry; Hells Canyon	Court of St. James's
Masters, Mates & Pilots' Association	St. Peter's Church
	St. Elizabeths Hospital
Dentists' Supply Co. of New York	Johns Hopkins University

International Ladies' Garment Workers' Union
Freedmen's Hospital
Hinds' Precedents

5. Generally the apostrophe should not be used after names of countries and other organized bodies ending in *s*, or after words more descriptive than possessive (not indicating personal possession), except when plural does not end in *s*.

United States control
United Nations meeting
Southern States industries
Massachusetts laws
Bureau of Ships report
Actors Equity Association
House of Representatives session
Teamsters Union
Congress attitude
editors handbook
sirup producers manual
technicians guide
teachers college
merchants exchange
children's hospital
Young Men's Christian Association
but Veterans' Administration (in conformity with enabling statute) when specifically requested on copy.

6. Possessive pronouns do not take an apostrophe.

its   theirs

7. Possessive indefinite or impersonal pronouns require an apostrophe.

each other's books
one's home
someone's pen
but somebody else's proposal

8. The singular possessive case is used in such general terms as the following:

arm's length
author's alterations
confectioner's sugar
cow's milk
distiller's grain

fuller's earth   printer's ink   writer's cramp
miner's inch   traveler's checks

9. An apostrophe is used to indicate contractions, the omission of figures or letters, and the coined plurals of letters, figures, and symbols.

don't	49'ers	a's; ¶'s; 7's
I've	TV'ers	T's, Y's
ne'er	B.t.u.'s	2 by 4's (lumber)
it's (it is)	OK's	
class of '92	MC'ing	*but* 10s (yarn and thread)
spirit of '76	YMCA's	
three R's	ABC's	4½s (bonds)
		3s (golf)

10. The apostrophe is omitted in abbreviations, and also in shortened forms of certain other words.

Danl., *not* Dan'l	coon	Halloween
Sgt., *not* Sg't	possum	copter
phone	Frisco	*but* ma'am

11. The plural of spelled-out numbers, of words referred to as words, and of words already containing an apostrophe is formed by adding *s* or *es;* but *'s* is added to indicate the plural of words used as words if the omission of the apostrophe would cause difficulty in reading.

twos	ins and outs	yeses and noes
threes	ups and downs	*but* do's and don'ts
sevens		
ands, ifs, and buts	whereases and wherefores	which's and that's

12. The possessive case is often used in place of an objective phrase even though ownership is not involved.

1 day's labor (labor for 1 day)   5 or 10 billion dollars' worth

2 hours' traveltime   for charity's sake
a stone's throw   for pity's sake
2 weeks' pay

13. The possessive case is not used in such expressions as the following, in which one noun modifies another.

    day labor (labor by   State prison
      the day)   State rights
    quartermaster stores

14. For euphony, nouns ending in *s* or *ce* and followed by a word beginning with *s* form the possessive by adding an apostrophe only.

    for old times' sake   for goodness' sake
    for acquaintance' sake   Mr. Hughes'
    for conscience' sake   service

15. A possessive noun used in an adjective sense requires the addition of *'s*.

    He is a friend of   Stern's is running a
      John's   sale

16. A noun preceding a gerund should be in the possessive case.

    in the event of   the ship's hovering
      Mary's leaving   nearby

The dash is used—

1. To mark a sudden break or abrupt change in thought.

    He said—and no one contradicted him—"The battle is lost."
    If the bill should pass—which God forbid!—the service will be wrecked.
    The auditor—shall we call him a knave or a fool?—approved an inaccurate statement.

2. To indicate an interruption or an unfinished word or sentence.

> "Such an idea can scarcely be———"
> "The word 'donation'———"
> "The word 'dona———' "
> He said: "Give me lib———"
> The bill reads "repeal," not "am———"
> Q. Did you see———A. No, sir.

3. Instead of commas or parentheses, if the meaning may thus be clarified.

> These are shore deposits—gravel, sand, and clay—but marine sediments underlie them.

4. Before a final clause that summarizes a series of ideas.

> Freedom of speech, freedom of worship, freedom from want, freedom from fear—these are the fundamentals of moral world order.

5. After an introductory phrase reading into the following lines and indicating repetition of such phrase.

> I recommend—
> That we accept the rules;
> That we also publish them; and
> That we submit them for review.

6. With a preceding question mark, in place of a colon.

> How can you explain this?—"Fee paid, $5."

7. To precede a credit line or a run-in credit or signature.

> Still achieving, still pursuing,
> Learn to labor and to wait.
> *—Longfellow.*
> Every man's work shall be made manifest.—I Corinthians 3: 13.
> This statement is open to question.—GERALD H. FORSYTHE.

8. To separate run-in questions and answers in testimony.

   Q. Did he go?—A. No.

9. In bibliographies to indicate repetition.

   Powell, James W., Jr., Hunting in Virginia's lowlands 1972, 200 pp.
   ——Fishing off Delmarva. 1972. 28 pp.

10. In a combination of figures, letters, or figures and letters.

exhibit 6–A	WTOP–AM–FM–TV
5–20 bonds	4–H Club
DC–14; *but* Convair 340	LK–66–A(2)–74
	$15–$20
Public Law 85–1	CBS–TV network
301–942–8367 (telephone number including area code)	AFL–CIO merger

11. In the absence of the word *to* when denoting a period of time.

    1935–37   January–June   Monday–Friday

The dash is not used—

1. For *to* when the word *from* precedes the first of two related figures or expressions.

   From January 1 to June 30, 1951; *not* from January 1–June 30, 1951.

2. For *and* when the word *between* precedes the first of two related figures or expressions.

   Between 1923 and 1929; *not* between 1923–29

3. At the beginning of any line of type.

4. Immediately after a comma, colon, or semicolon.

Hyphen

The hyphen is used—

1. To connect the elements of certain compound words.

2. To indicate continuation of a word divided at end of a line.

3. Between the letters of a spelled word.

    c-e-n-t-s   h-o-l-d-u-p

4. To separate elements of chemical formulas.

5. To represent letters deleted or illegible copy.

    d--n   h-ll   Leroy Joseph B---

Question mark

The question mark is used—

1. To indicate a direct query, even if not in the form of a question.

    Did he do it?
    He did what?
    Can the money be raised? is the question.
    Who asked, "Why?" (Note single question mark)
    "Did you hurt yourself, my son?" she asked.

2. To express more than one query in the same sentence.

    Can he do it? or you? or anyone?

3. To express doubt.

    He said the boy was 8(?) feet tall.
    The statue(?) was on the statute books.
    The scientific identification *Dorothia*? was noted.

The question mark is omitted—

1. After a question that is a request.

    > Would you please sign the statement.
    > Would you kindly send me three copies of the speech.

Quotation Marks

Quotation marks are used—

1. To enclose direct quotations. (Each part of an interrupted quotation begins and ends with quotation marks.)

    > The answer is "No."
    > He said, "John said 'No.' "
    > "John," said Henry, "why do you go?"

2. To enclose any matter following the terms *entitled, the word, the term, marked, designated, classified, named, endorsed,* or *signed;* but are not used to enclose expressions following the terms *known as, called, so-called,* etc., unless such expressions are misnomers or slang.

    > Congress passed the act entitled "An act * * *."
    > After the word "treaty," insert a comma.
    > Of what does the item "Miscellaneous debts" consist?
    > The column "Imports from foreign countries" was not * * *.
    > The document will be marked "Exhibit No. 21"; *but* The document may be made exhibit No. 2.
    > The check was endorsed "John Adamson."
    > It was signed "John."
    > Beryllium is known as glucinium in some European countries.
    > It was called profit and loss.
    > The so-called investigating body.

262 CORRECT ENGLISH USAGE

3. To enclose titles of addresses, articles, books, captions, chapter and part headings, editorials, essays, headings, headlines, motion pictures and plays (including TV and radio programs), papers, short poems, reports, songs, subheadings, subjects, and themes. All principal words are to be capitalized.

>An address on "Uranium-235 in the Atomic Age"
>The article "Germany Revisited" appeared in the last issue.
>"The Conquest of Mexico," a published work (book)
>Under the caption "Long-Term Treasuries Rise"
>The subject was discussed in "Courtwork" (chapter heading)
>It will be found in "Part XI: Early Thought"
>The editorial "Haphazard Budgeting"
>"Compensation," by Emerson (essay)
>"United States To Appoint Representative to U.N." (heading or headline)
>In "Search for Paradise" (motion picture); "South Pacific" (play)
>A paper on "Constant-Pressure Combustion" was read
>"O Captain! My Captain!" (short poem)
>The report "Atomic Energy: What It Means to the Nation"; *but* annual report of the Public Printer
>This was followed by the singing of "The Star-Spangled Banner"
>Under the subhead, "Sixty Days of Turmoil," will be found * * *
>The subject (or theme) of the conference is "Peaceful Uses of Atomic Energy"

also Account 5, "Management fees."

>Under the heading "Management and Operation."
>Under the appropriation "Building of ships, Navy."

4. If poetry is quoted, each stanza should start with quotation marks, but only the last stanza should end with them.

> "Danger is not past while despots use
>   Men as mere creatures, puppets only for
>   their needs.
> Danger is not past till all can choose
>   And freely live according to their creeds.
>
> "We cannot claim that our United States
>   Excels all other ways of life,
> While we have slums and gangs and hates,
>   And headlines scream of racial strife."
>   —C. H. BLATCHFORD.
>   NORTH TARRYTOWN.

5. At the beginning of each paragraph of a quotation, but at the end of the last paragraph only.

6. To give greater emphasis to a word or a phrase.

7. To enclose misnomers, slang expressions, sobriquets, or ordinary words used in an arbitrary way.

> He voted for the "lameduck" amendment.
> His report was "bunk."
> It was a "gentlemen's agreement."
> The "invisible government" is responsible.
> George Herman "Babe" Ruth.

Quotation marks are not used—

1. To enclose names of newspapers or magazines.

2. To enclose extracts that are indented or set in smaller type, or solid extracts in leaded matter; but indented matter in text that is already quoted carries quotation marks.

3. In indirect quotations.

> Tell her yes.
> He could not say no.

4. Before a display initial which begins a quoted paragraph.

5. The comma and the final period will be placed inside the quotation marks. Other punctuation marks should be placed inside the quotation marks only if they are a part of the matter quoted.

> Ruth said, "I think so."
> "The President," he said, "will veto the bill."
> The trainman shouted, "All aboard!"
> Who asked, "Why?"
> The President suggests that "an early occasion be sought * * *."
> Why call it a "gentlemen's agreement"?

6. In work showing amendments, and in courtwork with quoted language, punctuation marks are printed after the quotation marks when not a part of the quoted matter.

> Insert the words "growth", "production", and "manufacture".
> To be inserted immediately after the words "cadets, U.S. Coast Guard;".
> Change "February 1, 1951", to "June 30, 1951".
> "Insert in lieu thereof 'July 1, 1953,'."

7. When occurring together, quotation marks should precede the footnote reference number.

> The commissioner claimed that the award was "unjustified."[1]
> His exact words were: "The facts in the case prove otherwise."[2]

Parentheses

Parentheses are used—

1. To set off matter not intended to be part of the main state-

ment or not a grammatical element of the sentence, yet important enough to be included.

> This case (124 U.S. 329) is not relevant.
> The result (see fig. 2) is most surprising.
> The United States is the principal purchaser (by value) of these exports (23 percent in 1955 and 19 percent in 1956).

2. To enclose a parenthetic clause where the interruption is too great to be indicated by commas.

> You can find it neither in French dictionaries (at any rate, not in Littré) nor in English.

3. To enclose an explanatory word not part of the statement.

> the Erie (Pa.) News; *but* the News of Erie, Pa.
> Portland (Oreg.) Chamber of Commerce; *but* Washington, D.C., schools.

4. To enclose letters or numbers designating items in a series, either at beginning of paragraphs or within a paragraph.

> The order of delivery will be: (a) Food, (b) clothing, and (c) tents and other housing equipment.
> You will observe that the sword is (1) old fashioned, (2) still sharp, and (3) unusually light for its size.
> Paragraph 7(B)(1)(a) will be found on page 6.

5. To enclose a figure inserted to confirm a statement given in words if double form is specifically requested.

> This contract shall be completed in sixty (60) days.

6. A reference in parentheses at the end of a sentence is placed before the period, unless it is a complete sentence in itself.

> The specimen exhibits both phases (pl. 14, *A*, *B*).

The individual cavities show great variation. (See pl. 4.)

7. If a sentence contains more than one parenthetic reference, the one at the end is placed before the period.

This sandstone (see pl. 6) occurs in every county of the State (see pl. 1).

8. When a figure is followed by a letter in parentheses, no space is used between the figure and the opening parenthesis; but if the letter is not in parentheses and the figure is repeated with each letter, the letter is closed up with the figure.

15(a). Classes, grades, and sizes.
15a. Classes, grades, and sizes.

9. If both a figure and a letter in parentheses are used before each paragraph, a period and a space and a half are used after the closing parenthesis; if the figure is not repeated before each letter in parentheses but is used only before the first, the period is placed after the figure.

15(a). When the figure is used before the letter in each paragraph—
15(b). The period is placed after the closing parenthesis.
15. (a) When the figure is used before letter in first paragraph but not repeated with subsequent letters—
(b) The period is used after the figure only.

10. Note position of period relative to closing parenthesis:

The vending stand sells a variety of items (sandwiches, beverages, cakes, etc.).
The vending stand sells a variety of items (sandwiches, beverages, cakes, etc. (sometimes ice cream)).
The vending stand sells a variety of items. (These include sandwiches, beverages, cakes, etc. (6).)

11. When matter in parentheses makes more than one paragraph, start each paragraph with a parenthesis and place the closing parenthesis at end of last paragraph.

Ellipses

1. Three asterisks (preferred form) are used to denote an ellipsis within a sentence, at the beginning or end of a sentence, or in two or more consecutive sentences.

    > He called * * * and left. * * * When he returned the * * *.
    > * * * called * * * and left. * * * he returned the * * *.
    > He called * * * and * * *. When he returned the * * *.
    > He called * * * and * * * he returned the * * *.
    > [Two or more consecutive sentences, including intervening punctuation]

2. Three periods may be used to indicate ellipsis; four periods, when sentence is brought to a close.

    > He called . . . and left. . . . When he returned the . . . .
    > . . . called . . . and left. . . . he returned the . . . .
    > He called . . . and . . . . When he returned the . . . .
    > He called . . . and . . . he returned the . . . . [Two or more consecutive sentences, including intervening punctuation]

3. A line of asterisks (or periods) indicates an omission of one or more entire paragraphs.

    > *   *   *   *   *   *   *
    > .   .   .   .

Exclamation Point

1. The exclamation point is used to mark surprise, incredulity, admiration, appeal, or other strong emotion, which may be

expressed even in a declarative or interrogative sentence.

> He acknowledged the error!
> How beautiful!
> "Great!" he shouted. [Note omission of comma.]
> What!
> Who shouted, "All aboard!" [Note omission of question mark.]

2. In direct address, either to a person or a personified object, *O* is used without an exclamation point, or other punctuation; but if strong feeling is expressed, an exclamation point is placed at the end of the statement.

> O my friend, let us consider this subject impartially.
> O Lord, save Thy people!

3. In exclamations without direct address or appeal, *oh* is used instead of *O*, and the exclamation point is omitted.

> Oh, but the gentleman is mistaken.
> Oh dear; the time is so short.

Brackets

1. In transcripts, congressional hearings, testimony in courtwork, etc., brackets, not parentheses, are used to enclose interpolations that are not specifically a part of the original quotation, corrections, explanations, omissions, editorial comments, or a caution that an error is reproduced literally.

> He came on the 3d [2d] of July.
> Our conference [lasted] 2 hours.
> The general [Washington] ordered him to leave.
> The paper was as follows [reads]:
> I do not know. [Continues reading:]
> [Chorus of "Mr. Chairman."]
> They fooled only themselves. [Laughter.]
> Our party will always serve the people

[applause] in spite of the opposition [loud applause]. (If more than one bracketed interpolation, both are included within the sentence.)

The W<small>ITNESS</small>. He did it that way [indicating].

Q. Do you know these men [handing witness a list]?

The bill had *not* been paid. [Italic added.] *or* [Emphasis added.]

The statue [sic] was on the statute books.

The W<small>ITNESS</small>. This matter is classified. [Deleted.]

[Deleted.]

Mr. J<small>ONES</small>. Hold up your hands. [Show of hands.]

Answer [after examining list]. Yes; I do.

Q. [Continuing.]

A. [Reads:]

A. [Interrupting.]

[Discussion off the record.]

[Pause.]

The W<small>ITNESS</small> [interrupting]. It is known * * *.

Mr. J<small>ONES</small> [continuing]. Now let us take the next item.

Mr. S<small>MITH</small> [presiding].

Mr. J<small>ONES</small> [interposing].

[The matter referred to is as follows:]

The C<small>HAIRMAN</small> [to Mr. Smith].

The C<small>HAIRMAN</small> [reading]:

Mr. K<small>ELLEY</small> [to the chairman]. From 15 to 25 percent.

[Objected to.]

[Mr. Smith nods.]

[Mr. Smith aside.]

[Mr. Smith makes further statement off the record.]

Mr. J<small>ONES</small> [for Mr. Smith].

2. In bills, contracts, etc., to indicate matter that is to be omitted.

13. Spelling

Spelling Guidelines

When to double the final consonant. If you are in doubt as to whether to double the final consonant of a word before adding a suffix like *-ed, -ing,* or *-ence,* double the consonant only if *all* of the following conditions are met:

1. The word must end in a single consonant.
2. The single consonant must be preceded by a single vowel.
3. The accent must fall on the last syllable of the word.

If any of these conditions are not met, do not double the final consonant.

Examples of consonants not doubled:

travel, traveled (accent does not fall on last syllable)
careen, careening (final consonant not preceded by a *single* vowel)
exert, exerted (word does not end in a *single* consonant)

Exceptions to this rule occur when the syllabification of the new word changes and the accent is thrown back upon the first syllable, as in *defer, deference.*

Spelling

Plurals. Plural forms which often cause problems are as follows. Nouns ending in *o* preceded by a vowel add *s* to form the plural; nouns ending in *o* preceded by a consonant add *es* to form the plural, except as indicated in the following list.

albinos	Eskimos	magnetos	salvos
armadillos	falsettos	mementos	sextodecimos
avocados	gauchos	merinos	sextos
banjos	ghettos	mestizos	siroccos
cantos	gringos	octavos	solos
cascos	halos	octodecimos	tangelos
centos	inamoratos	pianos	tobaccos
didos	indigos	piccolos	twos
duodecimos	juntos	pomelos	tyors
dynamos	kimonos	provisos	virtuosos
escudos	lassos	quartos	zeros

Plurals of compound terms. The significant word in the compound takes the plural form.

Significant word first:
 aides-de-camp
 ambassadors at large
 attorneys at law
 attorneys general
 billets-doux
 bills of fare
 brothers-in-law
 chargés d'affaires
 commanders in chief
 courts-martial
 crepes suzette
 daughters-in-law
 grants-in-aid
 heirs at law
 men-of-war
 ministers-designate
 mothers-in-law
 notaries public
 pilots-in-command
 postmasters general
 presidents-elect
 prisoners of war
 rights-of-way
 secretaries general
 sergeants at arms

Significant word in middle:
 assistant attorneys general
 deputy chiefs of staff

Significant word last:
 assistant attorneys
 brigadier generals
 deputy judges
 general counsels
 judge advocates
 judge advocate generals
 lieutenant colonels
 trade unions

under secretaries
vice chairmen

Both words of equal significance:
Bulletins Nos. 27 and 28; *but* Bulletin No. 27 or 28
coats of arms
masters at arms
men buyers
men employees
secretaries-treasurers
women aviators
women students
women writers

No word significant in itself:
forget-me-nots
hand-me-downs
jack-in-the-pulpits
man-of-the-earths
pick-me-ups
will-o'-the-wisps

When a noun is hyphened with an adverb or preposition, the plural is formed on the noun.

comings-in
fillers-in
goings-on
hangers-on
listeners-in
lookers-on
makers-up
passers-by

When neither word is a noun, the plural is formed on the last word.

also-rans
come-ons
go-betweens
higher-ups
run-ins
tie-ins

Plurals of nouns ending with *ful*. The plural is formed by adding *s* at the end; if it is necessary to express the idea that more than one container was filled, the two elements of the solid compound are printed as separate words and the plural is formed by adding *s* to the noun.

Five bucketfuls of the mixture (one bucket filled five times)
five buckets full of earth (separate buckets)
three cupfuls of flour (one cup filled three times)
three cups full of coffee (separate cups)

Other plurals which may cause difficulty.

addendum, addenda
adieu, adieus
agendum, agenda
alga, algae
alumnus, alumni (masc.); alumna, alumnae (fem.)
antenna, antennas (antennae, zoology)
appendix, appendixes
aquarium, aquariums
automaton, automatons
axis, axes
bandeau, bandeaux
basis, bases
beau, beaus
cactus, cactuses
calix, calices
chassis (singular and plural)
cherub, cherubs
cicatrix, cicatrices
Co., Cos.
coccus, cocci
crisis, crises
criterion, criteria
curriculum, cirriculums
datum, data
desideratum, desiderata
dilettante, dilettanti
dogma, dogmas
ellipsis, ellipses
equilibrium, equilibriums (equilibria, scientific)
erratum, errata
executrix, executrices
flambeau, flambeaus
focus, focuses
folium, folia
formula, formulas
fungus, fungi
genius, geniuses
genus, genera
gladiolus (singular and plural)
helix, helices
hypothesis, hypotheses
index, indexes (indices, scientific)
insigne, insignia
Kansas Citys
lacuna, lacunae
larva, larvae
larynx, larynxes
lens, lenses
lira, lire
locus, loci
madam, mesdames
Marys
matrix, matrices
maximum, maximums
medium, mediums *or* media
memorandum, memorandums
minimum, minimums
minutia, minutiae
monsieur, messieurs
nucleus, nuclei
oasis, oases
octopus, octopuses
opus, opera
parenthesis, parentheses
phenomenon, phenomena
phylum, phyla
plateau, plateaus
podium, podiums
procès-verbal, procès-verbaux
radius, radii
radix, radixes

referendum, referendums
sanatorium, sanatoriums
sanitarium, sanitariums
septum, septa
sequela, sequelae
seraph, seraphs
seta, setae
ski, skis
stadium, stadiums
stimulus, stimuli
stratum, strata
stylus, styluses
syllabus, syllabuses

symposium, symposia
synopsis, synopses
tableau, tableaus
taxi, taxis
terminus, termini
testatrix, testatrices
thesaurus, thesauri
thesis, theses
thorax, thoraxes
vertebra, vertebras (vertebrae, zoology)
virtuoso, virtuosos
vortex, vortexes

List of Words Commonly Misspelled

absence
accept
accident
accidentally
accommodate
acknowledgment
acquaint
acquaintance
across
affect
aggravate
all right
amateur
appearance
argument
around
athletic
auxiliary

beginning
believe
believed
beneficial

benefit
benefited
benefiting
buoyant
business
busy

capital
career
catalog
cemetery
certain
character
chief
choose
chosen
coming
commit
commitment
committed
committee
committing
competition

complete
comptroller
conscientious
conscious
consensus
convenience
convenient
coolly
council
counsel
criticize
criticism

deceive
decide
decision
definite
descend
descendant, or
descendent
describe
description
desert

Spelling

dessert
develop
difference
different
dining
disappear
disappoint
dividend
doesn't
don't
during

effect
eighth
embarrass
environment
equipment
equipped
escape
exaggerate
excellent
excite
excitement
exciting
exercise
existence
experiment

familiar
fascinate
February
finally
foreign
foreigners
forth
forty
four
friend

glamorous

glamour
government
grammar
grievance

hadn't
height
hero
heroes
heroine
humor
humorous

image
imaginary
imagination
imagine
immediate
immediately
individual
interest
interested
it's (contraction)
its (possessive)

judgment

knowledge
knowledgeable

laboratory
latter
literature
lonely
loose
lose
losing

maintenance
marriage

marries
marry
meant
mischievous
monetary
municipal

necessary
necessity
noticeable

occasion
occasionally
occur
occurred
occurrence
occurring
o'clock
omitted
opinion
opportunity

parallel
parliament
performance
perhaps
personal
personnel
pleasant
possess
precede
prejudice
president
principal
principle
probably
proceed
professor
promissory
promotional

pronunciation
prophecy
prophesy
purchasable

quiet
quite

receive
recommend
referred
regrettable
relieve
responsibility
restaurant
rhythm

salable, or
saleable
schedule
seize
sense
separate
shining
similar
simplify
society

speech
stationary
stationery
stop
stopped
stopping
strength
studied
studies
study
studying
succeed
success
successful
superintendent
supersede
surprise

technicality
tendency
than
then
their
there
they're
thousandth
to

together
too
tragedy
transferred
transient
tries
tried
truly
two

until

villain

Wednesday
weird
where
whether
woman
writ
writer
writing
written

yield
you're
your

14. Abbreviations

Standard Usage

In ordinary business writing and in the body of letters, abbreviations should be used as sparingly as possible. Abbreviations may be used more freely in texts of legal and technical matter and in tables, footnotes, and bibliographies.

When you use an abbreviation that may be unfamiliar to the reader, give the full form first, followed by the abbreviation in parentheses, as

> The Board of Tax Appeals (BTA) met to discuss . . .

and in subsequent references use just the abbreviation, as

> It was decided that all further BTA business . . .

Plurals of abbreviations. Most abbreviations form the plural by adding *s* to the singular form; however, abbreviations which might otherwise be confusing form their plurals by adding *'s*.

gals.	yds.	C.O.D.s
OKs	Drs.	Ps and Qs
IOUs	CPAs	Depts.

but

| f.o.b.'s | a.m.'s | Btu's |

The following form their plurals by doubling.

pp. (pages) vv. (verses) MM. (Messieurs)
SS. (Saints) ff. (following pages)

These abbreviations are the same in both singular and plural.

ft. oz. deg.
enc. mi. (miles) sec.
kg., ml., mm. and all other metric abbreviations

Possessives of abbreviations. These are formed in the same way as other possessives. If the abbreviation is singular, add *'s*. If the abbreviation is plural, add only an apostrophe.

Singular	*Plural*
Dr.'s	Drs.'
Co.'s	Cos.'
M.D.'s	M.D.s'
CPA's	CPAs'
Bro.'s	Bros.'

French abbreviations. No period is used after French abbreviations if the last letter of the abbreviation is the last letter of the word; but if the last letter of the abbreviation is not the last letter of the word, the period is used.

Mme (Madame) St (Saint) Cie (Compagnie)

but

M. (Monsieur) MM. (Messieurs) fr. (franc)

Abbreviations

United States. United States may be abbreviated when it is used as an adjective, but when it is used as a noun, it should usually be typed in full.

U.S. Department of Agriculture
U.S. foreign policy

but

foreign policy of the United States

States of the United States and Their Abbreviations

STATE	OFFICIAL TEXT	ZIP CODE	STATE	OFFICIAL TEXT	ZIP CODE
Alabama, State of	Ala.	AL	Nevada, State of	Nev.	NV
Alaska, State of	Alas.	AK	New Hampshire, State of	N.H.	NH
Arizona, State of	Ariz.	AZ	New Jersey, State of	N.J.	NJ
Arkansas, State of	Ark.	AR	New Mexico, State of	N.M.	NM
California, State of	Calif.	CA	New York, State of	N.Y.	NY
Canal Zone	CZ.	CZ	North Carolina, State of	N.C.	NC
Colorado, State of	Colo.	CO	North Dakota, State of	N.D.	ND
Connecticut, State of	Conn.	CT	Ohio, State of	Ohio	OH
Delaware, State of	Del.	DE	Oklahoma, State of	Okla.	OK
District of Columbia	D.C.	DC	Oregon, State of	Oreg.	OR
Florida, State of	Fla.	FL	Pennsylvania, Commonwealth of	Pa.	PA
Georgia, State of	Ga.	GA	Puerto Rico	P.R.	PR
Hawaii, State of	Hawaii	HI	Rhode Island and Providence Plantations, State of	R.I.	RI
Idaho, State of	Ida.	ID	South Carolina, State of	S.C.	SC
Illinois, State of	Ill.	IL	South Dakota, State of	S.D.	SD
Indiana, State of	Ind.	IN	Tennessee, State of	Tenn.	TN
Iowa, State of	Iowa	IA	Texas, State of	Tex.	TX
Kansas, State of	Kans.	KS	Utah, State of	Utah	UT
Kentucky, Commonwealth of	Ky.	KY	Vermont, State of	Vt.	VT
Louisiana, State of	La.	LA	Virgin Islands	V.I.	VI
Maine, State of	Maine	ME	Virginia, Commonwealth of	Va.	VA
Maryland, State of	Md.	MD	Washington, State of	Wash.	WA
Massachusetts, Commonwealth of	Mass.	MA	West Virginia, State of	W.Va.	WV
Michigan, State of	Mich.	MI	Wisconsin, State of	Wis.	WI
Minnesota, State of	Minn.	MN	Wyoming State of	Wyo.	WY
Mississippi, State of	Miss.	MS			
Missouri, State of	Mo.	MO			
Montana, State of	Mont.	MT			
Nebraska, State of	Nebr.	NE			

280 CORRECT ENGLISH USAGE

Canadian Provinces and Their Abbreviations

PROVINCE	OFFICIAL TEXT	ZIP CODE
Alberta	Alta.	AB
British Columbia	B.C.	BC
Manitoba	Man.	MB
New Brunswick	N.B.	NB
Newfoundland	Nfld.	NF
Northwest Territories	N.W.T.	NT
Nova Scotia	N.S.	NS
Ontario	Ont.	ON
Prince Edward Island	P.E.I.	PE
Province of Quebec	Que. *or* P.Q.	PQ
Saskatchewan	Sask.	SK
Yukon Territory	Y.T.	YT

Short Abbreviations for Months and Days

Special short abbreviations for the months of the year and the days of the week may be used in tabular work or in library material where space is at a premium.

Months

January	Ja.
February	F.
March	Mr.
April	Ap.
May	My.
June	Je.
July	Jy.
August	Ag.
September	S.
October	O.
November	N.
December	D.

Days

Monday	M.
Tuesday	Tu.
Wednesday	W.
Thursday	Th.
Friday	F.
Saturday	Sat.
Sunday	S.

Academic Degrees and Honors

A

A.B. *or* B.A.	Bachelor of Arts
A.B.A.	Associate in Business Administration
A.B.Ed.	Bachelor of Arts in Education
Ae.E.	Aeronautical Engineer
Ag.E.	Agricultural Engineer
A.F.D.	Doctor of Fine Arts
A.G.E.	Associate in General Education
A.I.Ed.	Associate in Industrial Education
A.H.E.	Associate in Home Economics
A.M. *or* M.A.	Master of Arts
A.M.S.W.	Master of Arts in Social Work
Ar.M.	Master of Architecture

B

B.A. *or* A.B.	Bachelor of Arts
B.A.A.	Bachelor of Applied Arts
B.Acc.	Bachelor of Accounting
B.Ag. *or* B.Agr	Bachelor of Agriculture
B.A.M.	Bachelor of Applied Mathematics; Bachelor of Arts in Music
B.Ar. *or* B.Arch.	Bachelor of Architecture
B.A.S. *or* B.A.Sc.	Bachelor of Applied Science
B.B.A.	Bachelor of Business Administration
B.C. *or* B.Ch.	Bachelor of Chemistry
B.C.E.	Bachelor of Chemical Engineering; Bachelor of Christian Education
B.C.L.	Bachelor of Civil Law
B.D.	Bachelor of Divinity
B.D.S.	Bachelor of Dental Surgery
B.E.	Bachelor of Engineering
B.E.E.	Bachelor of Electrical Engineering
B.E.P.	Bachelor of Engineering Physics

282 CORRECT ENGLISH USAGE

B.F.	Bachelor of Finance; Bachelor of Forestry
B.F.A.	Bachelor of Fine Arts
B.J.	Bachelor of Journalism
B.L. or LL.B.	Bachelor of Laws
B.Litt. or B.Lit.	Bachelor of Letters; Bachelor of Literature
B.L.S.	Bachelor of Library Science
B.M.	Bachelor of Medicine
B.M.E.	Bachelor of Mechanical Engineering; Bachelor of Mining
B.M.E. or B.Mus.	Bachelor of Music
B.P.	Bachelor of Pharmacy
B.P. or B.Ph. or B.Phil.	Bachelor of Philosophy
B.Pd. or B.Pe.	Bachelor of Pedagogy
B.P.E.	Bachelor of Physical Education
B.S. or B.Sc.	Bachelor of Science
B.S.Ed.	Bachelor of Science in Education
B.S. in Ch. or B.S. in Ch.E.	Bachelor of Science in Chemical Engineering
B.S.A.	Bachelor of Science in Agriculture
B.S. in L.S.	Bachelor of Science in Library Service
B.T. or B.Th.	Bachelor of Theology
B.V.Sc.	Bachelor of Veterinary Science

C

C.A.	Chartered Accountant
C.E.	Civil Engineer
Ch.D.	Doctor of Chemistry
Ch.E. or Chem.E.	Chemical Engineer

D

D.C.L.	Doctor of Civil Law
D.D.	Doctor of Divinity
D.D.S.	Doctor of Dental Surgery
D.F.A.	Doctor of Fine Arts

D.Lit(t)	Doctor of Literature, or Letters
D.L.S.	Doctor of Library Science
D.M.D.	Doctor of Dental Medicine
D.Mus.	Doctor of Music
D.O.	Doctor of Osteopathy
D.P.H.	Doctor of Public Health
D.S. *or* D.Sc.	Doctor of Science
D.Th. *or* D. Theol.	Doctor of Theology
D.V.M.	Doctor of Veterinary Medicine

E

Ed.B.	Bachelor of Education
Ed.D.	Doctor of Education
Ed.M.	Master of Education
E.E.	Electrical Engineer
E.M.	Engineer of Mines
Eng.D.	Doctor of Engineering

F

F.A.C.P.	Fellow of the American College of Physicians
F.A.C.S.	Fellow of the American College of Surgeons
F.A.G.S.	Fellow of the American Geographical Society
F.A.I.A.	Fellow of the American Institute of Architects
F.B.A.	Fellow of the British Academy
F.C.A.	Fellow of the (Institute of) Chartered Accountants
F.C.I.S.	Fellow of the Chartered Institute of Secretaries
F.C.S.	Fellow of the Chemical Society
F.I.C.	Fellow of the Institute of Chemistry
F.S.A.	Fellow of the Society of Antiquaries; Fellow of the Society of Actuaries

J

J.C.B.	Bachelor of Canon Law; Bachelor of Civil Law
J.C.D.	Doctor of Canon Law; Doctor of Civil Law
J.D.	Doctor of Law; Juris Doctor; Doctor of Jurisprudence
Jur.D.	Doctor of Law

L

L.B.	Bachelor of Letters
L.H.D.	Doctor of Humanities
Lit(t).B.	Bachelor of Literature; or of Letters
Lit.D.	Doctor of Literature, or Letters
Litt.D.	Doctor of Letters
LL.B. *or* B.L.	Bachelor of Laws
LL.D.	Doctor of Laws
LL.M.	Master of Laws

M

M.A.	Master of Arts
M.Agr.	Master of Agriculture
M.B.	Bachelor of Medicine
M.B.A.	Master in, *or* of, Business Administration
M.C.L.	Master of Civil Law
M.D.	Doctor of Medicine
M.D.S.	Master of Dental Surgery
M.E.	Mechanical Engineer
M.Ed.	Master of Education
M.F.A.	Master of Fine Arts
M.L.S.	Master Library Science
M.Pd.	Master of Pedagogy
M.P.E.	Master of Physical Education
M.R.C.P.	Member of the Royal College of Physicians
M.R.C.S.	Member of the Royal College of Surgeons

M.S. *or* M.Sc.	Master of Science
M.S.E.	Master of Science in Engineering
Mus.B. *or* Mus.Bac.	Bachelor of Music

N

N.E.	Naval Engineer

P

Pd.B.	Bachelor of Pedagogy
Pd.D.	Doctor of Pedagogy
Pd.M.	Master of Pedagogy
Pe.B.	Bachelor of Pediatrics
Phar.B.	Bachelor of Pharmacy
Phar.D.	Doctor of Pharmacy
Phar.M.	Master of Pharmacy
Ph.B.	Bachelor of Philosophy
Ph.C.	Pharmaceutical Chemist
Ph.D.	Doctor of Philosophy
Ph.G.	Graduate in Pharmacy
Pod.D.	Doctor of Podiatry

R

R.A.	Royal Academician
R.N.	Registered Nurse

S

S.B. *or* Sc.B.	Bachelor of Science
Sc.D. *or* S.D.	Doctor of Science
Sc.M.	Master of Science
S.J.D.	Doctor of Juridical Science
S.M. *or* Sc.M.	Master of Science
S.T.B.	Bachelor of Sacred Theology
S.T.D.	Doctor of Sacred Theology
S.T.M.	Master of Sacred Theology

T

Th.D.	Doctor of Theology

V

V.M.D.   Doctor of Veterinary Medicine

U.S. Government Agencies

ACDA	Arms Control and Disarmament Agency
AEC	Atomic Energy Commission
AID	Aid for International Development
ARC	American Red Cross
ARS	Agricultural Research Service
BEC	Bureau of Employees' Compensation
BLS	Bureau of Labor Statistics
CAB	Civil Aeronautics Board
CAP	Civil Air Patrol
CCC	Commodities Credit Corporations
CEA	Council of Economic Advisors
CIA	Central Intelligence Agency
CMS	Consumer and Marketing Services
CSC	Civil Service Commission
FAA	Federal Aviation Agency
FAS	Foreign Agricultural Service
FBI	Federal Bureau of Investigation
FCA	Farm Credit Administration
FCC	Federal Communications Commission
FDA	Food and Drug Administration
FDIC	Federal Deposit Insurance Corporation
FHA	Federal Housing Administration
FMC	Federal Maritime Commission
FMCS	Federal Mediation and Conciliation Service
FNMA	Federal National Mortgage Association
FPC	Federal Power Commission
FRB	Federal Reserve Board
FRS	Federal Reserve System
FSA	Federal Security Agency
FTC	Federal Trade Commission
GAO	General Accounting Office
GPO	Government Printing Office
GSA	General Services Administration
HHFA	Housing and Home Finance Agency
ICC	Interstate Commerce Commission

IRS	Internal Revenue Service
MA	Maritime Administration
NASA	National Aeronautics and Space Administration
NATO	North Atlantic Treaty Organization
NBS	National Bureau of Standards
NIH	National Institutes of Health
NLRB	National Labor Relations Board
NSC	National Security Council
NSF	National Science Foundation
OAS	Organization of American States
OEO	Office of Economic Opportunity
PHA	Public Housing Administration
PHS	Public Health Service
REA	Rural Electrification Administration
RRB	Railroad Retirement Board
SBA	Small Business Administration
SEC	Securities and Exchange Commission
SSA	Social Security Administration
SSS	Selective Service System
TVA	Tennessee Valley Authority
USES	United States Employment Service
USIA	United States Information Service
VA	Veterans Administration
VISTA	Volunteers in Service to America

General Abbreviations

A

a   are (metric); ampere
@   at
A, A., A.U.   angstrom unit
A.   Army; acre(s); absolute (temperature); area
a.a.   author alterations
A-1   first-class
a.a.r.   against all risks (ins.)
ab.   about; absent
abbr., abbrev.   abbreviation; abbreviated
ab ex.   from without (ab extra)
ab init.   from the beginning (ab initio)
abr.   abridged; abridgment
abs.   absolute; abstract; absent

Abs., A. absolute (temperature)
abs.re. the defendant being absent (absente reo)
abst. abstract
abt., ab. about
a.c., ac alternating current
a/c, A/C, acct. account
A.C. Air Corps; account current
accum. accumulative
ack. acknowledgment
acpt. acceptance
acre-ft., AF., Ac-ft., A-ft. acre-foot
act. active; actual
Actg. Acting [officer]
ad advertisement
a.d. before the day (ante diem)
a/d after date
A.D. in the year of our Lord (anno Domini)
ADC Aide-de-Camp
add. addition
addl., additional
ad fin. to the end (ad finem)
ad h.l., a.h.l. at this place or on this passage (ad hunc locum)
ad inf. to infinity (ad infinitum)
ad init. at the beginning (ad initium)
ad int., a.i. in the meantime or meanwhile (ad interim)
adj. adjective; adjustment (bonds)
Adj. Adjutant
Adj.Gen., A.G. Adjutant General
ad lib. at pleasure (ad libitum)
ad loc. at the place (ad locum)
Adm. Admiral, -ty; administration, -tive
Admr. Administrator; **Admx.,** -trix
ads. address
ad us. according to custom (ad usum)
adv. adverb; advance(s)
ad val., adv., a/v according to the value (ad valorem)
adv.chgs. advance charges
advt., ad advertisement
advtg. advertising
ae., aet. aged; of age (L. aetatis)

a.f., AF audio frequency
Af., Afr. African; Africa
aff. affirmative; **Aff.** Affairs
afft. affidavit
A.F.T.R. American Federal Tax Reports
A1C, A/1c Airman 1st Class; **A2C; A3C**
AG, Adj.Gen., TAG Adjutant General
a.g.b. a good brand
agcy., agy. agency
agr., ag., agri. agriculture; agricultural
agt. agent; against; agreement
a-h ampere-hour
aj., adj. adjustment (bonds)
a.k.a also known as (law)
alt. altitude; alternate, -ing; alteration
a.m. before noon (ante meridiem)
Am. American; America
AM, a.m. amplitude modulation (radio)
A.M. Associate Member
Amb. Ambassador
amd. amended
amp., a ampere
amp-hr. ampere-hour
amt. amount
A.N. arrival notice
anal. analysis; analytic; analogy
anon. anonymous
ans. answer, -ed; **A.** in court writings
a/o account of
A to O.C. attached to other correspondence
A-OK, A-Okay all perfect
ap. according to (apud); apothecaries'; approximate, -ly; airplane
AP Associated Press
A.P. accounts payable
A/P authority to pay, or purchase
Apd. assessment paid
app. appendix; applied; apparatus
appl. application; appliance
approx., ap. approximate, -ly

appt. appointed; appointment
Apr. April
Apt. Apartment
aq. water (aqua); aqueous
ar. arrive, -al
Ar. Arabian; Arabic; Arabia
A.R. accounts receivable; all risk (ins.); return receipt
ARC American National Red Cross
arch. architect, -ure; archaic
arr. arranged
art. article; artist
a.s. at sight
as., asst., ast. assented (securities), assistant
A.S. Academy of Science; Apprentice Seaman; account sales
asd. assumed; assented (securities)
asgd. assigned
asgmt. assignment
Asle., A.S. account sales
asmt. assortment; assessment
assd. assessed; assigned
Assn. Association
asso., assoc. associate; associated
asst., ast. assented; assessment
Asst. Assistant
AST, AT Atlantic standard time
astd., asstd. assorted; assented
astron., astr. astronomy, -er, -ical
AT Am. Terms (grain); assay ton; atomic
athl. athlete, -ic, -ics
Atl. Atlantic
atm. atmosphere(s); atmospheric
att., attm. attach, -ed, -ment
Attn., Att., Atten. Attention
Atty. Attorney
Atty.Gen. Attorney General
at.wt. atomic weight
Au. Author
Aug. August
Aus., Austl. Australian; Australia
aux. auxiliary

av., avdp.   avoirdupois
A.V.   authorized version
Ave., Av.   Avenue
avg., av.   average
avn.   aviation
A/W   actual weight; all water (transportation)
A.W.G.   American wire guage
AWOL   absent without leave

B

b.   base; bay; bond; battery; born
b7d   buyer 7 days to take up (securities)
B., Be.   Baumé (hydrometer)
B.A.   Bachelor of Arts; (Br.) Business Administration; British Academy; British Association
bal.   balance
bar.   barometer; barometric
bat.   battery
BBC   British Broadcasting Corporation
bbl.   barrel
bbls/day, b/d   barrels per day
B.C.   before Christ
bch.   bunch
bd.   board; bond; bound
bd.ft., b.ft.   board foot or feet
bdl.   bundle
bd.rts.   bond rights (securities)
bds.   [bound in] boards (bookbinding)
bdy.   boundary
Be., B.   Baumé (hydrometer)
bet.   between
b.f.   brought forward; board foot; bold face
bg.   bag; building
Bhn   Brinell hardness number (metals)
b.hp., bhp   brake horsepower
bk.   bank; book
bkg.   banking
bkt., bsk.   basket
bl.   bale; block; black; boulevard

B/L, b/l bill of lading (pl. Bs/L, bs/l)
B/L Att. bill of lading attached
Bldg., Bg. Building
bldr. builder
blk. block; black; bulk
Blvd., Bl., Bv. Boulevard
b.m. board measure
B/M bill of material(s)
b.o. buyer's option; back order
B.O. branch office
Bor. Borough
bot. bottle (pl. bots.); bottom; bought
B.O.T. Board of Trade
bp., Bp., BP blueprint
b.p., bp boiling point; boiler pressure
B.P., p.p., b.pay. bills payable
b.p.d., bpd, b/d barrels per day
Br. British; Branch; Brother
B.R., b.r., b.rec. bills receivable
Brig. Gen. Brigadier General
Brit. British; Britain
Bro. brother
brt.fwd., b.f. brought forward
B.S. balance sheet
B/S bill of sale
B&S Brown and Sharpe wire gauge
bsk., bkt. basket
B.S. & W. basic sediment and water
bt. brought; boat
B.t.u., Btu British thermal unit
bu. bushel(s)
bull., bul. bulletin
Bur., Bu. Bureau
bus. business; bushels
b.v. book value
Bv., Blvd., Bl. Boulevard
B.W.G., Bwg Birmingham wire gauge
bx., x box
BX Base Exchange(s)

C

c carat (metric); cycle (elec.); candle
c. coupon; cent; cash; cost; carat; chapter
c., C. cup(s)
c., ca. about (L. circa)
C 100 (L. centum); gallon, apothecaries' (L. Congius)
C. Centigrade (Celsius); Congress; cup
©, **Copr.** copyright
ca centare (metric); about (L. circa)
C.A. Chief Accountant; capital, credit, or current account; Central America
c.a.f., caf, c. & f. cost and freight
cal. small calorie; calendar; caliber
Can. Canadian; Canada
canc. canceled; cancellation
Cantab. of Cambridge University (L. Cantabrigiensis)
cap. capital; capacity
caps capital letters
Capt. Captain
car., c. carat
cat. catalogue
CATV community antenna (cable) TV
c.b. currency bond
C/B cash book
CBD, c.b.d. cash before delivery
cc, c.c. carbon copy; cubic centimeter
CCC Commodity Credit Corporation
cd. cord
c/d carried down
CD, C/D certificate of deposit
Cdr., Cmdr., Comdr. Commander
c.e. at buyer's risk (L. caveat emptor)
C.E. Civil Engineer; Canada East
Cel. Celsius
cem. cement
cen. center; central; century
Cen.Am., C.A. Central America
cert., ct., ctf. certificate, -tion; certified
cf. compare (L. confer); certificate

c/f carried forward
c. & f., caf cost and freight
Cfa. company (Sp. Compañía)
C.F.C. Consolidated Freight Classification
cfm (cfs) cubic feet per minute (or second)
c.f.o. cost for orders
CFR Code of Federal Regulations
cg centigram(s)
c.g. center of gravity
C.G. Consul General; Commanding General; Coast Guard
CGS, cgs centimeter-gram-second [system]
ch. chain; choice; chests; chief; channel (television); chemical; chart
c.h. candle hours
Ch. Chinese; China; Chaplain; Church
CH. Customhouse; Courthouse
C.H. Clearing House
chap., ch., C. chapter
Ch.Clk. Chief Clerk
chem., ch. chemical; chemistry
chf. chief
chg. charge; change
Chin., Ch. Chinese
Chm., Chmn. Chairman
chron. chronological
cht., ch. chart
C.I. consular invoice
Cie, C[ie] company (Fr. Compagnie)
c.i.f., cif cost, insurance, and freight
cir. circle; circular; circumference
cir. mils, c.m. circular mils (wire measure)
cit. citation; citizen
civ. civil; civilian
ck. cask; check
ckt. circuit
cl centiliter
cl. class, -ification; carload; clause; claim
cl., CL, center line
C/L cash letter
cld. colored; cleared; called (securities)

clfd. classified
clk. clerk; clock
clr. color; clear, -ance
C.L.U. Chartered Life Underwriter; Civil Liberties Union
cm centimeter
cm. cumulative (interest or dividends)
c.m., cir.mils circular mils (wire measure)
cml. commercial
cm.pf. cumulative preferred (stocks)
cn. consolidated (bonds)
C.N., c.n. cover note (ins.)
C/N credit note; consignment note; circular note
c/o, %, c.o. care of; carried over
Co. Company; Coast; County
C.O. Commanding Officer; cash order
C/O certificate of origin
c.o.d. certificates of deposit (securities)
C.O.D., c.o.d. collect, or cash, on delivery
coef. coefficient (math.)
C. of C. Chamber of Commerce
C. of S. Chief of Staff
col. column; colony
Col. Colonel; College
coll. collection; collateral
colloq. colloquial
coll.tr., clt collateral trust (bonds)
Colo. Colorado (official);
com., comm. commerce; commission, -er; committee; common; communication; commonwealth
comb. combine, -ing, -ation
Comdr., Cmdr., Cdr. Commander
Comdt. Commandant (Navy and Marine)
coml., cml. commercial
Como. Commodore
con., cons., consol. consolidated
Con. Consul; continued
conc. concentrate
cond. conductivity (elec.); condition
Cong., C. Congress; Congressional
cons. consolidated; consign, -ed, -ment

const. constant; construction
cont. contract; contents; continent
contd., cont., con. continued
Contl. Continental
conv. convertible
co-op co-operative
Copr., © copyright
cor. corner; correct, -ed
Corp. Corporation
corr. corrected; corresponding, -ence
Cor.Sec. Corresponding Secretary
cp. compare; coupon; candlepower
cp., corp. corporation
c.p., cp chemically pure; center of pressure
CP Central Press; Canadian Press
CPA, C.P.A. Certified Public Accountant
cpd. compound
CPFF, C.P.F.F. cost-plus-fixed-fee [job]
Cpl. Corporal
CPLS Certified Professional Legal Secretary
cpm (cps) cycles per minute (or second)
cpn., cp. coupon
CPO, C.P.O. Chief Petty Officer
CPS Certified Professional Secretary
cq sic; that's right (press copy)
cr. credit; creditor
C.R., c.r. company's risk (ins.)
crt. crate
cs centistere
cs. cases
C.S.T., CST Central standard time
ct. cent; count; certificate
Ct. Court
C.T. Central time
C.T.A. with the will annexed (L. cum testamento annexo)
ctf., ct., cf. certificate
ctg. cartage
ctn. carton
c. to c., c-c center-to-center
ctr. center; counter

ct.stp.   certificate stamped (securities)
cu.   cubic
cu.ft., ft³   cubic foot or feet
cu.in., in³   cubic inch or inches
cum., cm.   cumulative
cum d., cum div.   with dividend (L. cum dividendo)
cum.pfd., cu.pf.   cumulative preferred (stocks)
cur.   current; currency
cust.   customer
cu.yd.   cubic yard or yards
c.v.   chief value
cv., cvt.   convertible (securities)
cv.db.   convertible debenture (securities)
cv.pf.   convertible preferred (securities)
C.W.   Canada West
c.w.o.   cash with order
C.W.O.   Chief Warrant Officer
cwt.   hundredweight
cy.   currency; copy; cycle; capacity; city
cyl.   cylinder, -rical

D

d   dyne; deficit
d.   date; died; dose; density; distance; penny (L.denarius); pence; daughter
d., da.   day(s)
D.   Democrat; diameter
d/a   days after acceptance
D.A.   District Attorney
D/A   documents upon acceptance of draft
Dan., Da.   Danish
DAR   Daughters of the American Revolution
db   decibel
d.b.a.   doing business as [company name]
D.B.N.   of the goods not [yet administered] (L. de bonis non)
db.rts.   debenture rights (securities)
d.c., dc   direct current
D.C.   District of Columbia
D/C   deviation clause

dd. delivered
D/D demand draft; delivered at docks; delivered at destination; dock dues
D/d days after date
d.d. in d. from day to day (L. de die in diem)
D.D.Sc. Doctor of Dental Science
D.E., D. Eng. Doctor of Engineering
deb. debenture
dec. decrease; deceased; decimal; declination
def. defense; definition; deferred (securities)
deg.,° degree or degrees
del. deliver, -y; he drew it (L. delineavit)
Dem., D. Democrat
Den. Denmark
dep. deposit; deputy; depot
dep.ctfs. deposit certificates (securities)
Dept. Department
der. derived, -ation
det. detached; detachment; detective
dev. deviation
d.f. dead freight
D.F. Distrito Federal (Mexico City is a Federal District, like D.C.)
dft., Dft. draft; defendant
dg decigram
D.G. by the grace of God (L. Dei gratia)
DH. deadhead (freight)
DHQ Division Headquarters (Army)
dia., diam., D. diameter
diag. diagram; diagonal
dict. dictionary
Dir. Director
dis. discount; discharge
disch. discharge
dist. district; distance; distribution
distr. distributed, -tion, -tor
dit called (Fr., said)
div. dividend; division
DJ Dow Jones; District Judge; disk (disc) jockey; dust jacket
dk. dock; deck; dark

dkg, dag dekagram or deca-
dkl, dal dekaliter or deca-
dkm, dam dekameter or deca-
dl deciliter
DL demand loan
D.L.O. dead letter office
dlvd., dld. delivered
dlvy., dly., dy. delivery
dm decimeter
DM Deutsche mark
dn. down
D/N debit note
do. ditto (It., the same)
D.O. delivery order; diesel oil; defense order
DOA dead on arrival
doc. document
DOD, DoD Department of Defense
dol., dl., $ dollar
dom. domestic; dominion; domicile
doz. dozen
d.p., dp, DP dew point
DP displaced person
D/P documents upon payment of draft
DPL, dpl. diplomat, -ic; diploma
D.Q. direct question
D/R deposit receipt
dr. dram; drum; debtor; debit
Dr. doctor; Drive
Dra. doctora (Sp., doctress)
dr.ap. dram apothecaries'
dr.av. dram avoirdupois
ds decistere (metric)
D/s days after sight
D.S.C. Distinguished Service Cross
D.S.M. Distinguished Service Medal
D.S.O. Distinguished Service Order (Br.)
d.s.p. died without issue (L. decessit sine prole)
D.S.T. daylight saving time
dstn. destination
dtd. dated

DTs, D.T.s, d.t.'s delirium tremens
Du. Dutch
D.V. God willing (L. Deo volente)
d.w. dead weight
D.W. dock warrant
d.w.c. dead weight capacity
dwg. drawing
dwt. pennyweight; deadweight
d.w.t.f. daily and weekly till forbidden (advertising)
DX [long-]distance (radio transmission)
dy. delivery; day; duty; deputy

E

e erg; error(s)
E. East; Engineer, -ing; English; excellent
ea. each
E.A.O.N. except as otherwise noted
EB eastbound
eccl. ecclesiastic, -al
econ. economy, -ics, -ist
Ed. Editor; Edition; Education
EDP electronic data processing
E.D.T., EDT., e.d.t. Eastern daylight time
educ. educated; education, -al
e.e. errors excepted
eff. efficiency; effect, -ive
e.g. for example (L. exempli gratia)
el., elev. elevation, -ted
elct. electronics
elec., el. electric, -al, -ian, -ity
elem. element(s), -ary
E.Long. east longitude
emf, e.m.f., EMF electromotive force
e.m.p. end of month payment
enc. enclosure(s); **ency.,** encyclopedia
end. endorsed; endorsement
Eng. English; England; Engineer, -ing
Engr. Engineer; Engraved, -er, -ing
Ens. Ensign
entd. entered

env., ep   envelope
e.o.d.   every other day (advertising)
E. & O.E.   errors and omissions excepted
e.o.m., EOM   end of month
e.p., ep   end point (distillation)
eq.   equal; equivalent; equipment; equation; equator
equip., eq., eqt., eqpt.   equipment
equiv.   equivalent
erron.   erroneous, -ly
esp.   especially
ESP   extrasensory perception
Esq.   Esquire
est   established, -ment; estimate; estate
E.S.T., EST   Eastern standard time
esu   electrostatic unit(s)
ET   Eastern time; elec. transcription
ETA, e.t.a.   estimated time of arrival
et al   and others (L. et alii)
etc., &c   and so forth (L. et cetera)
etq.   etiquette
et seq., seq., sq.   and the following (L. et sequens) (pl. et seqq.)
et ux   and wife (L. et uxor)
et vir   and husband (L., and man)
Eur.   Europe; European
ex.   example; exchange; exercise; express; exception; extra; executive
exam.   examined; examination
exc., exch.   exchange
Exec., Ex.   Executive
ex.fcy.   extra fancy
exp.   express; expense; export; expiration
expt., exp.   experiment, -al
Exr.   Executor;   **Exrx.,** Executrix
ex rel.   by relation (L. ex relatione)
ext.   exterior; extended; extension; extract; external; extinct
exx.   examples

F

f   farad; force
f.   and the following [page] (pl. ff.); folio; female; fathom

F., Fahr. Fahrenheit
f.a.a. free of all average (ins.)
f.a.c. fast as can
f.a.q. fair average quality; free at quay
f.a.q.s. fair average quality of season
f.a.s. free alongside ship
fath., fm., f. fathom
f.b. freight bill
f.b.m., fbm feet board measure
fcp. foolscap
f.c. & s. free of capture and seizure (ins.)
fcy.pks. fancy packs
fd. fund; funding
f. & d. freight and demurrage
fdg. funding (bonds)
Fdy. foundry
fec. he, or she, made it (L. fecit)
Fed. Federal; Federated; Federation
fem., f. female
F.E.T., FET Federal excise tax
ff. and the following [pages]; folios
f.f.a. free from alongside; free foreign agency
f.i.a. full interest admitted
Fid. Fidelity; Fiduciary
fifo first-in, first-out
fig. figure
fin. financial; finance; finish
Fin. Finnish; Finland
Fin.Sec. Financial Secretary
f.i.o. free in and out
f.i.t. free of income tax; free in truck
f.i.w. free in wagon
fl. fluid; floor
fl.dr. fluid dram, apothecaries'
F.L.N. following landing numbers
fl.oz. fluid ounce, apothecaries'
Flt. fleet; flight; filing time
flts., fts. flats
fm. fathom; from; form
FM, f.m. frequency modulation (radio)

fn., ftnt. footnote
fn.p., fnp fusion point
fo., f°, fol., f. folio (pl. ff.)
f.o. firm offer; free overside
F.O. Foreign Office
f.o.b. free on board
f.o.c. free on car; free of charge
f.o.d. free of damage
f.o.f. free on field
fol. folio; follow, -ing
f.o.q. free on quay
for. foreign; forestry
4-H Head, Heart, Hands, and Health
F.P. floating policy; fully paid
f.p., fp freezing point
f.p.a. free of particular average (ins.)
f.pd full paid
f.p.m., fpm, f/m feet per minute
FPO Fleet Post Office
f.p.s, fps, f/s feet per second
F.P.S., f.p.s., f-p-s., fps foot-pound-second [system]
fr., fm. from
Fr. French; France; francs; Father (Catholic); Frau (Ger.)
FR full-rate (cables)
F/R freight release
F.R., FR, FRS Federal Reserve System
Fra friar
freq. frequent, -cy, -ly
Fri. Friday; **F.** or **Fr.** in tabulations
Frl. Fräulein (Ger., Miss)
F.R.S. Fellow of the Royal Society
frt. freight
Frwy., Fy. freeway
FS field or foreign service; filmstrip
ft. foot or feet
Ft. Fort
ft-c foot-candle; **ft-l,** foot-lambert
ftd. fitted
ft-lb. foot-pound(s)
ft/sec., fs feet per second

ft-tn. foot-ton
fur. furlong
furn. furnished; furniture
fut. futures (exchange)
f.v. on the back of the page (L. folio verso)
f.w.d. fresh-water damage
fwd. forward
FX foreign exchange
FYI, fyi, f.y.i. for your information

G

g gram(s)
g. gold; gauge; gulf; gravity
g.a. general average (ins.)
Ga. Georgia (official)
GA General Agent; General Assembly
gal. gallon
gar. garage
GAW guaranteed annual wage
G.B., Gt.Br. Great Britain
g-cal., cal. gram-calorie (small calorie)
GCD, gcd greatest common divisor
GCT, G.C.T., G.c.t. Greenwich civil time
gd(s). good(s)
gen. general; generator; genus or kind
Gen. General
geog. geography
geol. geology
Ger. German; Germany
g.f.a. good fair average
G.F.A. general freight agent
g.gr. great gross (144 dozen)
GHQ General Headquarters
gi. gill or gills
GI Government Issue
Gk. Greek
gm general mortgage (bonds)
GM general manager; guided missile
G.m.a.t., GMAT Greenwich mean astronomical time
G.m.b.H., GmbH, GMBH corporation with limited liability

(Ger. Gesellschaft mit beschränkter Haftung)
GMT, G.m.t. Greenwich mean time
gn., gen. general
G.N. Graduate Nurse
GNP gross national product
G.O., GO general orders (military)
G.O.P. Grand Old Party (Republican)
Gov. Governor
govt. government
gp. group
G.P.A. general passenger agent
g.p.m., gpm, g/m gallons per minute, or mile
GPO Government Printing Office
gr. gross; grade; grain (spelled out for weight); gravity; graph; great
Gr. Greece; Grecian
grad. graduate, -ed, -tion
gr.wt. gross weight
g.s. ground speed
GSA General Services Administration
gt. drop (L. gutta) (pl. gtt.); great
GTC good till canceled (brokerage order)
gtd. guaranteed
G.T.M. good this month
G.T.W. good this week
gu., guar. guarantee; guaranteed

H

h henry (elec.); hours, as 12^h or 12h
ha hectare; in this year (L. hoc anno)
har., h. harbor
H.C. held covered; House of Commons
hdbk. handbook
hdlg. handling [charge]
hdw. hardware
H.E., HE His Excellency; high explosive
hf. half
h-f., HF high-frequency
H.F.M. hold for money
hg hectogram

hhd.   hogshead(s)
hist.   history, -ical
hl   hectoliter
hm   hectometer
H.M.S.   His, or Her, Majesty's Ship, or Service
hol.   holiday
Hon.   Honorable
Hosp.   hospital
hp., hp, HP   horsepower
h.p.   high pressure
hp-hr.   horsepower-hour
HQ, Hq.   Headquarters
hr.   hour
H.R.   House of Representatives
H.R.H.   His, or Her, Royal Highness
hs., hse.   house; **hsg.,** housing
HS   hydrofoil ship
HST, HT   Hawaiian [standard] time
ht.   height; heat
Hts., Hgts.   Heights
hund., C   hundred
Hung.   Hungary; Hungarian
hvy., (H)   heavy
H.W.   high water
H.W.M.   high-water mark
Hwy., Hy.   Highway
Hz.   hertz

I

I.   Island(s); Isle(s)
Ib., ibid.   in the same place (L. ibidem)
I.B.   invoice book; in bond
I.B.I.   invoice book, inwards
I.B.O.   invoice book, outwards
ICBM   intercontinental ballistic missile
I.C. & C.   invoice cost and charges
id.   the same (L. idem)
i.d., ID   inside diameter; identification
i.e.   that is (L. id est)
ign.   unknown (L. ignotus); ignites, -tion
i.hp., ihp, IHP   indicated horsepower

IHS monogram for Greek word for Jesus
ill., illus. illustration; illustrated
imp. improvement; implement; imperial; import, -ed
in.," inch
Inc. Incorporated; increase; income, -ing
incl. inclusive; including
incog. in secret; unknown (It. incognito)
ind. industry, -ial; independent
Ind. Indian; India
inf. inferior; below (L. infra)
info information
infra dig undignified (L. infra dignitatem)
init. initial
in-lb. inch-pound
in lim. at the outset (L. in limine)
ins. insurance; inspector; insulated
inst. instant, -aneous; installment
Inst. Institute; Institution, -al
instr. instructor, -tion(s); instrument
int. interest; interior; international; interstate; internal; intermediate
Intl., Int. International
(int.) n.mi. international nautical mile
inv. invoice; investment; inventor, -tion
invt. investment; inventory
IOU I owe you
i.p., ip intermediate pressure
i.p.s., ips inches per second
i.q. the same as (L. idem quod)
IQ intelligence quotient
Ir. Irish
Ire. Ireland
Is., Isl., I. Island
iss. issue
It. Italian; Italy
i.v. invoice value; increased value
Ix. index

J

j joule (elec.)

J. Judge; Justice (pl. JJ.)
J.A. Judge Advocate
J/A joint account
Jap. Japanese; Japan
Jc., Jct., Junc. Junction
JJ. Justices
jnt.stk. joint stock
Jour., J., Jr. Journal
J.P. Justice of the Peace
Jr. Junior; journal
jt. joint
junc. junction

K

k., kn. knot
K karat (gold measure); kilo
K. Kelvin
kc kilocycle
K.C. Knights of Columbus
kcal. kilocalorie
K.C.B. Knight Commander of the Bath
kcps, kc/s kilocycles per second
K.D. knocked down (freight)
kg kilogram
kg. keg or kegs
K.G. Knight of the Garter (Br.)
kg-cal. kilogram-calorie or kilocalorie (large calorie)
kgm, kg-m kilogram-meter
kg/m³ kilograms per cubic meter
kgps, kg/s kilograms per second
kip thousand (kilo) pounds
K.K.K. Ku Klux Klan
kl kiloliter
km kilometer
kmps, km/s kilometers per second
K.O. keep off; knockout
Kr. krone
kt., K. karat (gold)
Kt. karat
kv kilovolt

kva, kv-a   kilovolt-ampere
kvar   kilovar (reactive kilovolt-ampere)
kvarh   kilovarhour (reactive kilovolt-ampere-hour)
kw   kilowatt(s)
kwh, kw-hr., kwhr   kilowatt-hour

L

l   liter; lumen
l.   line (pl. ll.); left; league; leaf; length
L   listed (securities); lire (Italian money); lambert (unit of brightness)
L.   Latin; law; ledger
L/A   letter of authority; Lloyd's agent; landing account
la., lge.   large
lab.   laboratory; labor
lang.   language
lat.   latitude
lb.   pound (L. libra); labor
lb.ap.   pound, apothecaries'
lb.av.   pound avoirdupois
lb.-ft.   pound-foot
lb/ft^2   pounds per square foot
lb-in.   pound-inch
lb/in^2   pounds per square inch (See p.s.i.)
lbr.   lumber
lb.t.   pound, troy
lc., l.c.   lower case (printing); left center
LC   deferreds (cables)
L/C   letter of credit
LCD, lcd   least common denominator
LCdr, Lt.Comdr.   Lieutenant Commander
LCL(s), l.c.l.('s)   less-than-carload lot(s)
LCM, lcm   least common multiple
L.c.t., LCT   local civil time
lea.   league; leather
L.Ed.   Lawyers Edition
Leg.   Legislature, -tive, -tion; (lc) legal
Les.   Lesson
l-f., LF   low-frequency
lge., lg, L   large
l.h., LH   left hand

l-hr. lumen-hour
li. link
L.I. Long Island
lib. library; book (L. liber)
Lic. Licenciado (Sp., attorney)
Lieut., Lt. Lieutenant
lifo last-in, first-out
lin.ft. linear foot
L.I.P. life insurance policy
liq. liquid
lit. literature; literally
ll. lines; leaves
LL leased line (securities)
Ll. & Co.'s Lloyd's and Companies
L.M.S.C. let me see correspondence
ln. lien; loan
loc. location; local
loc.cit. in the place cited (L. loco citato)
log logarithm
long. longitude
l.p., lp low pressure; long-playing
lpw, l/w lumens per watt
l.s. left side
L.S. place of the seal (L. locus sigilli)
£ s. d. pounds, shillings, pence (British)
L.S.T., LST, LT local standard time
lt. light; left
LT letter message
Lt., Lieut. Lieutenant
Lt. Col. Lieutenant Colonel
Lt. Cmdr., LCdr Lieutenant Commander
Ltd. limited
Lt. Gen. Lieutenant General
Lt. Gov. Lieutenant Governor
Lt. (jg) Lieutenant (junior grade)
LTL(s), l.t.l.('s) less-than-truckload(s)
ltr. letter; lighter
lub. lubricate, -ing, -cant
lv. leave(s)

M

m minutes; meter (metric)
m² square meter
m. mass; mile; noon (L. meridies); month; male; masculine; married; mill; model
M 1000 (L. mille) as **2M;** medium [size]
M, min. minim or drop, apothecaries'
M. Monsieur (pl. MM.); Master; Monday
ma milliampere
m/a my account
M.A. Master of Arts (Br.)
mach. machine; machinery
mag. magazine; magnitude
Maj. Major; majority
Maj. Gen. Major General
Man. Manhattan; Manitoba
mar. market; maritime; married
Mar. Marine
mas., masc., m. masculine
mat. maturity (bonds); matinee
math. mathematics
MATS Military Air Transport Service
max. maximum
mb millibar
Mbm, M.B.M., MBM thousand [feet] board measure (lumber)
mc megacycle
m.c. market capacity
M.C. Master of Ceremonies (or emcee[s]); Member of Congress; Military Cross
M/C marginal credit
Mcf 1000 cubic feet
mch., mach. machine
m/d months after date
M/D memorandum of deposit
Mdm. Madam
mdnt., mid. midnight
mdse. merchandise
Me. Maine
M.E. Mining Engineer; Managing Editor

meas. measure, -ment
mech. mechanic, -ics
med. medium; medicine; medical
memo memorandum
m.e.p., mep mean effective pressure
mer. mercantile; meridian
Messrs., MM. Messieurs
met. metropolitan; meteorological; metal
metal., met. metallurgy
Mex. Mexican; Mexico
mf millifarad
M/F, M&F, m/f male or female (advtg.)
mfg. manufacturing
mfr. manufacture, -r
mfst. manifest
mg milligram
m.g.d., mgd million gallons per day
Mgr Monseigneur (Fr., My lord)
Mgr. Manager
mgt., mgmt. management
mh millihenry
M.H., MH Medal of Honor
mhcp mean horizontal candlepower
mi. mill; mile(s)
Mich. Michigan (official)
mid., mdnt. midnight
Midn., Mid. Midshipman
mil. military; mileage; million
min. minute(s); minimum; mineral; mining; minim, apothecaries'; minister
M.I.P. marine insurance policy
misc. miscellaneous
mk. mark
mks. MKS meter-kilogram-second [system]
mkt., mar. market
ml milliliter
mL millilambert
Mlle Mademoiselle (Fr., Miss)
mm millimeter
m.m. with the necessary changes (L. mutatis mutandis)

MM. Messieurs
Mme Madame (Fr.)
Mmes Mesdames (Fr.)
mmf, MMF magnetomotive force
m mu, mμ millimicron
Mn House (Fr. Maison)
mng. managing
mo. month(s)
m.o. money order; mail order
mod. modified (securities); moderate
mol. molecule
mol.wt. molecular weight
mot. motor
m.p., mp melting point
M.P. Member of Parliament; mounted police; military police
M.P.C. Member of Parliament, Canada
m.p.g., mpg, m/g miles per gallon
m.p.h., mph, m/h miles per hour
mphps, m/h/s miles per hour per second
Mr. Mister
Mrs. Mistress
ms., MS. manuscript (pl. mss., MSS.)
Ms. Miss or Mrs.
m/s meters per second
M/s months after sight
MS. motorship; manuscript
m.s.cp., mscp mean spherical candlepower
msg. message
Msgr. Monsignor (It., My lord); messenger
M.Sgt., M/Sgt. Master Sergeant
m.s.l. mean sea level
M.S.T., MST Mountain standard time
Mt. mount; mountain; material
M.T., MT Mountain time; empty
mt.ct.cp. mortgage certificate coupon (securities)
mtg. mortgage; mounting; meeting
mu micron
mu a microampere
mu f microfarad
mu mu micromicron

mun. municipal
mus. music, -al, -ian; museum
mu w microwatt
mv millivolt
m.v. market value
M.V. motor vessel

N

n. note; net; new; noun; noon; name
n/30 net in 30 days
N. north; Navy; noon
n.a. no account (bank); not available
N/A no advice
NA nonacquiescence; not available
N.A., N.Am. North America
NANA North American Newspaper Alliance, Inc.
Nat., Natl. national
naut. nautical
nav. naval; navigation
n.b., N.B. note well (L. nota bene)
NB northbound
NBS National Bureau of Standards
NC, n-c non-callable (bonds)
N.C. no charge
N/C new charter
n.c.u.p. no commission until paid
N.C.V. no commercial value
n.d. no date; next day's delivery
NE. northeast
N.E. New England
N/E no effects
n.e.c. not elsewhere classified
neg. negative, -ly
nem.con. none contradicting; unanimously (L. nemine contradicente)
n.e.s. not elsewhere specified or stated
Neth., Neld. Netherlands
N.F. no funds (banking)
n.g. no good, or "out"
N.G., NG National Guard; narrow gauge

n.hp., N.HP nominal horsepower
n.l. it is not permitted (L. non licet); it is not clear (L. non liquet); new line
NL night letter
N.Lat., NL north latitude
n mi, nm nautical mile(s); no middle initial
nn, NN noon; notes
no. number
No., N. North; northern
n/o in the name of (finance)
N.O.E. not otherwise enumerated
N.O.H.P. not otherwise herein provided
N.O.I.B.N. not otherwise indexed by name
nol.pros. to be unwilling to prosecute (L. nolle prosequi)
non pros. he does not prosecute (L. non prosequitur)
non seq. it does not follow (L. non sequitur)
Nor. Norwegian; Norway
n.o.s., NOS not otherwise specified
np nonparticipating
n.p. no place [of publication]; net proceeds
N.P. Notary Public; no protest (finance)
N.P.L. nonpersonal liability
NPO Navy Post Office
n.p.t. normal pressure and temperature
n.r. no risk; net register
nr. near; **NR,** no ranking or rating
NS, N.S. nuclear ship
N.S. not specified; new style
N.S.F. not sufficient funds (banking)
N.T.O. not taken out (insurance)
n.t.p. no title page; normal temperature and pressure
nt.wt., n.wt. net weight
n.u. name unknown
nuc. nuclear
NV no value, -ation; nonvoting
N.V. limited-liability company (Dutch Naamloze Vennootschap)
N.V.D., nvd no value declared
NW. northwest
N.Y.C. New York City
N.Z. New Zealand

O

o. off; old; only; order; out
O pint, apothecaries' (L. Octarius)
O. Ohio
oa., OA overall
o/a on account; on or about
ob. he, or she, died (L. obiit); obstetrics
obit. obituary
O.B./L, ob/l order bill of lading
obs. obsolete; observation, -tory
ob.s.p. died without issue (L. obiit sine prole)
oc. overcharge; ocean
o/c overcharge
o.d. outside diameter; on demand; over-draft
o.e omissions excepted
OED Oxford English Dictionary
ofc., off. office; official; officer
O/o order of
op. opera; work (L. opus); overproof
o.p., OP out of print; open policy
op.cit. in the work cited (L. opere citato)
opd. opened (stocks)
opp. opposite
opr. operate, -ing, -tion(s)
opt. optional; optician
o.r. owner's risk (shipping)
Or. Oriental
O.R.C., ORC Officers' Reserve Corps
ord. ordinance; order; ordinary
Org., Orgn. Organization
orig. original,- ly
o/s, OS out of stock
o.w., OW one way [fare]
Oxon. Oxford University (L. Oxonia)
oz. ounce or ounces
oz.ap. ounce, apothecaries'
oz.av. ounce, avoirdupois
oz-ft. ounce-foot
oz-in. ounce-inch
oz.t. ounce, troy

P

p. page (pl. pp.); per; pressure; population; power; pole; past; pitch
¶ paragraph
pa. paper
p.a., per an. per annum (by the year)
P.A. Purchasing Agent; Press Agent; private account; personal appearance; public-address system
P/A power of attorney
Pac. Pacific
p.a.e. equal parts (L. partes aequales)
pam. pamphlet
par. paragraph; parallel
paren., par. parenthesis
part. participating (securities); particular
pat. patent, -ed
Pat.Off. Patent Office
payt. payment
PBX private branch exchange (telephone)
pc. piece
pc., pct. percent
pcl. parcel
pd. paid
P.E. Professional Engineer
P/E, p/e (ratio) price ÷ earnings
P.E.G. prior endorsement guaranteed
perf. perforated; perfect; performer, -ance
perm. permanent
perp. perpetual (bonds); perpendicular
pet., petr. petroleum
petn. petition
pf., pfd., pref. preferred (securities)
p.f., PF power factor
Pfc. Private, first class
Pg. Portuguese; Portugal
ph., PH phase
P. & i. protection and indemnity
pinx., pxt. he, or she, painted it (L. pinxit)
pix pictures
pk. pack, -ing; park; peak; peck

pkg. package; pkgd., packaged
pkt. packet
Pkwy. parkway
pl. place; plural; plate
P.L. public law; partial loss; price list
P. & L. profit and loss
Plf., Ptf. plaintiff
PLS Professional Legal Secretary
pm., prem. premium
p.m. afternoon (L. post meridiem)
pmt., payt. payment
p.n., PN promissory note
P.O. post office; Petty Officer
P.O., Per Pro. by authorization; by proxy (L. per procurationem)
p.o.d. pay on delivery; payable on death
p.o.e., POE port of entry
Pol. Polish; Poland; (lc) politics, -al
pop. population; popular, -ly
p.o.r., P.O.R. pay on return (express); payable on receipt
Port. Portuguese; Portugal
pos. positive; possessive; position
pot. potential
pow. power; powder
pp. pages; prepaid; postpaid
p.p. parcel post; privately printed
ppd. postpaid; prepaid
p.p.i. parcel post, insured
p.p.m., ppm parts per million
pr. price; present; pair; prior; province; printed; printing; prime; power
PR payroll
P.R. Puerto Rico (official)
pref., pf. preferred; preference; preface
prem., pm. premium
prep. preposition; preparation
Pres. President
prim. primary
prin. principal
p.r.n. as the occasion arises (L. pro re nata)

prob. problem
prod. product; produce; produced
Prof. Professor
pron. pronunciation; pronounced; pronoun
prop. property; proposition
Prot. Protestant
pro tem. temporarily (L. pro tempore)
prov. province; provision, -al
prox. of the next month (L. proximo)
pr.pf. prior preferred (stocks)
prs. pairs
Ps. Psalm
PS. postscript
P/S public sale
Psgr., Pass. Passenger
p.s.i., psi pounds per square inch
P.S.T., PST, PT Pacific [standard] time
pstg. postage
pt. part; payment; pint; point; port
PT Pacific time; private terms; pro tempore
ptc. participating (securities)
ptg. printing
pt.pf. participating preferred (stocks)
Ptr. printer
Pty. proprietary
PU pickup; **PUD,** pickup and delivery
pub. public, -ation; published, -ing, -er
pur. purchaser; purchasing
Pvt. Private (Army and Marines)
pwr., pow. power
PX Post Exchange

Q

q quintal
Q. question; query (pl. QQ.); Quebec
q.d.a. quantity discount agreement
Q.E.D. which was to be proved (L. quod erat demonstrandum)
Q.E.F. which was to be done (L. quod erat faciendum)
qly. quality
QM. Quartermaster

qn. quotation
QQ. questions; queries
qr. quarter; quarterly; quire
q.s. quarter section; a sufficient quantity
qt. quart
q.t., Q.T. [on the] quiet; in secret (slang)
qtr., quar., qu. quarter, -ly
qty. quantity
qu., Q., ques. question
quad. quadrant; quadrangle
q.v. which see (L. quod vide) (pl. qq.v.)
Qy., Q. query

R

r. right; road
R. Range; Republic, -an; reports; registered; river; rule; radius; Réaumur (thermometric scale); Regina
R.A. Rear Admiral; Royal Academy
R/A refer to acceptor
rad. radio; radiant
R.A.F. Royal Air Force
RB Renegotiation Board
R.C. Red Cross; Roman Catholic
R/C reconsigned
rct. receipt; (cap) recruit
rd. road; rod; round
R/D refer to drawer
r.d. running days
R&D, Rand Research and Development
rdp., red. redemption
re in regard to
R.E. real estate
Rear Adm., RAdm Rear Admiral
rec. record, -ed, -er; recipe; receipt; reclamation (bonds)
recd., rcd. received
Rec.Sec. Recording Secretary
ref. reference; referee; refining; refunding
refr. refrigerate, -ed, -ing, -tor
reg. register, -ed; regulation; regular
REIT real estate investment trust

R.E.O. real estate owned (banking)
rep. repeat; report; repair
Rep. Republic, -an; Representative
rept., rpt., rep. report
req. requisition; required
res. reserve; residence; resort; resolution
ret. retired; return
retd. returned
rev. review; revenue; reverse; revise, -ed, -ion; revolve, -ing, -ution
Rev. Reverend
Rev.Stat., R.S. Revised Statutes
rf., rfg. refunding (bonds); refining (oil)
r.f., RF radio frequency
R.F. French Republic
R.F.D. rural free delivery
rg., reg. registered (bonds)
r.h. right hand; relative humidity
rhp, RHP rated horsepower
R.I. Republik Indonesia
R.I.P. may he, or she, rest in peace (L. requiescat in pace)
rm. ream; room
r.m.s., rms root mean square
R.N. Registered Nurse; Royal Navy
R.N.R. Royal Naval Reserve
R.O.G. receipt of goods
Rom. Roman; Romance
r.o.p. run of paper (advertising)
Rp., Rep., R. Republic, -an
RP reply paid; reprint, -ing
R.P. return premium
R/p return of post for orders
r.p.m., rpm, r/m revolutions per minute
r.p.s. rps, r/s revolutions per second
rpt. report
RR. railroad
R.R. rural route
r.s. right side
R.S. Revised Statutes; Recording Secretary
R.S.V.P. Reply, if you please (Fr. Répondez, s'il vous plait)
rt. right; round trip

Rte., Rt. Route
Rt. Hon. Right Honourable (Br.)
Rt. Rev. Right Reverend
Rus. Russian; Russia
rva reactive volt-ampere
R/W right of way
Ry. railway

S

s stere; seconds
s7d seller 7 days to deliver (securities)
s. silver; stock; steamer; shillings; son
S. south; science; Senate; mark prescription (L. signa); Saint, - e; small
s/a subject of approval
S.A. South America; South Africa; Salvation Army; an incorporated company (Fr. Société Anonyme); stock company (Sp. Sociedad Anónima)
SAE Society of Automotive Engineers
S.Afr. South Africa, -n
S.A.I. an incorporated company (It. Società Anonima Italiana)
S.Am. South America, -n
s.ap., sc. scruple, apothecaries'
Sav. Savings
SB southbound
S.B. Senate bill (state)
S/B statement of billing
s. & c. shipper and carrier
sc., sci. science
sc., scil., sct. namely or to wit
sc., sculp. he or she, carved or engraved it (L. sculpsit); sculptor
sch. school; schooner; schedule
Scot., Sc. Scottish; Scotch; Scotland
s.cp., scp spherical candlepower
Script. Scripture(s)
s.d. without a day [being named] (l. sine die); sight draft; special delivery
SDRs Special Drawing Rights
SE. southeast
sec. section; second(s); security; secured

Secy., Sec. Secretary
sel. select, -ed, -tion
Sen. Senate; Senator; Senior
sep. separate; **sepd.; sepg.; sepn.**
seq. the following (L. sequens) (pl. seqq.)
ser. series; serial; service; sermon
serv., svc., svce. service
sess. session
s.f. sinking fund; near end (L. sub finem)
S. & F.A. shipping and forwarding
S1c Seaman, first class
Sfc. Sergeant first class
Sgd., /S/, (s) signed
Sgt. Sergeant; **Sfc,** Sergeant first class
sh. share; sheet
shp shaft horsepower; shipping
shpt. shipment; **shpg.,** -ing; **shpd.; shpr.**
shtg. shortage
sh.tn., s.t. short ton
sic so written; thus (L.)
sig., sg. signature; write [on medicine]
Sig. Signor (It., Mr.)(pl. Sigg.)
Sig.ra Signora (It., Mrs.) (pl. Sig.re)
sim. similar
sing. singular
s.i.t. stopping in transit
S.J. Society of Jesus (the Jesuits)
sk. sack
sked schedule
S&L Savings and Loan
S.Lat., SL south latitude
sld. sailed; sealed; sold
sltx, SLTX sales tax
sm small; statute mile
Sn., SN Seaman
S/N shipping note
s.o. seller's option; shipping order
So., S. South; southern
Soc. Society; Sociology
Sol. solution; soluble; solicitor
S.O.L. shipowner's liability

S.O.P.   standard operating procedure
SOR   stockholder of record
SOS   distress signal (no periods)
sp.   species; special; spelling; specimen
s.p.   without issue (L. sine prole); singlephase
Sp.   Spanish; Spain; Specialist
S.p.A.   a corporation (It. Società per [for] Azioni [shares])
spec.   specification; specimen(s)
spg.   spring
sp.gr., s.g., sg   specific gravity
sp.ht.   specific heat
s.p.s.   without surviving issue (sine prole superstite)
spt.   seaport
sq.   square
sq.   the following (L. sequens)
Sq.   square (a block or street); Squadron
sq.ft.   square foot or feet
sq.in.   square inch or inches
Sr.   Senior; Sister; Sir; Señor
S.R.   shipping receipt; star route
Sra.   Señora
Sres.   Señores
S.R.O., SRO   standing room only (theater)
Srta.   Señorita
ss.   sections; namely or to wit
SS.   steamship; supersonic
S.Sgt., S/Sgt.   Staff Sergeant
SSR, S.S.R.   Soviet Socialist Republic
SST   supersonic transport
St.   Street; State; Store; Strait; Statute(s); Saint (pl. SS.)
Sta.   Station; Santa; stamped; stationary
stat.   statistics; statutes
std.   standard; seated
Ste   Sainte (Fr., feminine of Saint)
stg.   storage (or **stge.**); sterling (or **ster.**)
stk.   stock
Stk.Ex., St.Ex.   Stock Exchange
Stk.Mkt.   Stock Market
st.mi., sm   statute [legalized] mile(s)
stmt.   statement
stp., st., sta.   stamped (securities)

str. steamer; store; strength
stud. student
S.U. set up (freight); service unit
sub. substitute; subway; subscriber, -ption substance; submarine; suburb
subj., sub. subject
subs. subsidiary; subscription; subsistence
sup. superior; supply; above (supra)
supp., sup. supplement, -ary
Supt. Superintendent
sur. surface; surplus
surg. surgeon; surgery; surgical
surv., svy. survey, -ing, -or; surviving
s.v. under the word (sub verbo)
svc., svce., serv. service
svgs. savings
sw. switch; **swbd.,** switchboard
Sw., Swed. Swedish; Sweden
SW. southwest; seawater; short-wave
S.W.G., SWG standard wire gauge
sx sacks
syl. syllable(s)
sym. symbol; symmetrical; symphony; symptom
synd. syndicate, -ed
syst., sys. system

T

t metric ton
t. temperature; town; troy; time; teaspoon
T., Tp., Twp. township
tab. table(s)
T.A.G. The Adjutant General
t.a.w. twice a week (advertising)
TB tuberculosis
T.B. trial balance
tbsp., tbs., T. tablespoon(s)
T/C until countermanded
T.D. trust deed
T/D time deposit
T.E. trade expenses

tech.   technical
tel.   telephone; telegraph; telegram
temp.   temperature; temporary
Ter.   Territory; territorial; Terrace
t.f.   till forbidden (advertising)
tg.   telegraph; **tgm.,**   telegram
thou.   thousand; **M** in lumber, etc.
tkr.   tanker
TLO, t.l.o.   total loss only (ins.)
t.m.   true mean; trademark
TM, Tmk.   trademark
tn., T.   ton; town; train
tn.mi.   ton-mile
T/O   transfer order
tonn.   tonnage
tp   title page; telephone; (cap.) township
tph   tons per hour; **tpm,** tons per minute
tr.   trust; trustee; transit; transfer; transpose; translated, -tion, -tor; treasurer
T.R.   tons registered
trans., tr.   translated, -tion, -tor
Treas., Tr.   Treasurer; Treasury
t.s., ts   tensile strength
T.Sgt., T/Sgt.   Technical Sergeant
tsp., t.   teaspoon(s)
TT   teletype
T.T.s   telegraphic transfers (of money)
Turk.   Turkish; Turkey
TV   television; terminal velocity
TVA   Tennessee Valley Authority
Twad., Tw.   Twaddell (hydrometer)
Twp.   township
TWS   timed wire service
TWX   teletypewriter exchange
tx.   tax or taxes; text, -book

U

U., Univ.   University
UFO   unidentified flying object
UGT   urgent

UHF ultra-high frequency
u.i. as below (ut infra)
U.K. United Kingdom
UL Underwriters' Laboratories
ult. last month (ultimo); ultimate
un. unifying or unified (bonds)
Un. Union; United
U.N., UN United Nations
Univ. University; Universal
unl. unlimited; unlisted (securities)
up., UP underproof (alcohols); upper
u.s. as above (ut supra)
U.S.A.F., USAF United States Air Force
U.S.A.R., USAR U.S. Army Reserve
U.S.C. U.S. Code; under separate cover
U.S.C.G. United States Coast Guard
U.S.D.J. United States District Judge
U.S.M.C. United States Marine Corps
U.S.N. United States Navy
U.S.N.R. United States Naval Reserve
U.S.P. United States Pharmacopoeia
U.S.R.S. U.S. Reclamation Service
U.S.S. United States Senate; United States Ship
U.S.S.R. Union of Soviet Socialist Republics
ut. utilities
U.T., UT, u.t. Universal time
ut dict., u.d. as directed (ut dictum)
U/w underwriter

V

v volt
v. verse (pl. vv.); verb; volume; versus
V. valve; velocity
va, v-a volt-ampere
vac. vacuum
val. value; valuation
var reactive volt-ampere
var. variety; various; variant; variation
V.C. Victoria Cross (Br.); Vice Consul
vel. velocity

Ven. Venerable
vert. vertical
v.f., VF video frequency; very fine
V.G. Vicar General; very good
VHF very high frequency
v.i. see below (L. vide infra)
Vice Adm., V.A., VAdm Vice Admiral
Vice Pres., V.P., V.Pres. Vice President
VIP very important person
vis. visibility (aviation); visual; (cap) Vista
visc. viscosity
viz namely (videlicet)
vol. volume; volunteer
vou. voucher
voy. voyage
v.p., vt.pl. voting pool (stocks)
V.P. Vice President
vs., v. against (versus); verse
v.s. see above (vide supra); volumetric solution
V.S. Veterinary Surgeon
Vt. Vermont (official)
v.t.c., vtc voting trust certificates (stocks)
vtg., vt. voting (stocks)
vv. verses
v.v. vice versa

W

w watt; week
W. west
W.a. with average (ins.)
WAC Women's Army Corps
war., wt., w. warrant (securities)
wb. wheelbase
WB waybill; westbound
w.d., wd when distributed (securities)
w.g. wire gauge
wh, w-hr., whr. watt-hour
whf. wharf
whge. wharfage
whs. warehouse
whsle. wholesale

whs.rec., W.R.   warehouse receipt
w.i., wi   when issued (securities)
W.I.   West Indies
Wis.   Wisconsin (official)
wk.   work; week
w.l.   wave length; water line
W.Long.   west longitude
w/m   weight and/or measurement
W.O., WO   Warrant Officer; wait order
w.p.   without prejudice; weather permitting
wpc., w/c   watts per candle
wpm   words per minute
w.p.p.   waterproof paper packing
w.r., wr   with rights (securities)
W.R., whs.rec.   warehouse receipt
wt.   weight; warrant
w.w., ww   with warrants (securities)
W/W   warehouse warrant

X

x   box(es); by; cross, as **X-roads, x-ref.**; extension (phone); extra, as **x-hvy., XL**
xc, xcp.   ex or without coupon (bonds)
Xch., X   exchange
xd. xdiv.   ex or without dividend (stocks)
x in.   ex or without interest (securities)
Xn.   Christian; **Xnty.**, Christianity
XP   monogram for Greek word for Christ
x pr.   ex or without privileges (securities)
XQ.   cross-question
xr, x rts.   ex or without rights (securities)
Xtal, xtl   crystal
xw   ex or without warrants (securities)

Y

yb.   yearbook
yd.   yard
yr., y.   year; your; younger

Z

z., Z   zone; zero; zenith distance

15. Troublesome Words and Phrases

About. *He will arrive at about nine o'clock* is not a correct sentence. Use at or about, but not both.

Adapt, Adopt. Adapt means to adjust. Adopt means to take as one's own.

> We must adapt to the changed conditions.
> The Board adopted the suggestion unanimously.

Adverse, Averse. Adverse means opposed or unfavorable; averse means disinclined toward.

> The Board's decision was adverse to the interests of labor.
> The Chairman is averse to criticism.

Affect, Effect. Affect is always a verb meaning to modify or influence. Effect may be noun or verb. As a verb it means to accomplish or bring about; as a noun, outcome or result. Both affect and effect are overworked, correctly and incorrectly.

All-around is not correct. Use all-round.

All of. Say *all the workers*, not *all of the workers*.

All Ready, Already. The first is an adjective phrase, correctly used in this sentence: *When the hour came, they were all ready*. The second is an adverb that oftener than not should be omitted: *We have (already) written a letter.*

Alternative, Choice. Alternative refers to two only; choice, to two or more. Since there is only one alternative to another, don't say *the only other alternative;* simply say *the alternative.*

Among, Between. Choose between two persons, but choose among three or more.

Amount, Number are often used loosely. An amount is a sum total; number, as a noun, refers to collective units. You have *an amount of money,* and *a number of errors.*

Anticipate means to foresee or prevent by prior action. Don't use it when you actually mean expect.

Anxious is proper only when anxiety actually exists. We are eager to write good letters, not anxious.

Any. Don't follow superlatives with any, as *Lincoln's letters are the best of any.* When used in a comparative statement, any must be followed by other, as *that letter is better than any other he has written.*

Any Place is not good usage. Say *anywhere.*

Appear. A woman appears to be young, but she seems to be intelligent. Appear usually suggests that which is visible.

Apt, Liable, Likely. Apt suggests a predisposition or tendency; liable implies unpleasant consequences; likely indicates simple probability. *A tactless person is apt to write a blunt letter,* but *a dishonest merchant is liable to be sued. Company presidents are likely to be male.*

Balance. You may have a balance on an account, but that which is left after something is taken away is a remainder, as *the remainder of the year, the remainder of the office force.*

Beside(s). Beside means at the side of; besides means in addition to.

Biannual, Biennial. Biannual, like semiannual, means twice a year. Biennial means every two years.

Bimonthly means every two months. Semimonthly is used to express twice monthly.

Bring, Take. Bring the book to me, but take the book to her.

Capital, Capitol. The capital is a city, the capitol a building. *Boston is the capital of Massachusetts, and the capitol has a gold dome.*

Claim. Do not use claim as an intransitive verb. Claim ownership, but don't claim to be efficient.

Compare, Contrast. Compare apples with oranges by noting that they are both round; contrast them by noting that they are of different colors.

Compare to, Compare with. Compare one person with another to note their similarities; contrast one person to another to note their differences.

Continuously, Continually. The first word means without interruption; the second, intermittently, at frequent intervals. *A man may drive continuously for ten hours,* but *he looks continually at his watch.*

Correspondent, Corespondent. A correspondent writes letters; a corespondent is a party in a divorce suit.

Council, Counsel. A council is a group or assembly; a counsel is a legal adviser or legal advice.

Different is superfluous in this sentence: *Six (different) plans were discussed at the meeting.*

Disinterested, Uninterested. Disinterested means impartial; uninterested means not interested. *A judge is disinterested while in court; he is uninterested in hockey.*

Disburse, Disperse. The first is to give or pay out; the second, to scatter. *The police disburse directions to travelers, but they disperse crowds of rioters.*

During suggests continuously, throughout. *In* (not during) *the meeting, he brought up the question of pay raises.*

Each, Every. You can't get between an *each* or an *every*. Say *between paydays,* not *between every payday.*

Each Other, One Another. Use each other when only two things are referred to; one another when more than two are referred to.

Emigrate, Immigrate. A man emigrates from a country, immigrates to a country.

Ended, Ending. Ended indicates past time; ending indicates present or future time: *the week ended March 31; the week ending today.*

Everyone, Every One. Use everyone only when everybody is meant. *Everyone attended the meeting, and they approved every one of the motions.*

Except, Accept. Except is to leave out, as *to except them from consideration.* Accept is to receive, as *to accept an appointment.*

Exceptional, Exceptionable. Exceptional means unusual; exceptionable means objectionable. *He is an exceptional man,* but *his drunken rantings are exceptionable.*

Expect, Suspect. Expect refers to likely occurrences; suspect indicates doubt or uncertainty. *We expect the truth in court,* but *we suspect a liar's testimony.*

Extant, Extent. Extant means still existing; extent refers to measurements of length.

Farther, Further. Farther indicates distance, further quantity or degree. You go *farther* away; you hear nothing *further.*

Few, Less. Few is for numbers; less is for quantities or amounts. *Write fewer pages and say less.*

First is both an adjective and an adverb. Don't say *firstly.*

Flammable and Inflammable are synonymous.

Following. *He retired after* (not following) *an outstanding career.*

Forward, Foreword. A foreword appears in the front of a book.

Full, Fulsome. Full means complete or up to the brim. Fulsome means stupid or offensive, as *fulsome comments* or *fulsome praise.*

Guarantee, Guaranty. For the verb, always use guarantee. As nouns, the two words can be used interchangeably.

Imply, Infer. The speaker implies, the hearer infers.

Ingenious, Ingenuous. An ingenious person is clever; an ingenuous one is naive and guileless.

Insure, Ensure. Insure refers to insurance, as health or life insurance. Ensure means to make sure. My home is insured for its full purchase price; this ensures my peace of mind.

Its, It's. The first is a possessive; the second a contraction. *Its highways are crowded: it's (it is) the rush hour.*

Kind, Sort. Avoid *kind of a* and *sort of a.* Instead of *kind of a machine* and *sort of a trap,* refer to a class of objects as *kind of machine* and *sort of trap.*

Kindly should not be used for please. *Please reply,* not *kindly reply.*

Last and Latest are not interchangeable. Last means final; latest, most recent. *The last page* of a book, but *the latest book on the market.*

Least is used when more than two persons or things have been mentioned. Use *less* when only two persons or things have been mentioned: *He is the less* (not *least*) *forceful of the two speakers.*

Like. Never use like to introduce a subject and its verb. *He wrote as* (not like) *he spoke.*

Meritorious, Meretricious. The first means praiseworthy; the second, tawdry or blameworthy.

Myself is a reflexive pronoun properly used in referring back to *I*. *I will do it myself,* but *He selected Joe and me* (not *myself*) *for the job.*

Near is incorrectly used in this sentence: *There is not near enough.* Use *nearly.*

None as a subject is usually plural unless a singular subject is clearly indicated. *None of the jobs are open. None of the work is done.*

Number. Treat *a number* as a plural noun and *the number* as a singular noun; *a number were,* and *the number was.*

One should be omitted in sentences like this: *The error is not the first one.*

Official, Officious. Official means authorized; officious, meddlesome or pompous.

Over should be avoided when you mean *more than* in referring to a number. *There were more than* (not *over*) *five hundred people at the meeting.*

Past. Say *last year,* not *past year,* if you mean the preceding year.

Perquisite, Prerequisite. Perquisites are privileges of office, such as limousines and stock options. Prerequisites are required preliminaries: *gumption is a prerequisite for success.*

Personnel, Personal. Personnel are the staff of an organization. Personal means private.

Practical, Practicable. A practicable plan is one that is capable of being accomplished. A practical plan is one that is accomplished efficiently and easily.

Precede, Proceed. Proceed at your own pace, but precede me into the building.

Prescribe, Proscribe. To prescribe is to order or dictate, as *a medical prescription.* To proscribe is to prohibit: *smoking in theatres is proscribed.*

Principal, Principle. The noun principal means head or chief, as well as capital sum. The adjective principal means highest or best in rank or importance. Principle means truth, belief, policy, conviction, or general theory.

Proven should not be used as the past participle of prove. Use proved. Proven may be used as an adjective.

Providing should not be used for if or provided. *Providing low-*

cost houses is a problem but *we will meet the problem provided the builders get supplies.*

Quite means really, truly, wholly, positively. Avoid its use in phrases like *quite a few* and *quite some*.

Rarely Ever, Seldom Ever. Ever is superfluous in phrases like these. Say *we seldom fail,* not *we seldom ever fail.*

Reason Is Because. Redundant. Say *because* or *reason is.*

Sensuous, Sensual. Sensuous appeals to the finer senses, sensual to the baser: sensuous poetry, sensual dancing.

Simple, Simplistic. Simple means easy. Simplistic means foolishly simple and unrealistic; *the junior congressman offered a simplistic plan for balancing the budget.*

Stationary, Stationery. The first means standing still; the second is writing paper.

Their, There, They're. They're (they are) going there (to that place) in their car.

Valuable, Invaluable. Valuable means worth a lot. Invaluable means worth even more, priceless.

Whose, Who's. Whose is a possessive; who's, a contraction. *Who's* (who is) *going to the store? Whose car shall we take?*

Your, You're. Your is a possessive; you're, a contraction. *You're* (you are) *carrying your suitcase.*

16. Numbers

When Numbers Should Be Spelled Out.

1. In modern business usage, most numbers are written as figures, not spelled out.

    24 cases 200 reams
    in 90 days not more than 3
    9 times 3 or 4 meetings

2. The number one is often written out to prevent confusion with the letter *I.*

    questionable: I ordered 1 lamp.
    better: I ordered one lamp.

3. If two sets of figures occur in a sentence, one set may be spelled out to differentiate it from the other.

    Three men worked 20 hours each; five worked 30 hours; and nine worked 35 hours.

4. When two numbers come together in a sentence, one of them may be spelled out to prevent confusion.

    I ordered 200, one hundred of which . . .

not
I ordered 200, 100 of which . . .

5. When two numbers apply to the same item, one of them is usually spelled out.

    two 5-inch pipes   three ⅜-inch tubes
    five $1 bills   2,750 three-way valves
    one 13¢ stamp   391 thirteen-cent stamps

6. Million and billion are often written out to avoid too many zeroes.

    2½ billion   *not* 2,500,000,000
    1.75 million   *not* 1,750,000

7. Legal documents often include both words and figures.

    fifteen (15) dollars, *not* fifteen dollars (15)
    twenty dollars ($20), *not* twenty ($20) dollars

8. Fractions standing alone are usually spelled out.

    three-fourths of an inch
    one-half inch, *or* half an inch
    one-third of a ream
    three-tenths of a mile

But when fractions do not stand alone, i.e., when they occur with other numerals or are used as modifiers, they are not spelled out.

    ½-inch tubing   ¾-point rise
    2½-yard penalty   ½ to 2½ months
    4¼ gallons   1½ times

Measurements and Time

Age:

52 years old
52 years 9 months 5 days (*no commas*)
a 5-year-old

a 10½-year-old edition
at the age of 15
when he died, aged 87
an 800-year-old statue

but

in her thirties
midforties
the eighties

Clock time:

5:30 p.m.
10 a.m., *not* 10:00 a.m.
3 in the afternoon, *not* 3 p.m. in the afternoon
10:35 in the morning
in the evening at 6, *not* in the evening at 6 p.m.
12 noon
12 midnight
7-o'clock train
7:00 train
half past 2
a quarter to 11
three-quarters of an hour

Periods of Time:

3 years 300 days 34 minutes
2 days 5 hours 55 minutes
90-day notes
5-year warranty
8-day-long strike
24-hour-a-day radio station
4½-hour meeting *or* four-and-one-half-hour meeting
6-day-a-week job

Dollars:

$750, *or* $750.00 (for exactness)
$10 bill, *not* 10-dollar bill
$250-a-week salary

$7 million investment
$10–$20, *not* $10–20
from $2 to $3
between $150 and $200
$13 million, *rather than* $13,000,000
$2.5 billion, *rather than* $2,500,000,000
$500,000 to $1 million
$100,000, *not* $100 thousand
$¾ million to $1½ million

Dates:

March 1980, *not* March, 1980
1960's or 1960s
the sixties, *preferred to* the '60s
the late fifties
the midforties
the summer of '45

Weight and Volume:

8 lbs. 5 oz. *or* 8 pounds 5 ounces (formal)
10-lb. sack *or* 10-pound sack
2-ton shipment
4½-ton truck
8-lb.-7-oz. baby
5-gal.-2-qt. container
6-cylinder engine
2000-bbl.-a-day flow *or* 2000-barrel-a-day flow

Percent:

10% *or* 10 percent (formal)
½ of 1%
20% pay raise
50% to 60% *preferred to* 50 to 60%

Dimensions:

6 by 9 inches *or* 6 × 9 in. *or* 6" × 9"
5 ft. 10 in. *or* 5'10"

10 ft. 6 in. *or* 10 feet 6 inches (formal)
10-foot pole, *not* 10' pole
one-inch screw, *preferred to* 1-inch screw
7-foot-long board
3-foot-deep snow
5-inch-diameter pipe *or* 5"-diameter pipe
6-foot-3-inch man
6-footer
3-mile-long runway
12-inch-wide paper *or* 12"-wide paper
½-inch pipe *or* ½" pipe
5-by-8-foot rectangle *or* 5' by 8' rectangle
3" × 5" cards *or* 3 × 5-inch cards
16-in.-by-5-ft. mirror

Plurals of Numbers

Plurals are formed by adding *s*.

2×4s *or* 2 × 4s
6s and 7s
L1101s; 767s
1950s
AT&T 8½s

Plurals of written-out numbers are formed regularly, not with *'s*.

two-by-fours, *not* two-by-four's
sixes and sevens, *not* six's and seven's
fifties

In formal or legal documents. When dates are written out in formal or legal documents, they follow the same rule.

nineteen hundred and eighty-one
seventeen hundred and seventy-six

Hyphenation of Written-out Numbers

In general. Numbers below 100 are hyphenated when written out, but hundreds and thousands are not hyphenated.

>twenty-five
>seventy-six
>sixty-seven thousand
>thirty-eight million
>eight hundred sixty-five
>two million forty-seven thousand

Hundreds and thousands *are* hyphenated when they appear in a modifier before a noun.

>a six-hundred-foot tower
>two-thousand-year-old scroll
>fifty-millionth hamburger
>two-hundred-and-seventy-fifth anniversary

Ordinals

Ordinal numbers are those ending with *th, rd, st,* etc. In normal business usage, they are not spelled out.

>1st
>2nd or 2d
>3rd or 3d
>4th
>   etc.

In formal usage, ordinals are often spelled out.

>the Eighty-seventh Congress
>the Fourteenth Amendment
>paragraph the fifth

Dates may be written as ordinals only when the number of the day precedes the month.

30th of June, *not* June 30th
1st of September, *not* September 1st
June 30 *rather than* June 30th
September 1 *rather than* September 1st

Special Secretarial Functions

17. Keeping Minutes of Meetings

The Purpose of Minutes

What the minutes contain. Minutes are records of meetings and of actions taken in them. Minutes are not a verbatim transcript of every word spoken at a meeting. They are a concise documentation of the essential matter discussed at each meeting. They tell where and when the meeting was held; those in attendance; motions made and voted upon; special elections; and the date of the next meeting.

Meetings requiring minutes. Minutes are kept of many meetings of corporations, professional organizations, civic organizations, and clubs. As a rule, the more important the meeting, the more necessary it is that accurate minutes be taken.

Assembling the Minutes of a Meeting

Note taking. The minutes are drafted from the notes which the secretary has taken during the meeting. Since the minutes are primarily concerned with what was done or accomplished at the meeting—not what was said—the secretary will often find much extraneous matter in his or her notes. The notes must be sifted carefully so that only the truly important matter is contained in the final draft of the minutes. The secretary should be alert to recognize and record all definite decisions; all actions taken and by whom; and all business left pending.

Obtaining information before the meeting. The secretary will find it easier to take the minutes if he or she has obtained relevant information before the meeting. Know the purpose of the meeting. Read copies of reports and resolutions to be presented at the meeting—so as to be familiar with all of the items on the agenda.

The secretary should also have a list of the persons to be present at the meeting. Simply check the names "p" or "a" (for present or absent) when the roll is called.

Information included in the minutes. The form of minutes varies from organization to organization. Corporate minutes follow the form set forth in the corporation's bylaws; or sometimes they follow the instructions given in corporation minute books. However, certain general information is included in almost all minutes:

1. Name of organization or body holding the meeting
2. Type of meeting: board, stockholders, annual, regular, committee, etc.
3. Place, date, and hour
4. Presiding officer
5. Names or number of those present. For small meetings—under 20 persons—the name of every member present is listed. For large meetings, the officers' names are listed, with a statement that the members present constitute a quorum.
6. Approval of the minutes of the previous meeting
7. Reports
8. Unfinished business
9. Elections
10. New business, such as motions made and resolutions adopted
11. Date and time of next meeting
12. Adjournment

Resolutions. Resolutions are made according to the rules of parliamentary procedure, that is, they are made, seconded, and voted on.

Resolutions can follow either a formal or an informal form. The formal form includes both a WHEREAS clause and a RESOLVED clause, while the informal form includes only the RESOLVED clause. WHEREAS and RESOLVED are always set in full capitals. The first word following WHEREAS is not capitalized, nor does any punctuation follow WHEREAS unless the sense of the sentence requires it. RESOLVED is followed by a comma, and the first letter of the following word is capitalized. The "Therefore be it" phrase is always set on the line above RESOLVED.

This is an example of a formal resolution:

WHEREAS it is now necessary ....; and
WHEREAS conditions warrant that ....; and
WHEREAS, in addition, the party ....; Therefore be it
RESOLVED, That .... ; and be it
RESOLVED further, That ....

Resolutions are always recorded verbatim.

An informal resolution dispenses with the WHEREAS clause and "Therefore be it." A simple statement is made to give the facts or events leading to the resolution, as follows:

...... after consideration, the following resolution was unanimously adopted:
RESOLVED, That ....

(or)

...... On motion duly made and seconded, the following resolution was made and adopted (with one abstention):
RESOLVED, First, that ....
              Secondly, that ....

Motions. Motions are made according to the rules of parliamentary procedure; that is, they are made, seconded, and voted upon.

The name of the person making the motion is usually recorded in the minutes (although some organizations dispense with this practice), but the name of the seconder is omitted. The secretary records whether the motion was carried, lost, referred to a committee, or tabled. If a motion is not seconded, it is not recorded. Only the main motions need be recorded verbatim.

If desired, you may also note the manner in which the motion was voted upon. Voting methods, in decreasing order of formality, are as follows: proxy; secret ballot; roll call; standing or rising to be counted; show of hands; voice ("All in favor say 'aye'."); and general assent. If the vote was by ballot or roll call, the secretary should record the number who vote, the number for the affirmative, and the number for the negative.

Reports. Note who presented the report and record the final action taken. The report itself is entered in the minutes in one of three ways, depending on the importance of the subject of the report:

1. A concise summary, with the name of the presenter of the report
2. A verbatim transcript of the report (usually used only for very short reports)
3. Reference to the subject of the report and notation that the entire report may be found in a certain file

Discussions and debates. If a discussion or debate takes place at the meeting, the secretary summarizes the main points—such as the principal "for" and "against" arguments. The names of the debaters may also be recorded.

Tone of the minutes. As the minutes are a brief and totally factual record of a meeting, they should contain no editorial comment by the secretary. Be objective; make no references to "heated" debate, "moving" addresses, or "lengthy" discussion.

Typing the minutes. The format of the minutes varies from organization to organization; minutes are occasionally typed on special preprinted forms. The following is a list of rules relating to the format of most minutes:

1. Capitalize and center the heading: date, time, place, and organization.
2. Indent the "present" and "absent" section 12 to 15 spaces.
3. Indent all paragraphs.
4. Double space the text.
5. Double space between paragraphs.
6. Triple space between each item in the order of business.
7. Single space resolutions and indent them 12 to 15 spaces.
8. Proper names are usually capitalized: Board, Directors, Corporation, Company, Committee, President, Chairman, Treasurer, Secretary.
9. Sums of money should be written first in words and then in figures in parentheses.
10. Number each page at the bottom of the page in the center.

After the Minutes Are Written

The minute book. Any looseleaf binder may be used to hold the minutes. However, the minutes of important meetings are usually kept in a regular locking minute book, available at office supply stores. The minute book should also contain a copy of the organization's Charter or Constitution; its Bylaws; and its Policies and Plans, if any.

Important minutes should be typed on special 28-lb. bond paper which may be printed on both sides. If you are using lighter paper, such as 20-lb. bond, type on one side of the paper only.

Distribution of the minutes. The secretary may duplicate and distribute the minutes before the next meeting if this is deemed desirable. Before duplication, the minutes are submitted to the presiding officer for a check of their accuracy and completeness. They are then distributed to all members of the group or committee. Thus, members who were absent from the meeting are informed of actions taken, and each member is reminded of the job he was assigned.

When minutes are distributed, there is then no need to spend time reading the minutes at the next meeting. The minutes may be approved immediately, either "as distributed" or "as corrected."

Approval of the minutes. If the minutes have not already been distributed, they are read aloud at the next meeting for the approval of the members. Corrections are then suggested, if necessary. If the meeting approves these corrections, they are inserted in the minutes in red ink. The minutes are then approved "as corrected."

Once the minutes have been approved, the secretary signs his or her name. (The words Respectfully Submitted are usually omitted today.) In addition, the word Approved, along with the date, is written at the left margin on the line below the signature.

Once the minutes have been approved and signed, they must never be changed or rewritten.

Sample Minutes

Below is an example of the minutes of a corporate board meeting. This will give you an idea of the general format for all typed minutes.

International Factors Corporation
Minutes of the Quarterly Meeting of the Board of Directors
Held, pursuant to due notice, in Board Room, Company Headquarters
Cincinnati, Ohio
Monday, January 14, 19—, 11:30 a.m.

Presiding: Mr. Alex J. Houghton, Chairman
Secretary: Leslie Michaelson

Present (constituting a quorum)

Messrs. Alvin R. Allen
George Peabody
Melville Bell
Ms. Nancy H. Dowd
Joseph Donaldson
Franklin Jones
Jay Erie Mathison
(left at 12 noon)

Absent

Messrs. Roger Forsythe
　　　　Peter J. Wilson
　　　　Henry Willingham
Also in attendance: Robert J. Townsend, Financial Consultant (12–12:30)

Minutes. The minutes of the quarterly Board meeting of October 15, 19— were approved as read (as previously circulated) (as corrected).

First Quarter Earnings Report. The Vice-President for Finance, Mr. Bell, reviewed the earnings statement for January 30. Earnings per share were $3.56 as compared to $3.06 for the comparable quarter last year, an increase of 16%. (Complete report in Finance files.)

Dividend. The Chairman suggested a dividend increase of 5 cents per share. Following discussion, the following resolution was adopted (with Mr. Bell dissenting, preferring no dividend increase):

　　RESOLVED, That a regular quarterly dividend of forty-five (45) cents per share be and hereby is declared on the common stock of the Corporation, payable April 15, 19— to stockholders of record at the close of business March 31, 19—.

Mr. Bell then left the room to notify the Exchange of said dividend action and to release it to the press.

New Accounting System. Mr. Townsend, the Financial Consultant, was then invited in by the Chairman to present his recommendation concerning the proposed change of FIFO to LIFO accounting. Mr. Townsend recommended that the change be made. (Complete report in Finance files.)

New Director. Mr. Peabody made a motion that Mr. Thomas J. French be elected the new member of the Board of Directors. The motion duly seconded, Mr. French was elected unanimously.

　　The Secretary was instructed to notify Mr. French of his election.

　　The meeting was adjourned at 2 p.m.

　　　　　　　　　　　　　　　　　　　　　　　　Secretary

18. Legal Secretarial Practice

Basic Law Office Procedures

Incoming mail. The mail must be opened, read, and annotated carefully. This is especially important in a law office, as the mail often includes legal documents which may be crucial to the legal cases that the office is handling. Three important points to observe are as follows:

1. On all legal papers, mark the date they were received in the office. Do not discard the envelope; clip it to its respective letter. The postmark on the envelope may occasionally be important evidence when a case comes to trial.
2. If a letter mentions enclosures, but the enclosures were not included, make a clear notation on the letter that the enclosures were missing when the letter was received.
3. All checks received in the mail should be photocopied, front and back. The copies are placed in their respective files.

Standard legal forms. One of the most important duties of the legal secretary is to be familiar with the many standard forms used in the law office. These forms are available from office supply stores; they are usually purchased in pads. If you are responsible for keeping a supply of these forms, you will need a reminder system to ensure that you reorder them frequently enough to keep the office from running out. One good system is to staple a marker one-quarter of the way from the end of each pad, thus indicating when it is time to reorder.

Legal filing. Many large law offices use the numerical filing system. Each case is given a number, and these numbers are then filed numerically. A log book is kept to indicate the names of the clients for each numbered case:

7454	Finchley, Gerald
7455	American Lighting Co.
7456	Jones, Shirley

Certain important information regarding each case should be noted on the cover of the file folder. This makes for quick and easy reference. The following information should appear on each file folder, either on the outside of the front cover of the folder or on the inside.

1. Client's name, address, and telephone number.
2. Names and telephone numbers of the other important people in the case: opposing attorneys, persons being sued, witnesses, etc.
3. A notation to tell whether the action is JURY or NON-JURY.
4. A log of proceedings to tell when each legal document has been served.
5. A record of disbursements which lists all sums spent by the law office on a particular case. This record includes the cost of postage and certified or registered mail, cost of making photocopies of documents, cost of process-serving, etc.

Law library. Every law office contains a collection of legal books. This is called the law library. It contains the basic laws pertaining to the office's practice, all revisions and additions to the laws, digests and abstracts of cases, legal opinions and court's decisions, and any other texts and cross-references that will be valuable to the office's attorneys.

One of the secretary's principal duties is to keep the law library up to date. Revisions, supplements, and pamphlets called "pocket parts" are constantly received from the publisher and must be filed immediately. All new revisions contain instructions on the front page pertaining to the cases or laws with which they should be filed. Pocket parts contain the same information. There is a pocket in the back of law documents and texts to contain these pamphlets. New pocket parts replace the old ones in the back pocket.

Dealing with clients. In talking with clients in person or on the telephone, the secretary should keep in mind the following:

1. All client-attorney relationships are totally confidential. You should not discuss them, even obliquely, outside the office or mention them in the presence of other clients.
2. The client should talk only to the attorney about his case. If the client talks extensively to you about his problems, do not be abrupt or rude but try to suggest that he save his confidences for the attorney.
3. Because of the emergencies that often crop up in client's cases, you should always know where to reach the attorney. When the attorney leaves the office for any reason, the secretary should know where he is going.

Office diary. The office diary contains all the important dates in the attorney's cases. These include dates of appointments, examinations, office visits, court appearances, motion dates, real estate closings, and all deadlines for filing pleadings and briefs. The diary must be accurate and up-to-date, as a missed court appearance or delayed filing can jeopardize a case.

Make pencil notations in the diary several days prior to each of the attorney's appointments. This will remind you to confirm the date with the attorney, with the client, and with the opposing attorney, if necessary.

Letters and correspondence. Each letter you type should have a notation giving the name of the case or subject referred to in the letter. In legal correspondence, this notation is usually in the form of a subject line below the inside address and above the salutation, as Re: Johnson vs. Keyes, or Re: Codicil to Will.

In the case of an important letter, where you want to be sure that the addressee actually receives the letter, use certified mail. Mark the letter CERTIFIED MAIL—RETURN RECEIPT RE-

QUESTED. Certified mail cards and receipts may be procured from the post office. Keep a supply on hand so that you do not have to go to the post office every time you want to send a certified letter.

The procedure for using certified mail is as follows:

1. Paste the certified number coupon on the envelope.
2. Type the number of the coupon on the return receipt card.
3. Type the name and number of the action on the return receipt card so there will be no confusion when the card is returned. This name and number should be on the side of the card where your return address is printed, so that the addressee will not see who the letter is from. If the addressee knew who the letter was from, he might refuse it.
4. Tape the return receipt card to the back of the envelope.
5. Attach the stub from the certified number coupon to your file copy of the letter. When the return receipt card is received, match up the coupon numbers.
6. If the letter is returned marked REFUSED, attach it, *unopened*, to your file copy of the letter. The returned letter may be needed for evidence in a court case.

Personal tickler file. Whenever you type a letter that requires an answer, make a note of the date of the letter in your tickler file. Go through the tickler file regularly to see which letters have received replies. If no answer has been received in the specified time, write again.

The tickler file may also be used for any other reminders that you feel would be useful. It is a handy place to keep a record of books that have been borrowed from the law library.

Time sheets. You must keep a record of the time the attorney spends on each client's case—especially the time actually spent with the client—so that the attorney will know how much to bill the client. Note also the amounts of time the attorney spends on the telephone with the client. Small time sheets are available in pads from office supply stores. Write the time and date on the time sheet and put it, together with all other time sheets, in the proper file folder.

Notary public. The legal secretary can become a Notary Public by taking a test administered by the Department of State, Division of Licensing Services. Since there are many legal documents that have to be notarized, it is a great convenience if the secretary is able to notarize them in her own office. The Division of Licensing Services will provide you with an application for the test and also with a preparation booklet.

Conforming copies. The legal secretary is regularly given legal documents and told to "conform the copies." This means that all copies must be made exactly identical to the original, including any insertions or deletions. Using the original as a guide, make all corrections on the copies, note any additions, and delete indicated material, so that the copies are all exact duplicates of the original.

Standard Legal Forms

Three of the most common activities in the law office are (1) litigation (that is, when one person sues another), (2) preparation of wills, and (3) real estate closings. Each of these activities requires the preparation of numerous legal forms. The following is a listing of the most common of these forms. Many of these forms are available on preprinted pads.

Retainer statement. This is the form in which the client "retains" the attorney, that is, hires him to represent him for a specified fee. Type this statement in duplicate: one is for your files, one for the client.

Request for Medical Report. This form is often used in the case of accidents, illnesses, or insurance problems. It authorizes the attorney to receive medical information pertaining to his client's case. (No doctor or hospital will release such information without the written authorization of the client.)

Type as many copies of this form as are needed; there may be more than one doctor or hospital involved. Each copy must be individually signed by the client.

Motor vehicle report. Any auto accident involving death, injury, or damage in excess of $100 must be reported to the Motor Vehicle Bureau of the state in which the accident occurred. You will need three copies: one for your files, one for the Motor Vehicle Bureau, and one for the client's insurance company.

Police Report. Whenever the police have been present at the scene of an accident, their report is basic to the trial. The Police Report form requests a copy of the patrolman's records from the Police Department. It must be signed by the client.

Claim letter. This is *not* a preprinted form but a short letter that advises the addressee that the client is bringing an action against him. Many law offices have a basic form letter that may be easily adapted for each individual case. This is a common form:

> Please be advised that we are the attorneys for .... (name of client) .... who was caused to suffer personal injuries and/or property damage as a result of .... (describe accident or other problem) .... If you are insured, please turn this letter over to your insurer so that the matter may be adjusted amicably. If you are not insured, kindly contact us so we can discuss the matter.

Summons. The Summons notifies the person named therein, the defendant, that he is being sued. It commands him to appear in court to answer the charges.

There are many different forms of Summonses. They are all available in preprinted forms. If there is more than one defendant, type enough copies for all of them, as they must each be summoned individually. Depending on the state in which your law office is located, the Summons is either signed by the attorney or his name is simply typed in.

Complaint. The Complaint accompanies the Summons; it tells the defendant in detail why he is being sued. The Complaint is usually not a preprinted form. It is dictated by the attorney and follows a standard pattern. The parts of the Complaint are as follows:

1. Jurisdiction and Venue. These are the names of the court and the county in which the suit is to be tried. They differ in form in various states, but a sample jurisdiction line would be CIVIL COURT OF THE STATE OF NEW YORK and a sample venue line COUNTY OF RICHMOND. The jurisdiction and venue are typed in full capitals in the upper left corner of the Complaint.

2. Title of the Action. This gives the names of the plaintiff(s) and defendant(s). It appears below the jurisdiction and venue lines in the upper left corner of the Complaint. Personal names are typed in full capitals.
3. Title of the Pleading. This tells what the document is, i.e., a Complaint. The usual heading is VERIFIED COMPLAINT, and it is typed opposite the jurisdiction, venue, and title of the action in the upper right corner of the Complaint.
4. First paragraph of the Complaint. This is a brief introduction that starts the Complaint as follows:

> JOHN JONES, plaintiff, by HOWARD HINCHLEY, his attorney, complaining of SAM SMITH, defendant, herein alleges:

5. Body of the Complaint. This is the main part of the Complaint. It gives the full details of the action and is dictated by the attorney. Each basic detail of the action is numbered. If there is more than one plaintiff, there will be more than one "cause of action." Each cause of action has a separate heading typed in full capitals and centered on the page, as follows:

> AS AND FOR A FIRST CAUSE OF ACTION, PLAINTIFF JOHN JONES ALLEGES

6. WHEREFORE clause. This is the last paragraph of the Complaint, in which the plaintiff demands judgment against the defendant and states the amount of the damages that he is demanding. This paragraph is not numbered. WHEREFORE is always typed in full capitals.
7. Signature and date. The Complaint is signed by the attorney or the plaintiff. The date is included along with the attorney's telephone number, county, and state.

CIVIL COURT OF THE STATE OF -------
COUNTY OF ---------

JOHN JONES and SUSAN JONES,

                Plaintiff   VERIFIED COMPLAINT

    -against-

SAM SMITH,

                Defendant

    Plaintiff, by HOWARD HINCHLEY his attorney, complaining of the defendant, alleges:

AS AND FOR A FIRST CAUSE OF ACTION, PLAINTIFF JOHN JONES ALLEGES

1.
2.
3.

AS AND FOR A SECOND CAUSE OF ACTION, PLAINTIFF SUSAN JONES ALLEGES

1.
2.
3.

WHEREFORE, plaintiffs demand...........................
....

                    ....
                    Attorney for Plaintiffs

Verification. The verification is the form in which the plaintiff swears that his allegations, to the best of his knowledge, are true. The plaintiff must swear to the verification on oath before a Notary Public.

The *jurat* clause appears at the end of the verification and states when, where, and before whom the verification was sworn:

Sworn to before me this
_____day of_____, 19___.

Wills

There are many types of wills, but the formal will, drawn according to the laws of the state in which the testator resides, is the most common. To be legally valid, the will must be very carefully drawn up and typed. These are the points to keep in mind:

1. If at all possible, wills should be typed so that there are no erasures and corrections. If there are any erasures or corrections, they must be initialed by the testator (the person who makes the will) when he signs the will.
2. Type only the original of the will; type no copies. *After* the will is signed (executed), make two photocopies; one of these is for the office files, the other for the testator.
3. Double-check the spelling of all names and addresses. The will may not be valid unless these items are correctly spelled.
4. Do not staple the pages of the will together. After you have typed the will, give the loose pages to the attorney. He will staple them together after reading the will carefully. Once the will has been stapled together, it must NEVER be unstapled. A will that has been taken apart is liable to be contested.
5. The testator must read the will carefully before signing it. If any changes are to be made, the testator, the attorney, and the witnesses must initial each correction.
6. Wills are double-spaced, with triple-spacing between paragraphs.
7. Type all proper names in full capitals.
8. The usual heading, centered at the top of the first page and

typed in full capitals, is LAST WILL AND TESTAMENT.
9. Each paragraph of the body of the will is preceded, respectively, by *FIRST:*, *SECOND:*, *THIRD:*, etc. Note that each numbered word is typed in full capitals and followed by a colon.
10. Leave at least five spaces before the first word of the sentence which begins after *FIRST:*, *SECOND:*, *THIRD:*, etc.
11. The last sentence of the will concludes with a phrase giving the date of the signing of the will. Type it as follows: "This . . . . day of . . . ., 19 . . . . . " The testator will write in the date when he signs the will.
12. Three lines below the date, type a line for the testator's signature—use the underscore key.
13. The abbreviation (L.S.) in parentheses should immediately follow the signature line. It stands for *locus sigilli*, meaning "the place for the seal."
14. The "attestation clause" is the final portion of the will. It contains the space for the signatures of the witnesses. The attestation clause may sometimes be typed in single-space, unlike the body of the will. (The attorney will instruct you.)
15. If there is not room for the entire attestation clause on the final page of the will, include at least one line of the clause on this page and carry over the rest of it to another page. This guarantees continuity and indicates that no pages have been taken out or inserted.
16. After typing the will, proofread every word. The safest proofreading method is to have one person read aloud from the draft of the will while another simultaneously checks the original.

Real Estate

Representing the seller of a piece of property. When your client sells a piece of property, your office will be responsible for drawing up the contract of sale. Your file folder on the transaction should contain the name, address, and telephone numbers of the following people: the client (seller), the purchaser, the purchaser's attorney, and the broker (if any) who arranged the sale.

The Contract of Sale. The Contract of Sale is the principal legal document involved when a piece of property changes hands. Rules for typing a Contract of Sale are as follows:

1. Type one original, plus copies for: (1) your files, (2) the purchaser's attorney, (3) the title company, if any, and (4) the bank or other lending institution.
2. Type all proper names in full capitals.
3. Include zip codes with all addresses.
4. Type the description of the piece of property without errors exactly as it appears on the Deed. Descriptions tend to be complex and confusing; it may help to use a ruler to follow along, line by line, so that you do not make any transpositions or typographical errors.
5. Descriptions of property are usually typed single-space, with double-spacing between paragraphs.
6. Do not use abbreviations like *St.*, *Ave.*, or *Blvd.*, unless the document you are copying from uses these forms.
7. The description of the property on the Deed may not include the street address. If the attorney instructs you to add the street address to the description, it should be placed in a new paragraph, beginning as follows:

    SAID PREMISES being known as and by street number_____.

8. If the attorney dictates SUBJECT clauses to add to the Contract of Sale, each clause should form its own paragraph beginning with the words SUBJECT TO.
9. If the property is being sold by a corporation, prepare the signature as follows:

    ABC CORPORATION
    by_____
    (title of officer)

10. If you are using a printed form, do not forget to complete the back of the form.
11. Proofread the contract, especially the description of the property. Do not read it alone. Have someone else in the office read from your typed page while you compare it to the original.

Legal Terminology

Abstract of title
A chronological listing of all instruments and proceedings which affect the title to a piece of property.

Ad damnum
The "ad damnum" is that part of a writ which states the amount of money that the plaintiff is claiming in damages. (Ad damnum means "to the damage.")

Adverse possession
A conclusive presumption of title in the possessor from which he cannot be ousted.

Affiant
One who voluntarily swears to a written statement.

Affidavit
Any written declaration made voluntarily and sworn under oath.

Appeal
A petition by one party to a legal action to a higher court for a review of a decision made by a lower court.

Appellant
The person who appeals a case to a higher court.

Appurtenance
Anything which is annexed to, attached to, or closely related to a piece of real property.

Arraignment
The calling of the defendant to the court to answer the accusation contained in the indictment.

Assignee
A person to whom some right or property has been assigned.

Assignor
Any person who assigns some right or property.

Attachment
An authorization or an order for the seizure of an asset or property for the purpose of satisfying a court judgment.

Beneficiary
Any person who receives the benefits or advantages of some action, such as insurance policy or trust.

Binder
An agreement to pay a down payment for the purchase of real estate as evidence of good faith on the part of the purchaser.

Caveat
   A written warning to a judicial officer to suspend a proceeding until the notifier is given a hearing.
Certiorari
   A writ issued by a higher court directing a lower court to send to the higher court all records of a proceeding (either in process or terminated) so the higher court may review the legality of the procedure or decision of the lower court.
Chattel
   Any personal possession or movable goods.
Close
   To complete a transaction involving real property between buyer and seller.
Codicil
   An addition to a will which supplements or modifies its terms.
Complainant
   Any person who alleges that he has been damaged; plaintiff.
Conservator
   Any person or institution who protects and directs another's interests.
Consideration
   Anything of value which one person gives to another person to induce that person to enter into a contract.
Contest
   To dispute an action by another party.
Conveyance
   A transfer of title of property from one owner to another.
Countersign
   To add the signature of a second person to a document.
Court of record
   The particular court in which written documents are filed and where all proceedings are recorded.
Covenant
   A document promising performance or nonperformance of an action.

Defeasance
   Any instrument which voids another.
Defendant
   The person who is sued or called to answer in any civil or criminal action.

Demurrer
: A plea whereby the defendant admits the facts alleged by the plaintiff but denies that these facts constitute sufficient cause for action against him.

Deponent
: One who gives evidence or makes a sworn statement.

Deposition
: A witness' testimony taken by an officer of a court but not given in open court.

Detainer
: A writ or order which withholds property from its rightful owner.

Distributee
: An heir; one who receives a distribution from an estate.

Domicile
: A person's legal residence.

Dower rights
: A widow's rights to the estate of her late husband.

Duress
: Unlawful coercion to deprive a person of the use of his free will.

Earnest money
: Money paid by a purchaser of real estate as evidence of good faith.

Easement
: The right to use another's land for a special purpose.

Encumbrance
: Any charge, lien, or fee against real property.

Enjoin
: To order a person to perform or to cease performing any particular act.

Escheat
: The government's right to claim an estate when there is no one legally entitled to claim it.

Escrow
: An agreement delivered by a grantor to a third party, to be held by the third party until a certain action has been performed; then the agreement is delivered to the grantee.

Estoppel
: The prevention or barring of a person from asserting (or denying) a fact which is a result of his own prior statements or actions.

Fee simple
   Absolute title to land or property.

Garnishee
   A person who holds money or property which belongs to a defendant or to a debtor whose property has been attached.
General release
   An instrument which frees a party from all possible claims resulting from a legal action.
Guarantee
   A person who is assured as to the condition of property or goods he has received.
Guaranty
   An assurance as to the condition of property or goods.

Habeas corpus
   A writ commanding one who detains another to produce him before the court.
Habendum clause
   Also called the "to have and to hold" clause; defines the quantity of an estate granted in the premises of the deed.
Holograph
   Any legal document written entirely by hand of the testator.

In common
   Shared together; held by several for the equal use of all.
Instrument
   Any legal document designed to bring about the rights of the parties to an action.
Intervener
   A third party who becomes (voluntarily) a party to an action involving two other persons.
Intestate
   Deceased without making a will.

Joint tenancy
   Ownership of property by two or more persons, each of whom has an interest with the right of survivorship.
Jurat
   The final clause of an affidavit or will, which states when, where, and before whom the document was sworn.

Jurisdiction
: The territory over which a court has the legal authority to try a case, decide an issue, and enforce a decision.

Legatee
: A person who receives an inheritance from a will.

Lessee
: A renter of a piece of property.

Lessor
: Owner or landlord of a piece of property.

Lien
: A claim or other legal right which a creditor has against a specific piece of property of the debtor; the creditor may attach the property until the debt is satisfied.

Lis pendens
: A notice of warning that the title to a certain property is under litigation.

Mandamus
: A court order which orders an official to enforce a judgment of the court.

Metes and bounds
: The boundary line of pieces of property, including their terminating points or angles.

Nolo contendere
: A plea of no contest (meaning "I will not contest it").

Party of the first part
: The lessor or seller; the party named first in a contract.

Party of the second part
: The lessee or buyer; the party named second in a contract.

Per stirpes
: Distribution of the estate of a deceased heir.

Prima facie
: A piece of information presumed to be true unless disproved by an indication to the contrary.

Proviso
: A limitation or stipulation that qualifies the terms of a prior basic agreement.

Real property
: Land; and whatever is erected on it.

Recordation
: An official record in the county records of the full text of a legal document, especially regarding the sale of property.

Release
: A document by which a claim is surrendered or an obligation released.

Residuary
: The amount remaining in an estate after dispositions.

Res judicata
: A settled case (meaning "a suit already judged").

Restraining order
: A court injunction which forbids a person to do a certain thing.

Scilicet (ss)
: Latin for "that is to say."

Scire facias
: A writ requiring a defendant to show cause why the plaintiff should not have access to certain records.

Subrogation
: The substitution of one person for another.

Summons
: A document commanding a defendant to appear in court.

Testator
: The maker of a will.

Title
: Evidence of ownership.

Tort
: A wrong or injury to a person which provides grounds for legal action.

Venue
: The place where the case is to be tried.

Writ
: A legal instrument issued by a court in the name of the state; it commands the person named to appear in court or to perform some specific act.

19. Medical Secretarial Practice

Special Concerns of the Medical Secretary

Although many of the day-to-day duties of the medical secretary are the same as those of the regular office secretary, he or she also has certain additional important concerns. The medical secretary must work closely with doctors, either in private offices or in hospitals or public agencies, and must see to it that he or she has a clear understanding of the doctor's work.

Probably the single most important attribute of a good medical secretary is a thorough familiarity with medical terminology. Medical terms are often difficult and sometimes confusing, and a medical dictionary is the medical secretary's constant companion. A basic listing of medical terms may be found on pp. 370–77.

Medical ethics. The medical secretary must be familiar with (and always observe) certain principles of medical ethics. These are as follows:

1. Never discuss a patient's affairs outside the doctor's office. A patient's dealings with the doctor are completely confidential.
2. It is considered unethical for a doctor to treat a patient who is already being treated by another doctor for the same con-

Medical Secretarial Practice

dition. If you learn of such a situation, you should notify your employer at once.

3. If a patient is referred to your office by another doctor and the patient tells you that he does not intend to return to the doctor who referred him, tell your employer. It would be considered unethical for your employer to keep the patient under such conditions; he will have to discuss the matter with the patient.
4. Do not criticize a doctor to a patient.
5. Do not undertake any actions that might be construed as advertising your employer's services.

Medical etiquette. In addition to the rules of medical ethics, certain practices are traditionally observed by doctors in their dealings with other doctors. Several of these practices affect the medical secretary, as follows:

1. Do not send a bill to another doctor (or members of his family) unless your employer expressly tells you to do so; doctors traditionally do not charge each other for their services.
2. Do not keep a doctor waiting in your reception room. Let him see your employer as soon as possible, even if patients must be kept waiting.
3. When a doctor calls your office, do not ask him what he is calling about. Connect him immediately to your employer.

Medical Forms with Which You Should Be Familiar

The medical secretary is responsible for the preparation and/or typing of numerous medical forms and reports. Many of these forms, such as the medical history sheet or the blood pressure chart, are available in preprinted form and need only be filled in by the secretary. Others may be dictated in full by the doctor. The following are the most important of these forms and reports.

Admission Record. When a patient enters a hospital, an admission sheet is filled out. This sheet provides a record of basic information about the patient, such as his name, address, telephone number; resident doctor; insurance coverage; tentative diagnosis, etc. If the patient is under the age of twenty-one, the signature of a witness must appear along with that of the patient (the secretary often acts as witness).

Medical History. The secretary types the medical history from the doctor's notes; it is usually typed on a preprinted form. It contains all pertinent information about the patient's past health record; family and social history; findings of the current examination and any other current symptoms.

Physical Examination Record. A complete record of the patient's current condition.

Medical Summary. When a patient enters a hospital or is treated by a specialist, the hospital or specialist prepares a medical summary after the patient is treated and sends it to the doctor who referred the patient in the first place: it tells the doctor what happened to his patient. The Medical Summary is divided into the following sections: identifying data: final diagnosis: introductory sentence: history: physical examination: laboratory data: consultations: hospital course: final comment and recommendations. Each of these sections is typed as a single paragraph; at the end of the summary, type the dictating doctor's name for signature.

Treatment record. This is a chronological record of all treatments (including drugs) which a hospital patient has received. Dates and times are noted, as well as the initials of the nurse who administered the treatment.

Progress Notes. This is a record of the patient's day-by-day condition, including all hospital treatments and the patient's reactions.

Report on Electrocardiogram. This short report is usually dictated to the secretary by the cardiologist and contains all pertinent results of a patient's electrocardiogram.

Consultation Sheet. When the doctor in charge of a case wishes to get the opinion of another doctor, he completes a consultation sheet which gives details of the patient's condition. This sheet is then submitted to the consultant, who writes down his own opinion of the case.

Report of X-Ray Exam. When an x-ray examination is conducted by an x-ray technician or roentgenologist, a complete report of the findings is dictated to the secretary.

Pathology Report. After an operation, a sample of the organ or tissue involved is sent to the pathology lab for further testing or microscopic examination. This form records the results of that examination or test.

Operation and Anesthesia Record. A complete record is always made of a patient's condition before, after, and during the operation. It is then dictated to the secretary or recorded for her to transcribe.

Report of Postmortem Examination. When the coroner orders an autopsy in the case of unusual or suspicious death, the postmortem report is prepared by the examining doctor. It is then dictated to the secretary.

Problems in Medical Dictation

Since dictation is taken phonetically, the secretary may not know how to spell the words she has taken down in shorthand.

Many medical terms are derived from Latin and Greek roots, and their spelling may not follow their pronunciation. For example, the Greek letter rho is pronounced r in English but spelled rh, as in hemorrhage. In many cases when you cannot find a word in the dictionary spelled with an r, you will find it under rh.

The following list gives some other commonly encountered phonetic sounds and their proper spelling.

PHONETIC SOUND	SPELLING	EXAMPLES
i	y	cyst; cyanide
f	ph	phenol
k	c or ch	colon; choluria
loo	leu	leukocytes

370   SPECIAL SECRETARIAL FUNCTIONS

noo	pneu	pneumonia
r	rh or rrh	rheumatic; gonorrhea
s	c, sc, or ps	cilia; sciatica; psychosis
sh	sc	fascia
t	pt	ptomaine
th	phth	phthalate

Medical terms, Prefixes, and Suffixes

TERM	MEANING
acou-, acu-	Hear
aden-	Gland
-aemia	Condition of the blood
aesthesio	Sensation
-algia, -algy	Pain
aqua-	Water
anesthesiology	Branch of medicine dealing with anesthesia
alve-	Channel or cavity
amyl-	Starch
angi-	Vessel
ankyl-	Crooked or looped
arter(i)-	Artery
arth(r)-	Joint
articul-	Joint
aur-	Ear
-blast-	A growing thing in its early stages
blep-	Look or see
blep(har)-	Eyelid
brachi-	Arm
brachy-	Short
brady-	Slow
bronch-	Windpipe
bucc-	cheek
carcin-	Cancer

cardi-	Heart
cardiology	Branch of medicine dealing with the heart and its diseases.
-cele	Hernia
cente-	Puncture
cephal-	Head
cerebr-	Brain
cervic-	Neck
cheil-	Lip
cheir-, chir-	Hand
chol-	Bile
chondr-	Cartilage
-clasis	Breaking
-cleisis	Closure
coel-, cel-	Hollow
colp-	Vagina
cost-	Rib
crani-	Skull
cyst-	Bladder
-cyst	Sac containing water
-cyte	Hollow vessel
dacry-	Tear
dactyl-	Finger or toe
dent-	Tooth
derm-	Skin
dermatology	Branch of medicine dealing with the skin and its diseases
dextr-	Right hand
didym-	Twin
digit-	Finger or toe
diplo-	Double
-dynia	Painful
dys-	Difficult or painful
ect-	Outside
-ectasia, -ectasis	Dilation or stretching
-ectomy	Removal
ede-	Swell
end(o)-	Inside or within

372 SPECIAL SECRETARIAL FUNCTIONS

endocrinology	Branch of medicine dealing with the glands and their diseases
entero-	Intestine
epi-	Upon
erythr-	Red
eso-	Inside
-esthesia	Sensation
ex(o)-	Outside
fibr-	Fiber
fract-	Break
front-	Forehead or front
galact-	Milk
gangli-	Swelling
gastr-	Stomach
gastroenterology	Branch of medicine dealing with the stomach and intestines
gloss-, glott-	Tongue
glyc-	Sweet
-gram	Tracing or picture
gyn-	Woman
Gynecology	Branch of medicine dealing with diseases of women
haem-	Blood
hem-	Blood
hemi-	Half
hepat-	Liver
hetero-	Different
hex(a)-	Have, hold, or be
hist-	Tissue
homeo-	Similar
hydro-	Water
hyper-	Too much
hypn-	Sleep
hypo-	Lack of
hyster-	Uterus
-ia	Disease

Medical Secretarial Practice 373

ile-	Ileum (intestines)
infra-	Below
inter-	Between or among
intra-	Within or inside
is-	Equal
ischi-	Hip
-itis	Inflammation
jejun-	Hungry
kerat-	Cornea
labi-	Lip
lact-	Milk
laryng-	Windpipe
laryngology	Branch of medicine dealing with the throat and its diseases
leuk-	White
li-	Fat
lien-	Spleen
lig-	Bond or tie
-lith-	Stone
-logy	Study of
lumb-	Loin
lymph-	Water
-lysis	Disintegration or dissolving
macr-	Large
mal-	Bad
mania	Madness
mast-	Breast
mega-	Large
men-	Month
mening-	Membrane
mes-	Middle
metr-	Womb
micro-	Small
mon(o)-	Only
morph-	Form or shape
my(o)-	Muscle

SPECIAL SECRETARIAL FUNCTIONS

myel-	Marrow
myx-	Mucus
ne(o)-	New or young
nephr-	Kidney
neur-	Nerve
neurology	Branch of medicine dealing with the nerves and brain
obstetrics	Branch of medicine dealing with pregnancy
ocul-	Eye
odont-	Tooth
-oid	Like or similar
olig(o)-	Few; less than usual
-ology	Study of
-olus	Diminution
-oma	Tumor
oncology	Branch of medicine dealing with tumors
oo-	Egg
ophthalmology	Branch of medicine dealing with the eye and its deformities.
-opia	Sight or vision
or-	Mouth
orchi-	Testicle
-orexia	Appetite or desire
ortho-	Straight or normal
orthopedics	Branch of medicine dealing with the correction of deformities
-oscopy	Inspection of
-ose	Sugar
-osis	Disease
oss-	Bone
ost(e)-	Bone
-ostomy	Making an opening
ot-	Ear
otolaryngology	Branch of medicine dealing with the ear, nose, and throat
otology	Branch of medicine dealing with the ear

-otomy	Cutting or incision
ov-	Egg
pan-	All or every
par(a)-	Beside
path-	Disease
pathology	Branch of medicine dealing with disease
pediatrics	Branch of medicine dealing with children
per-	Through
peri-	Around
-pexy	Fixation
-phagia	Eating
pharmac-	Drug
pharyng-	Throat
-phasia	Speech
phleb-	Vein
-phobia	Fear of
phren-	Mind; midriff
-plasia	Excessive growth
-plasty	Forming or repair
-plegia	Paralysis
-pne(u)-	Breathing
pneumat-	Breath; air
pneumo(n)-	Lung
pod-	Foot
poly-	Many
post-	After
postero-	Behind
proct-	Rectum
proctology	Branch of medicine dealing with the rectum and its diseases
pseud-	False
psych-	Mind
-ptosis	Falling of
pulmo-	Lung
py(o)-	Pus
radiology	Branch of medicine dealing with x-rays

ren-	Kidneys
retro-	Backwards
rhin-	Nose
Rhinology	Branch of medicine dealing with the nose and its diseases
-(r)rhag-	Break or burst
-rhaphy	Sewing up
-(r)rhea	Discharge or flow
salping-	Tube
sanguin-	Blood
sarc-	Flesh
scler-	Hard
-scopy	Visual examination
-sect	Cutting
semi-	Half
spin-	Spine
splen-	Spleen
-spasm	Convulsion
sphygm-	Pulsation
-stasis	Stopping or stagnation
steno-	Narrow or contracted
stom(a)-	Mouth or orifice
-stosis	Standing still
-stomy	Opening
strep-	Twisted
sub-	Under or below
super-	Above; extreme
supra-	Above or upon
syn-, syl-, sym-	With or together
-taxis	Arrangement
therap-	Treatment
therm-	Heat
thorac-	Chest
thromb-	Clot
-tomy	Cutting or incision
tox-	Poison
-tripsy	Crushing
trache-	Windpipe
trans-	Across

trich-	Hair
-troph-	Nutrition
-ulent	Full of
ultra-	Beyond
-uria	Urine
urology	Branch of medicine dealing with urine and the urinary tract
vas-	Vessel
ventro-	Belly
zo-	Life
zyg-	Union or yoke

Medical Abbreviations

aa.	equal parts of each
a.c.	before meals (ante collation)
ad lib.	at pleasure
adv.	against
alt. dieb.	alternate days
alt. hor.	alternate hours
alt. noct.	alternate nights
a.p.	front to back (antero-posterior)
aq.	water
aq. dest.	distilled water
ASHD	arteriosclerotic heart disease
A.V.	atrioventricular; auriculoventricular
av.	average; avoirdupois
A.Z.	Aschheim-Zondek (test for pregnancy)
Baso.	Basophil
B.E.	Barium enema
bib.	drink
b.i.d.	twice a day
B.M.R.	basal metabolic rate
B.P.	blood pressure
B.S.	blood sugar
BSP	bromsulphalein
BUN	blood urea nitrogen

378 SPECIAL SECRETARIAL FUNCTIONS

C.	Centigrade; closure; contraction
c̄	with
Ca.	carcinoma
caps.	capsules
CBC	complete blood count
cc.	cubic centimeter
cf.	to bring together or compare
Cg., Cgm.	centigram
cm.	centimeter
C.M.	tomorrow morning
c.m.s.	to be taken tomorrow morning
C.N.	tomorrow night
C.N.S.	central nervous system
cont.	bruised
Contin.	let it be continued
coq.	boil
Cs.	conscious
C.S.F.	cerebrospinal fluid
CST	convulsive shock therapy
C.V.	cardiovascular; tomorrow evening
CVA	cerebrovascular accident
D.	dose; give; distal; dorsal; duration
d.	daily
d.d.	let it be given to
D&C	dilatation and curettage
decub.	lying down
dil.	dilute
div.	divide
D.O.A.	dead on arrival
dr.	dram(s)
D/S or D&S	dextrose and saline
d.t.d.	give of such a dose
DTRs	deep tendon reflexes
D/W or D&W	dextrose and water
Dx.	diagnosis
EEG	electroencephalogram
EENT	eye, ear, nose, and throat
EKG	electrocardiogram
EOM	extraocular muscles

Eos.	Eosinophils
ESR	erythrocyte sedimentation rate
ext. or extr.	extract
ext. fl.	fluid extract
F.	Fahrenheit; formula
FB	fingerbreadth
FBS	fasting blood sugar
fl.	fluid
fl. oz.	fluid ounce
f. pil	let pills be made
F&R	force and rhythm (pulse)
fract. dos.	in divided doses
ft.	let there be made
ft. pulv.	let a powder be made
FUO	fever of undetermined origin
G.	gram
G.B.	gall bladder
G.I.	gastrointestinal
gm.	gram
gr.	grain
gt., gtt.	drop, drops
GTT	glucose tolerance test
g.u.	genitourinary
GYN	gynecology
H.	hydrogen; hour
Hb.	hemoglobin
Hct.	hematocrit
h.d.	at bedtime
hpf.	high-power field
h.s.	at bedtime (hour of sleep)
I.M.	intramuscular
In.d.	daily
inj.	injection
I.V.	intravenous
kg.	kilogram
k.j.	knee jerk

SPECIAL SECRETARIAL FUNCTIONS

k.k.	knee kicks
K.U.B.	kidney, ureter, and bladder
L.	liter
LBD	left border dullness
L.D.	lethal dose
L.E.	left eye
lig.	ligament
L.L.Q.	left lower quadrant
L.U.Q.	left upper quadrant
L.M.P.	last menstrual period
Lymphs	lymphocytes
M.	mix
m.	meter; minimum
m.b.	mix well
mc.	milicurie
m.eq.	milliequivalents
mg.	milligram
mHg.	millimeters of mercury
min.	minim
M.L.	midline
ml.	milliliter
M.M.	mucous membranes
mm.	millimeter
M.S.L.	midsternal line
M.T.	membrana tympani
Muc.	mucilage
N.	nitrogen
N.A.D.	no appreciable disease
no.	to the number of
Noct.	at night
N.P.N.	nonprotein nitrogen
N.Y.D.	not yet diagnosed
O.	eye
O.B.	obstetrics
O.D.	right eye
o.h.	every hour

o.m.	every morning
omn. hor	every hour
o.n.	every night
O.P.D.	outpatient department
O.S.	left eye
ov.	ovum
oz.	ounce
P.	pulse
P.A.	postero-anteriorly
p.a.	in equal parts
P&A	percussion and auscultation
PBI	protein-bound iodine
p.c.	after meals
P.E.G.	pneumoencephalography
P.H.	past history
P.I.	protamine insulin
PID.	pelvic inflammatory disease
P.M.I.	point of maximal impulse
P.M.N.	polymorphonuclear neutrophil leukocytes
P.O.	orally
Polys.	polymorphonuclear cells
p.r.n.	as needed
PSP	phenolsulfonphthalein
P.X	physical examination
q.	every
q.d.	every day
q.h.	every hour
q.i.d.	four times a day
q.l.	as much as you please
q.p.	at will
q.q.h.	every four hours
q.s.	quantity sufficient
q.2h.	every two hours
R.	respiration
RBC	red blood count
R.L.L.	right lower lobe
RLQ	right lower quadrant

382 SPECIAL SECRETARIAL FUNCTIONS

R.M.L.	right middle lobe
RUQ	right upper quadrant
S. or Sig.	give the following directions
Sol.	solution
S.O.S.	if it is necessary
S.R. or Sed Rate	sedimentation rate
ss.	one half
stat.	immediately
syr.	syrup
T.	temperature
Tabs.	tablets
T&A	tonsils and adenoids
t.i.d.	three times daily
tr.	tincture
ult. praes.	last prescribed
URI	upper respiratory infection
U.S.P.	United States Pharmacopeia
var.	variety
W.B.C.	white blood count
W.R.	Wassermann reaction
Z.	contraction

Useful Information

20.

Weights and Measures

Avoirdupois Weight

(For all articles except drugs, gold, silver, and gems)

$27^{11}/_{32}$ grains	= 1 dram (dr.)
16 drams	= 1 ounce (oz.)
16 ounces	= 1 pound (lb.)
100 pounds	= 1 hundredweight (cwt.)
2,000 pounds	= 1 ton (T.)
1 lb.	= 1,000 grs.

Troy Weight

(For gold, silver, and gems)

24 grains (gr.)	= 1 pennyweight (pwt.)
20 pennyweights	= 1 ounce (oz.)
12 ounces	= 1 pound (lb.)

for diamonds only:

1 carat   = 3.168 Troy grains

USEFUL INFORMATION

Apothecaries' Weight

20 grains	= 1 scruple
3 scruples	= 1 dram
8 drams	= 1 ounce
12 ounces	= 1 pound

U.S. Liquid Measure

60 minims	= 1 fluid dram
8 fluid drams	= 1 fluid ounce
4 fluid ounces	= 1 gill
4 gills	= 1 pint
2 pints	= 1 quart
4 quarts	= 1 gallon
31½ gallons (sometimes 32)	= 1 barrel
42 gallons (petroleum)	= 1 barrel
2 barrels	= 1 hogshead

U.S. Dry Measure

2 pints	= 1 quart
8 quarts	= 1 peck
4 pecks	= 1 bushel

Apothecaries' Fluid Measure

60 minims (or drops)	= 1 fluid dram
8 fluid drams	= 1 fluid ounce
16 fluid ounces	= 1 pint
8 pints	= 1 gallon

U.S. Linear Measure

12 inches	= 1 foot
3 feet	= 1 yard
5½ yards	= 1 rod (or pole)
40 rods	= 1 furlong
8 furlongs	= 1 mile
5,280 feet	= 1 mile

U.S. Square Measure

144 square inches	= 1 square foot
9 square feet	= 1 square yard
30¼ square yards	= 1 square rod

16	square rods	= 1 square chain
160	square rods	= 1 acre
43,560	square feet	= 1 acre
640	acres	= 1 square mile
36	square miles	= 1 township

U.S. Cubic Measure

1728 cubic inches	= 1 cubic foot
27 cubic feet	= 1 cubic yard

Miscellaneous Measures

128 cubic feet	= 1 cord (of wood)
6 feet	= 1 fathom
6076.1155 feet	= 1 nautical mile
1 knot	= 1 nautical mile in 1 hour
12 dozen	= 1 gross
500 sheets	= 1 ream
500 pounds	= 1 bale (of cotton)
$1/_5$ gallon	= 1 fifth (wine measure)
4 inches	= 1 hand (horses' height)

METRIC TABLES

LENGTH

Myriameter	10,000 meters	6.2137 miles.
Kilometer	1,000 meters	0.62137 mile.
Hectometer	100 meters	328 feet 1 inch.
Dekameter	10 meters	393.7 inches.
Meter	1 meter	39.37 inches.
Decimeter	0.1 meter	3.937 inches.
Centimeter	0.01 meter	0.3937 inch.
Millimeter	0.001 meter	0.0394 inch.

AREA

Hectare	10,000 square meters	2.471 acres.
Are	100 square meters	119.6 square yards.
Centiare	1 square meter	1,550 square inches.

USEFUL INFORMATION

WEIGHT

Name	Number of grams	Avoirdupois weight
Metric ton, millier or tonneau	1,000,000	2,204.6 pounds.
Quintal	100,000	220.46 pounds.
Myriagram	10,000	22.046 pounds.
Kilogram or kilo	1,000	2.2046 pounds.
Hectogram	100	3.5274 ounces.
Dekagram	10	0.3527 ounce.
Gram	1	15.432 grains.
Decigram	.1	1.5432 grains.
Centigram	.01	0.1543 grain.
Milligram	.001	0.0154 grain.

CAPACITY

Name	Number of liters	United States measure
Kiloliter or stere	1,000	1.308 cubic yards
Hectoliter	100	2.838 bushels; 26.417 gallons
Dekaliter	10	1.135 pecks; 2.6417 gallons
Liter	1	0.908 dry quart; 1.0567 liquid quarts
Deciliter	.1	6.1023 cubic inches; 0.845 gill
Centiliter	.01	0.6102 cubic inch; 0.338 fluid ounce
Milliliter	.001	0.061 cubic inch; 0.271 fluid dram

Metric Equivalents

Common measure	Equivalent
Inch	2.54 centimeters.
Foot	0.3048 meter.
Yard	0.9144 meter.
Rod	5.029 meters.
Mile	1.6093 kilometers.
Square inch	6.452 square centimeters.
Square foot	0.0929 square meter.
Square yard	0.836 square meter.
Square rod	25.29 square meters.
Acre	0.4047 hectare.
Square mile	259 hectares.
Cubic inch	16.39 cubic centimeters.
Cubic foot	0.0283 cubic meter.
Cubic yard	0.7646 cubic meter.
Cord	3.625 steres.
Liquid quart, United States	0.9463 liter.
Dry quart, United States	1.101 liters.
Quart, imperial	1.136 liters.
Gallon, United States	3.785 liters.
Gallon, imperial	4.546 liters.
Peck, United States	8.810 liters.
Peck, imperial	9.092 liters.
Bushel, United States	35.24 liters.
Bushel, imperial	36.37 liters.
Ounce, avoirdupois	28.35 grams.
Pound, avoirdupois	0.4536 kilogram.
Ton, long	1.0160 metric tons.
Ton, short	0.9072 metric ton.
Grain	0.0648 gram.
Ounce, troy	31.103 grams.
Pound, troy	0.3732 kilogram.
Grain, Apothecaries'	0.0648 grams.
Dram, Apothecaries'	3.887 grams.

21. Signs and Symbols

Accents

- ´ acute
- ˘ breve
- ¸ cedilla
- ˆ circumflex
- ¨ dieresis
- ` grave
- ¯ macron
- ~ tilde

Measure

- ℔ pound
- ʒ dram
- ƒʒ fluid dram
- ℥ ounce
- ƒ℥ fluid ounce
- O pint
- ℈ scruple

Money

- ¢ cent
- ¥ yen
- £ pound sterling
- ₥ mills

Scientific

- ° ′ ″ degrees, minutes, seconds, as Longitude 30° 08′ 14″ W.
- °F degrees Fahrenheit
- °C degrees Centigrade
- ∥ parallel
- | | absolute value
- : is to; ratio
- ∴ therefore; hence
- ∵ because
- :: proportion; as
- > greater than
- ≷ greater than or less than
- ≯ is not greater than

< less than
≶ less than or greater than
≮ is not less than
⋖ smaller than
≤ less than or equal to
≧ greater than or equal to
⋜ equal to or less than
⋝ equal to or greater than
≠ not equal to
≡ identical with
≢ not identical with
≈ or ≒ nearly equal to
∼ difference
≃ perspective to
≅ congruent to approximately equal
≏ difference between
≎ equivalent to
π pi
ϵ base (2.718) of natural system of logarithms; epsilon
± plus or minus
∓ minus or plus
% percent
∫ integral
∮ contour integral
∝ variation; varies as
Π product
Σ summation of; sum; sigma

Miscellaneous

§ section
† dagger
‡ double dagger
℀ account of
℅ care of
¶ paragraph
∝ variation
℞ recipe
HP horsepower
⌀ diameter
☍ opposition
c̄ mean value
© copyright
® registered in U.S. Patent Office
¡ Spanish quote
¿ Spanish open quote

Sex

♂ or ♂ male
□ male, in charts
♀ female
○ female, in charts

22. Proofreading

Standard Proofreading Marks

⊙	Insert period	⊏⊐	Indent 2 ems
⌄	Insert comma	¶	Paragraph
:	Insert colon	no ¶	No paragraph
;	Insert semicolon	*tr*	Transpose—used in margin
?	Insert question mark	∽	Transpose—used in text
!	Insert exclamation mark	*sp*	Spell out
=/	Insert hyphen	*ital*	Italic—used in margin
˅	Insert apostrophe	___	Italic—used in text
˅˅	Insert quotation marks	*b.f.*	Boldface—used in margin
⊢⊣	Insert 1-en dash	~~~~	Boldface—used in text
⊢⊣	Insert 1-em dash	*s.c.*	Small caps—used in margin
#	Insert space	═══	Small caps—used in text
ld>	Insert lead	*rom.*	Roman type
shill	Insert virgule	*Caps.*	Caps—used in margin
˅	Superior	═══	Caps—used in text
˄	Inferior	c + sc	Caps & small caps—used in margin
(/)	Parentheses	═══	Caps & small caps—used in text
[/]	Brackets	*l.c.*	Lowercase—used in margin
☐	Indent 1 em	/	Used in text to show deletion or substitution

Proofreading

w.f.	Wrong font	⌣	Push down space
⌒	Close up	⌒	Use ligature
⌐|	Delete	*eq.#*	Equalize space—used in margin
⌐|	Close up and delete	✓✓✓	Equalize space—used in text
⊙	Correct the position	*stet.*	Let it stand—used in margin
⌐	Move right	....	Let it stand—used in text
⌐	Move left	⊗	Dirty or broken letter
⊓	Move up	*run over*	Carry over to next line
⊔	Move down	*run back*	Carry back to preceding line
‖	Aline vertically	*out, see copy*	Something omitted—see copy
=	Aline horizontally	?/?	Question to author to delete
⊐⊏	Center horizontally	∧	Caret—General indicator used to mark
⊔⊓	Center vertically		exact position of error in text.

Corrected Proof

Note: Marking proofs can be made easier by the use of an imaginary vertical line through the center of the page. Errors on the left side of the page are corrected in the left margin; errors on the right side of the page, in the right margin. However, if one margin is much wider than the other, use the wide margin for all corrections.

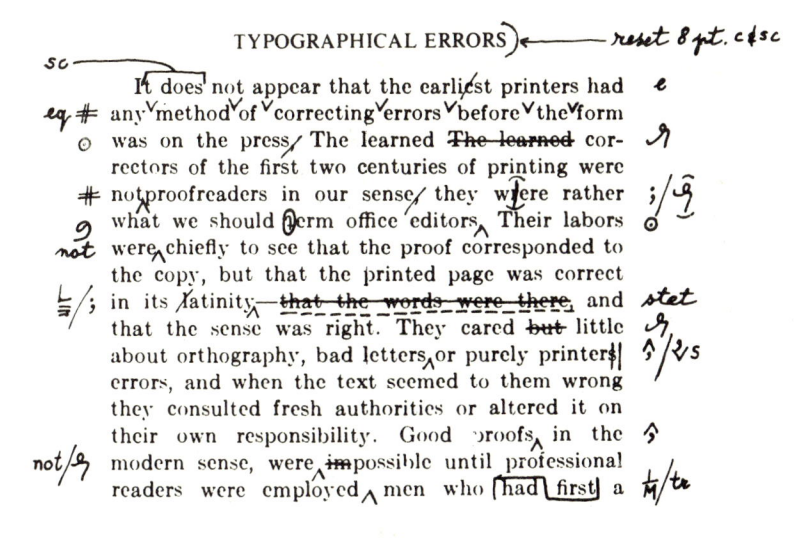

TYPOGRAPHICAL ERRORS

It does not appear that the earliest printers had any method of correcting errors before the form was on the press. The learned ~~The learned~~ correctors of the first two centuries of printing were not proofreaders in our sense; they were rather what we should term office editors. Their labors were chiefly to see that the proof corresponded to the copy, but that the printed page was correct in its latinity, ~~that the words were there~~, and that the sense was right. They cared ~~but~~ little about orthography, bad letters, or purely printers errors, and when the text seemed to them wrong they consulted fresh authorities or altered it on their own responsibility. Good proofs, in the modern sense, were ~~im~~possible until professional readers were employed men who had first a printer's education, and then spent many years in the correction of proof. The orthography of English, which for the past century has undergone little change, was very fluctuating until after the publication of Johnson's Dictionary, and capitals, which have been used with considerable regularity for the past 80 years, were previously used on the miss or hit plan. The approach to regularity, so far as we have, may be attributed to the growth of a class of professional proofreaders, and it is to them that we owe the correctness of modern printing. More errors have been found in the Bible than in any other one work. For many generations it was frequently the case that Bibles were brought out stealthily, from fear of governmental interference. They were frequently printed from imperfect texts, and were often modified to meet the views of those who publised them. The story is related that a certain woman in Germany, who was the wife of a Printer, and had become disgusted with the continual assertion of the superiority of man over woman which she had heard, hurried into the composing room while her husband was at supper and altered a sentence in the Bible, which he was printing, so that it read Narr instead of Herr, thus making the verse read "And he shall be thy fool" instead of "and he shall be thy lord." The word not was omitted by Barker, the king's printer in England in 1632, in printing the seventh commandment. He was fined £3,000 on this account.

23. Further Information

Greek Alphabet

A	α	**alpha**	N	ν	**nu**
B	β	**beta**	Ξ	ξ	**xi**
Γ	γ	**gamma**	O	o	**omicron**
Δ	δ	**delta**	Π	π	**pi**
E	ε	**epsilon**	P	ρ	**rho**
Z	ζ	**zeta**	Σ	σ	**sigma**
H	η	**eta**	T	τ	**tau**
Θ	θ	**theta**	Υ	υ	**upsilon**
I	ι	**iota**	Φ	φ	**phi**
K	κ	**kappa**	X	χ	**chi**
Λ	λ	**lambda**	Ψ	ψ	**psi**
M	μ	**mu**	Ω	ω	**omega**

The States of the United States and Their Capitals

State	Capital
Alabama	Montgomery
Alaska	Juneau

USEFUL INFORMATION

Arizona	Phoenix
Arkansas	Little Rock
California	Sacramento
Colorado	Denver
Connecticut	Hartford
Delaware	Dover
Florida	Tallahassee
Georgia	Atlanta
Hawaii	Honolulu
Idaho	Boise
Illinois	Springfield
Indiana	Indianapolis
Iowa	Des Moines
Kansas	Topeka
Kentucky	Frankfort
Louisiana	Baton Rouge
Maine	Augusta
Maryland	Annapolis
Massachusetts	Boston
Michigan	Lansing
Minnesota	St. Paul
Mississippi	Jackson
Missouri	Jefferson City
Montana	Helena
Nebraska	Lincoln
Nevada	Carson City
New Hampshire	Concord
New Jersey	Trenton
New Mexico	Santa Fe
New York	Albany
North Carolina	Raleigh
North Dakota	Bismarck
Ohio	Columbus
Oklahoma	Oklahoma City
Oregon	Salem
Pennsylvania	Harrisburg
Rhode Island	Providence
South Carolina	Columbia
South Dakota	Pierre
Tennessee	Nashville

Texas	Austin
Utah	Salt Lake City
Vermont	Montpelier
Virginia	Richmond
Washington	Olympia
West Virginia	Charleston
Wisconsin	Madison
Wyoming	Cheyenne

United States Territories and Their Capitals

Territory	*Capital*
American Samoa	Pago Pago
Guam	Agaña
Trust Territory of the Pacific Islands	—
Virgin Islands	Charlotte Amalie
Canal Zone	—
Puerto Rico, Commonwealth	San Juan

Canadian Provinces and Their Capitals

Provinces	*Capitals*
Alberta	Edmonton
British Columbia	Victoria
Manitoba	Winnipeg
New Brunswick	Fredericton
Newfoundland	St. John's
Nova Scotia	Halifax
Ontario	Toronto
Prince Edward Island	Charlottetown
Quebec	Quebec
Saskatchewan	Regina
Yukon Territory	Dawson
Northwest Territories	—

Appellations for Natives of the Several States

Alabamian	Louisianian	Ohioan
Alaskan	Mainer	Oklahoman
Arizonan	Marylander	Oregonian
Arkansan	Massachusettsan	Pennsylvanian
Californian	Michiganite	Rhode Islander
Coloradan	Minnesotan	South Carolinian
Connecticuter	Mississippian	South Dakotan
Delawarean	Missourian	Tennessean
Floridian	Montanan	Texan
Georgian	Nebraskan	Utahan
Hawaiian	Nevadan	Vermonter
Idahoan	New Hampshirite	Virginian
Illinoisan	New Jerseyite	Washingtonian
Indianian	New Mexican	West Virginian
Iowan	New Yorker	Wisconsinite
Kansan	North Carolinian	Wyomingite
Kentuckian	North Dakotan	

Wedding Anniversaries

1st—Paper
2d—Cotton
3d—Leather
4th—Linen (silk)
5th—Wood
6th—Iron
7th—Wool, copper
8th—Bronze
9th—Pottery (china)
10th—Tin (aluminum)
11th—Steel
12th—Silk
13th—Lace
14th—Ivory
15th—Crystal
20th—China
25th—Silver
30th—Pearl
35th—Coral
40th—Ruby
45th—Sapphire
50th—Gold
55th—Emerald
60th—Diamond

Birthstones

January	*Garnet*
February	*Amethyst*
March	*Bloodstone*
April	*Diamond*
May	*Emerald*
June	*Pearl*
July	*Ruby*
August	*Sardonyx*
September	*Sapphire*
October	*Opal*
November	*Topaz*
December	*Turquoise*

Roman numerals

I	1	XI	11	XXX	30	CCC	300
II	2	XII	12	XL	40	CD	400
III	3	XIII	13	L	50	D	500
IV	4	XIV	14	LX	60	DC	600
V	5	XV	15	LXX	70	DCC	700
VI	6	XVI	16	LXXX	80	DCCC	800
VII	7	XVII	17	XC	90	CM	900
VIII	8	XVIII	18	C	100	M	1,000
IX	9	XIX	19	CC	200	MM	2,000
X	10	XX	20				

Index

AAA, *see* American Automobile Association
Abbot, forms of address for, 169
Abbreviations, 277–329
  academic degrees and honors, 281–85
  Canadian provinces
    official, 280
    Zip Code, 45, 280
  days of week, 280
  French, 278
  list of, 287–329
  medical, 377–82
  months, 280
  plurals of, 277–78
  possessives of, 278
  postal, official, 45–47
  standard usage of, 277
  state
    official, 279
    Zip Code, 45, 279
  United States, 279
    government agencies, 286–87
About, use of word, 330
Academic degrees
  abbreviations, 281–85
  initials of, used in addresses, 124
Accept, use of word, 332
Accounting errors, letters regarding, 179
Acknowledgment letters, 176–77
Acting Governor, forms of address for, 153
Adapt, use of word, 330
Address, forms of, 144–75
  college and university officials, 164–67
  diplomats, 159–62
  government officials
    foreign, 158–62
    local, 157–58
    state, 153–56
    U.S., 145–53
  military, 162–64
  religious personages, 169–75
  United Nations officials, 167–68
Addresses
  envelopes and, 43–48, 135
  foreign, titles used in, 127
  inside (business letters), 122–27
Admiral, forms of address for, 162, 163
Admission Record, Hospital, 367–68
Adopt, use of word, 330
Adverse, use of word, 330
Aerogrammes, 61
Affect, use of word, 330
After, use of word, 333
Agencies, U.S. government, abbreviations for, 286–87
Agents, travel, use of, 72, 78
Airline letter codes, 73
Air mail, 54, 62, 63
Airplane travel, 72–74
Alderman, forms of address for, 157
All, use of word, 330
All-around, use of phrase, 330
All of, use of phrase, 330
All ready, use of phrase, 330

399

INDEX

All-round, use of phrase, 330
Alphabet, Greek, 393
Alphabetizing rules (filing), 12–17
Already, use of word, 330–31
Alternative, use of word, 331
Ambassadors, forms of address for, 159–60
American Automobile Association, 74–75
Among, use of word, 331
Amount, use of word, 331
Anesthesia Record, 369
Anticipate, use of word, 331
Anxious, use of word, 331
Any, use of word, 331
Any place, use of phrase, 331
Anywhere, use of word, 331
Apostolic Delegate, forms of address for, 169
Apostrophes, use of, 253–57
Apothecaries' weight, 384
   fluid measure, 384
Appear, use of word, 331
Appointment letters, 180
Appointment schedule for business trips, 77
Apt, use of word, 331
Archbishop, forms of address for
   Anglican, 172
   Catholic, 170
Archdeacon, forms of address for, 173
Area codes, telephone
   by number, 32
   by state, 33
   Canadian, 34
As, use of word, 333
Assembly, Speaker of the, forms of address for, 156
Assemblyman, state, forms of address for, 156
Assistant Secretary to the President, forms of address for, 152
Associate Justice, forms of address for
   state Supreme Court, 155
   U.S. Supreme Court, 146
At, use of word, 330
Attention line (business letters), 128
Attorney, City, forms of address for, 157
Attorney General, forms of address for
   state, 154
   U.S., 148
Auditor, state, forms of address for, 156
Automobile travel, 74–75
Averse, use of word, 330
Avoirdupois weight, 383

Balance, use of word, 331
Beside, use of word, 331
Besides, use of word, 331
Between, use of word, 331
Biannual, use of word, 331
Biennial, use of word, 331
Bimonthly, use of word, 331
Birthstones, 397
Bishop, forms of address for
   Anglican, 172
   Catholic, 170
   Methodist, 173
   Protestant Episcopal, 172, 173
Board of Commissioners, President of, forms of address for, 157
Brackets (punctuation), use of, 268–69
Bring, use of word, 331
Brother, forms of address for, 170
Business agreement letters, 182
Business hours (foreign countries), 99–103
Business titles, use of, 125

Cabinet officers, U.S., forms of address for, 146
   former, 147
Cablegrams, 35, 37–38
   determination of charges, 37–38
   how to send, 37
   types of, 37
Calendars, desk, 1–3
   employer's, 1–3
   next year's, 3
   recurring items on, 2–3
   secretary's, 1
Canadian provinces
   abbreviations
      official, 280
      Zip Code, 45, 280
   capital cities, 395
   list of, 395
Canon, forms of address for, 170
Capital, use of word, 331
Capitalization
   general rules for, 195–97
   guide to, 197–242
Capitals (cities)
   Canadian provinces, 395
   state, 393–95
   territories, U.S., 395
Capitol, use of word, 331
Captain, forms of address for, 163
Car travel, 74–75
Carbon copy notations (letters), 134
Cardinal, forms of address for, 169
Certificate of mailing, 56
Certified mail, 56, 122
   confidential material, 138
   law offices and, 351–52
Chaplain, forms of address for
   college or university, 167

INDEX

military, 164
Chargé d'Affaires, forms of address for, 161–62
Chief Justice, forms of address for
  State Supreme Court, 155
  U.S. Supreme Court, 146
Choice, use of word, 331
Cities
  capital, *see* Capitals
  foreign, variant spellings of, 87
Claim, use of word, 331
Claim letters, 182–84
  law office, 354
Classified information
  categories of, 138
  mailing of, 138
Clerk, court, forms of address for, 157
Clients, secretary's dealing with, in law office, 351
Close, complimentary (business letters), 129–31, 144
C.O.D. (mail), 57–58
College officials, forms of address for, 164–67
Colon, use of, 250–52
Colonel, forms of address for, 163
Comma
  omission of, 247–48
  use of, 243–46
Commander, forms of address for, 163
Commissioners, Board of, President, forms of address for, 157
Committee Chairman, U.S. Senate, forms of address for, 149
Commodore, forms of address for, 163
Compare, use of word, 332
Compare to, use of phrase, 332
Compare with, use of phrase, 332
Complaint (standard legal form), 354–56
Complaint letters, 182–84
  replies to, 184
Complimentary close (letters), 129–31, 144
Comptroller, state, forms of address for, 156
Comptroller General, U.S., forms of address for, 152
Condolence letters, 185–86
Conforming copies, 353
Confidential information, 138
Confidential mail, 42, 122
Congratulation, letters of, 186–88
Congressmen
  forms of address for, 150
  letters to, 188
  See also Representative, Senator
Consulates, U.S., 83–86
Consultation Sheet, 368–69

Contact file, 4–5
Continental Timetable, 74
Continually, use of word, 332
Continuously, use of word, 332
Contract of Sale, 359
Contrast, use of word, 332
Copies, conforming, 353
Corespondent, use of word, 332
Corporation Counsel, forms of address for, 157
Correspondence
  cutting costs, 110–13
  government, 137–38
  informal replies, use of, 113
  law office and, 351–52
  See also Letters; Mail; Stationery
Correspondent, use of word, 332
Council, use of word, 332
Counsel, City, forms of address for, 157
Counsel, use of word, 332
Countries, foreign
  business hours, 99–103
  capital cities, 88–95
  holidays, 99–103
  language, official, 88–95
  money, 96–99
  nationalities, 88–95
  variant spellings of, 87
Cross-references, filing and, 10
Customs, travel and, 80

Dash, use of, 257–59
Datagram, 39
Date line (letters), 122
Dates, writing, 339
Days of week, abbreviations for, 280
Dean, forms of address for, 173
Debates, minutes of meetings and, 345
Defense Department, letters to the, 137–38
Degrees, academic, *see* Academic degrees
Delegate, state, forms of address for, 156
Diary, office (law office), 351
Dictation
  of letters, 112
  medical, problems in, 369–77
Different, use of word, 332
Dimensions, writing numbers involving, 339–40
Diplomats, forms of address for, 159–62
Directors, forms of address for, 151
Directory of Post Offices, 49
Disburse, use of word, 332
Discussions, minutes of meetings and, 345
Disinterested, use of word, 332

Disperse, use of word, 332
District Attorney, state, forms of address for, 156
During, use of word, 332

Each, use of word, 332
Each other, use of phrase, 332
Eager, use of word, 331
Effect, use of word, 330
Electrocardiogram Report, 368
Ellipses, use of, 267
Embassies, U.S., list of, 83–86
Emigrate, use of word, 332
Enclosure notation (letters), 133–34
Ended, use of word, 332
Ending, use of word, 332
English usage, correct, 195–341
  abbreviations, 277–329
  capitalization, 195–242
  numbers, 336–41
  punctuation, 243–69
  spelling, 270–76
  words and phrases, troublesome, 330–41
Ensure, use of word, 333
Envelopes
  address formats for, 48
  addressing, 43–48, 135
  kinds of, 106
  sizes of, 104
  small, fitting large letters into, 136
  typing, 23
Errors in accounts, letters regarding, 179
Esquire, use as title, 125
Ethics, medical, principles of, 366–67
Etiquette, medical, 367
Every, use of word, 332
Every one, use of phrase, 332
Everyone, use of word, 332
Except, use of word, 332
Exceptionable, use of word, 332–33
Exceptional, use of word, 332–33
Exclamation point, use of, 267–68
Expect, use of word, 331, 333
Express mail, 54–55
  international, 63
Extant, use of word, 333
Extent, use of word, 333

Farther, use of word, 333
Few, use of word, 333
File
  contact, 4–5
  tickler, 3–4
    law office, 352
File guides, 8–9
File references on letters, 122

Files, control of material borrowed from, 11
Filing, 7–17
  alphabetical, 7
  alphabetizing rules, 12–17
  control of material borrowed from, 11
  cross-references and, 10
  geographic, 7–8
  indexing rules, 12–17
  legal, 350
  numeric, 8
  preparing material for, 10
  retention codes and, 10
First, use of word, 333
Flammable, use of word, 333
Folders, file, 8
Following, use of word, 333
Follow-up systems, 5–6
  indefinite dates and, 6
  large-scale, 5–6
  preparing material for, 6
  simple, 5
Foreign countries. *See* Countries, foreign
Foreign heads of state, forms of address for, 158–59
Foreign Minister, forms of address, 161
Foreign spellings of cities and countries, 87
Foreign titles, 127
Foreign travel, 78–83
Foreword, use of word, 333
Form letters, use of, 113
Forms
  legal, standard, 349–50, 353–57
  medical, 367–69
Forward, use of word, 333
Fulsome, use of word, 333
Further, use of word, 333

General, forms of address for, 162
Gifts, unsolicited, 80
Government agencies, U. S., abbreviations for, 286–87
Government correspondence, 137–38
Government officials, *see* Officials, government
Governor, state, forms of address for, 153
  Acting, 153
  former, 154
  Lieutenant, 154
Governor-elect, state, forms of address for, 153
Greek alphabet, 393
Guarantee, use of word, 333
Guaranty, use of word, 333

INDEX 403

High Commissioner, forms of address for, 161
Holiday notes, 184–85
Holidays (foreign countries), 99–103
Hotel reservations, 75
Hours, business (foreign countries), 99–103
House of Representatives, Speaker of the (state), forms of address for, 156
Hyphen, use of, 260
  written-out numbers and, 340–41

Identification initials (letters), 133
Immigrate, use of word, 332
Immunizations, 80–81
Imply, use of word, 333
Indexing rules (filing), 12–17
Infer, use of word, 333
Inflammable, use of word, 333
INFOCOM, 39
Information, classified, see Classified information
Ingenious, use of word, 333
Ingenuous, use of word, 333
Initials, identification (letters), 133
Inquiry letter, 181
Inside address (business letters), 122–127
Insurance, rain, travel and, 78
Insure, use of word, 333
International Mail (publication), 49, 59, 60, 63, 64
Introduction, letters of, 82, 192
Invaluable, use of word, 335
Invitations, formal, 193
  replying to, 193–94
Itineraries, 75, 76
Its (It's), use of, 333

Judges, forms of address for
  federal, 152
  local, 158
Justices, forms of address for
  State Supreme Courts, 155
  U.S. Supreme Court, 146

Kind, use of word, 333
Kindly, use of word, 333

Labels, thin, typing, 22–23
Last, use of word, 333
Latest, use of word, 333
Law library, 350–51
Law office procedures, basic, 349–53
Least, use of word, 333
Legal filing, 350
Legal forms, standard, 349–50, 353–57

Legal secretarial practice, 349–65
  conforming copies, 353
  correspondence, 351–52
  dealing with clients, 351
  incoming mail, 349
  law library, 350–51
  legal filing, 350
  letters, 351–52
  Notary Public, 352–53
  office diary, 351
  standard legal forms, 349–50, 353–57
  tickler file, personal, 352
  time sheets, 352
Legal terminology, 360–65
Less, use of word, 333
Letterheads
  printing and, 106–107
  samples, 108–110
  selecting, 108
  See also Stationery
Letters
  acknowledgment, 176–77
  addressing, 43–48
  appointment, 180
  attention line, 128
  business
    parts of, 122–34
    styles for, 114–21
    typing of, 121–34
  business agreement, 182
  carbon copy notations, 134
  claim, 182–84
    law office, 354
  complaint, 182–84
    replies to, 184
  complimentary close, 129–31, 144
  condolence, 185–86
  confidential, 42, 122
  congratulation, 186–88
  to Congressmen, 188
  continuation pages of, 114–15
  date line, 122
  to Department of Defense, 137–38
  dictation of, 112
  difficult, tips for writing, 139–40
  enclosure notation, 133–34
  form, 113
  forms of address for, 144–75
  good
    characteristics of, 138–43
    guidelines for, 104–43
  holiday notes, 184–85
  identification initials, 133
  inquiry, 181
  inside address, 122–27
  of introduction, 82, 192
  invitation, 193
    replying to, 193–94

404 INDEX

large, fitting into small envelopes, 136
law office, 351–52
model, 176–94
order, 178
personal, 42, 122
phrases, trite and outmoded, 140–43
positioning on page, 121
postscripts, 134
reference, 189–91
  criticism in, 191–92
reference line, 122
regarding errors in accounts, 179
reminder, 181
reservation, 177–78
resignation, 194
salutations, 128–29, 145–75
signature on, 131–33
special mailing notations on, 122
subject line, 129
time factors in writing, 111, 112
titles in inside address, 124–27
See also Correspondence; Envelopes; Letterheads; Mail; Stationery
Liable, use of word, 331
Librarian of Congress, forms of address for, 151
Library, law, 350–51
Lieutenant, forms of address for, 163 164
Lieutenant Governor, forms of address for, 154
Like, use of word, 333
Likely, use of word, 331
Local government officials, forms of address for, 157–58
Luggage limitations, travel and, 79–80

Mail, 42–71
  addressing, 43–48
  advertising, 53
  annotating, 42–43, 349
  C.O.D., 57–58
  certificate of mailing, 56
  certified, 56, 122, 138
    law offices and use of, 351–52
  classes of, 49–58
  classified information and, 138
  confidential, 42, 122
  domestic, 48–59
  first-class, 52
  fourth-class, 53–54
  handling, when employer is away, 43
  how to send specific items, 50–52
  incoming, 42–43
    law offices and, 349
  international, 59–64
    addressing, 59–60
    classes of, 60–64
    labeling, 60
    prohibited items, 64
    stamps for, 60
  insured, 56
  letters requiring attention by others than addressee, 43
  outgoing, 43–64
  packing and, 64, 65–71
  personal, 42, 122
  priority, 54
  prohibited items, 58, 64
  publication, 52
  recall of, 64–65
  registered, 55–56, 138
  second-class, 52–53
  sources of information about, 48–49
  special delivery, 57, 60, 61, 122
  special fourth-class, 54
  special handling, 57, 61
  third-class, 53
  See also Envelopes; Letters
Mailgrams, 36, 39, 58
Major, forms of address for, 163
Mayor, forms of address for, 157
Measurements, numbers and, 337–40
Measures (tables), 383–87
Medical abbreviations, 377–82
Medical dictation, problems in, 369–77
Medical ethics, principles of, 366–67
Medical etiquette, 367
Medical forms, 367–69
Medical History, 368
Medical secretarial practice, 366–82
  dictation problems, 369–82
  medical forms, 367–69
  special concerns, 366–67
Medical Summary, 368
Medical terms, prefixes and suffixes, 370–77
Meetings, minutes of. *See* Minutes of meetings
Memo book, pocket, employer's, 2
Meretricious, use of word, 334
Meritorious, use of word, 334
Messrs., use as title, 125
Meters, postage, setting of, 59
Metric Tables, 385–87
Military, forms of address for, 162–64
Minister, American, forms of address for, 160
Minister, Protestant, forms of address for, 174
Minute book, 346
Minutes of meetings, 342–48
  approval of, 347
  assembling, 342–46
  contents, 342, 343

INDEX 405

debates and, 345
discussions and, 345
distribution of, 346
form of, 343
information obtainable before meeting, 343
meetings requiring, 342
motions and, 344–45
note taking, 342–43
purpose of, 342
reports and, 345
resolutions and, 344
sample, 347–48
storage of, 346
tone of, 345
typing, 345–46
Money
 foreign, 96–99
 writing numbers out, 338–39
Money orders, postal, 58
 international, 63–64
Months, abbreviations for, 280
More than, use of phrase, 334
Mother Superior, forms of address for, 171
Motions, minutes of meetings and, 344–45
Motor vehicle report, 353
Myself, use of word, 334

Near, use of word, 334
Nearly, use of word, 334
None, use of word, 334
Notary Public, 352–53
Note taking, for minutes of meetings, 342–43
Number, use of word, 331
Numbers, 336–41
 measurements and, 337–40
 ordinal, 341
 plurals of, 340–41
 Roman numerals, 397
 time and, 338
 when to spell out, 336–37
 written-out, hyphenation of, 340–41

Office diary (law office), 351
Official, use of word, 334
Official Airline Guide, 74
Official Guide of the Railways, 74
Officials, government, forms of address for
 local, 157–58
 state, 153–56
 U.S., 145–53
Officious, use of word, 334
On call guides (filing system), 11
One, use of word, 334

One another, use of phrase, 332
Operation Record, 369
Order letters, 178
Ordinal numbers, proper usage of, 341
Other, use of word, 331
Out files, 11
Out guides (filing system), 11
Over, use of word, 334

Packaging for mailing, 64, 65–71
Parcel post, 53–54
 international, 63
Parentheses, use of, 264–67
Passports, 78–79
 lost or stolen, 79
Past, use of word, 334
Pathology Report, 369
Percent, writing numbers involving, 339
Period
 omission of, 250
 use of, 248–49
Perquisite, use of word, 334
Personal, use of word, 334
Personal mail, 42, 122
Personnel, use of word, 334
Phonetic sounds, common, and their proper spelling, 369–70
Phrases, trite and outmoded, list of, 140–43
Physical Examination Record, 368
Plane travel, 72–74
Please, use of word, 333
Plurals
 abbreviations, 277–78
 numbers, 340–41
 spelling, 271–74
Pocket memo book, employer's, 2
"Pocket papers," 350–51
Police Report form, 354
Pope, forms of address for, 169
Possessives of abbreviations, 278
Post Office, services available, 58–59
Postage meters, setting of, 59
Postal abbreviations, official, 45–47
Postal Bulletin, 49
Postal centers, self-service, 59
Postal money orders, 58
 international, 63–64
Postal Service Manual, 49
Postcards
 international, 61
 notices on, 194
Postmaster General, forms of address for, 148
Postmortem Examination Report, 369
Postscripts, 134
Practicable, use of word, 334
Practical, use of word, 334

INDEX

Precede, use of word, 334
Prefixes (medical terms), 370-77
Premier, forms of address for, 159
Prerequisite, use of word, 334
Prescribe, use of word, 334
President, U.S.
  Assistant Secretary to, forms of address for, 152
  former, forms of address for, 145
  forms of address for, 145
  Press Secretary to, forms of address for, 153
  Secretary to the, forms of address for, 152
President-elect, U.S., forms of address for, 145
President of a Republic, forms of address for, 159
Presiding Justice, State Supreme Court, forms of address for, 155
Press Secretary to the President, forms of address for, 153
Priest, forms of address for
  Catholic, 171
  Episcopal, 174, 175
Prime Minister, forms of address for, 158
Principal, use of word, 334
Principle, use of word, 334
Printing, letterheads and, 106-107
Priority mail, 54
Proceed, use of word, 334
Professional titles, use of, 126
Professor, forms of address for, 166
Progress Notes, 368
Proofreading, 390-92
Proscribe, use of word, 334
Proved, use of word, 334
Proven, use of word, 334
Providing, use of word, 334-35
Public Printer, U.S., forms of address for, 152
Punctuation, 243-69
  apostrophes, 253-57
  brackets, 268-69
  colon, 250-52
  comma, 243-48
  dash, 257-59
  ellipses, 267
  exclamation point, 267-68
  hyphen, 260
  parentheses, 264-67
  period, 248-50
  question mark, 260-61
  quotation marks, 261-64
  semicolon, 252-53

Queen, forms of address for, 159
Question mark
  omission of, 261
  use of, 260
Quite, use of word, 335
Quotation marks
  omission of, 263-64
  use of, 261-63

Rabbi, forms of address for, 175
Rain insurance, travel and, 78
Rarely ever, use of phrase, 335
Real estate, 358-59
Reason is because, use of phrase, 335
Reference letters, 189-91
  criticism in, 191-92
Reference line (letters), 122
Registered mail, 55-56
  secret information and, 138
Remainder, use of word, 331
Reminder letters, 181
Reminder systems, 3-5
  for indefinite dates, 4
  for standard legal forms, 349-50
Reports, minutes of meetings and, 345
Representative, forms of address for
  state, 156
  U.S., 150
  former, 150
Request for Medical Report, 353
Reservation letters, 177-78
Reservations, hotel, 75
Resident Commissioner, forms of address for, 151
Resignation letters, 194
Resolutions, minutes of meetings and, 344
Retainer statement, 353
Retention codes (filing), 10
Roman Numerals, 397

Sale, Contract of, 359
Salutations (business letters), 128-29, 145-75
Schedule, appointment, for business trips, 77
Secret information, 138
Secretary General (UN) forms of address for, 167
Secretary of State, forms of address for, 154
Secretary to the President, forms of address for, 152
Seldom ever, use of phrase, 335
Self-service postal centers, 59
Semicolon, use of, 252-53
Semimonthly, use of word, 331
Senate, state, President of, forms of address for, 155
Senate, U.S.

INDEX

Committee Chairman, forms of address for, 149
Subcommittee Chairman, forms of address for, 150
Senator, forms of address for state, 156 U.S., 149
  See also Congressmen
Senator-elect, U.S., forms of address for, 149
Sensual, use of word, 335
Sensuous, use of word, 335
Signature (letters), 131–33
Simple, use of word, 335
Simplistic, use of word, 335
Signs and symbols, 388–89
Sir, use as title, 128
Sister, forms of address for, 171
6-6-6 system (letter positioning), 121
Sort, use of word, 333
Speaker of the House of Representatives, forms of address for, 147
  former, 147
Special delivery mail, 57, 60, 61, 122
Special handling (mail), 57, 61
Spelling
  foreign, of cities and countries, 87
  guidelines for, 270
  numbers, when to write out, 336–37
  plurals, 271–74
  words commonly misspelled, list of, 274–76
Stamps
  international mail and, 60
  ordering by mail, 59
Standard legal forms, 349–50, 353–57
Standard time, *see* Time, standard
State, Secretary of, forms of address for, 154
State government officials, forms of address for, 153–56
States
  abbreviations for
    official, 279
    Zip Code, 45, 279
  appellations for natives of, 396
  capital cities of, 393–95
Stationary, use of word, 335
Stationery
  ordering, 107
  paper, 105–106
    content of, 105
    grain of, 105–106
    kinds of, 105
    weight of, 105
  sizes of, 104
  use of word, 335
  See also Envelopes; Letterheads; Letters
Subcommittee Chairman, U.S. Senate,
  forms of address for, 150
Subject line (business letters), 129
Suffixes (medical terms), 370–77
Summons, 354
Suspect, use of word, 333
Symbols, 388–89

Tables
  metric, 385–87
  typing of, 19–20
  weight, 383–84
Take, use of word, 331
Telegrams
  domestic, 35–36
    determinations of charges, 36
    types of, 35–36
  international, *see* Cablegrams
Telegraph channels, private leased, 39
Telephone, 24–34
  annoyed callers, soothing, 27
  appointment calls, 28
  area codes
    Canadian, 34
    listed by number, 32
    listed by states, 33
  calls employer doesn't want to take, 25–26
  conference calls, 27
  discretion on the, 26–27
  etiquette, 24–27
  international direct distance dialing, 28–30
  messenger calls, 27
  mobile calls (air-land-sea), 28
  placing employer's calls, 24–25
  screening calls, 25
  using, in place of letters, 112–13
Telepost, 39
Telex, 38
Terminology, legal, 360–65
Terms, medical, 370–77
Territorial Delegate, forms of address for, 151
Territories, U.S., and their capitals, 395
Their, use of word, 335
There, use of word, 335
They're, use of word, 335
Tickler file, 3–4
  law office, 352
Time, numbers and, 338
Time, standard, determining
  in foreign cities, 41
  overseas by country, 39–40
Time sheets, law office use of, 352
Titles
  business, 125
  Cabinet secretaries, 147
  complementary, 124

INDEX

Esquire (Esq.), 125
foreign, corresponding to "Mr.," "Mrs.," and "Miss," 127
inside address (letters) and, 124–25
Messrs., 125
professional, 126
Sir, 128
for women, 126–27
Top Secret information, 138
Train travel, 74
Travel, 72–103
  appointment schedule, 77
  automobile, 74–75
  customs and, 80
  foreign, 78–83
    checklist for, 81–82
  hotel reservations, 75
  immunizations and, 80–81
  itineraries, 75, 76
  luggage limitations, 79–80
  passports and, 78–79
  plane, 72–74
  rain insurance and, 78
  train, 74
  "unsolicited gifts" and, 80
  vaccinations and, 80–81
  visas and, 79
Travel agents, use of, 72, 78
Treasurer, state, forms of address for, 156
Treatment Record, 368
Trips, business, planning, 72–83
Troy weight, 383
TWX, 38–39
Typewriters, semi-automatic, 113
Typing, 18–23
  body position for, 23
  business letters, 121–34
  Contract of Sale, 359
  envelopes, 23
  insertion of carbon packs, 23
  labels, thin, 22–23
  making corrections, 21–22
  measurements, useful, 18
  minutes of meetings, 345–46
  same number of lines per page, 18
  semi-automatic typewriters and, 113
  separating carbon copies, 23
  spacing after punctuation, 20–21
  tables, 19–20
  vertical centering and, 19
  wills, 357–58

Under Secretary of a Department, forms of address for, 149
Uninterested, use of word, 332
United States
  abbreviation, use of, 279
  government agencies, abbreviations for, 286–87
  government officials, forms of address for, 145–53
University officials, forms of address for, 164–67
"Unsolicited gifts," sending, 80

Vaccinations, 80–81
Valuable, use of word, 335
Verification (legal form), 357
Vice-President, U.S., forms of address for, 145
Visas, 79
Volume, writing numbers involving, 339

Warrant officer, forms of address for, 164
Wedding anniversaries, 396
Weight, writing amounts of, 339
Weights (tables), 383–84
Who's, use of word, 335
Whose, use of word, 335
Wills, 357–58
Women, titles for, 126–27

X-Ray Examination Report, 369

Your, you're, proper use of, 335

Zip Code Directory, 49
Zip Code state abbreviations, 45, 279